OXFORD CONSTITUTIONAL THEORY

Series editors

MARTIN LOUGHLIN, JOHN P. MCCORMICK, AND NEIL WALKER

Legitimation by Constitution

OXFORD CONSTITUTIONAL THEORY

Series editors

Oxford Constitutional Theory has rapidly established itself as the primary point of reference for theoretical reflections on the growing interest in constitutions and constitutional law in domestic, regional, and global contexts. The majority of the works published in the series are monographs that advance new understandings of their subject. But the series aims to provide a forum for further innovation in the field by also including well-conceived edited collections that bring a variety of perspectives and disciplinary approaches to bear on specific themes in constitutional thought and by publishing English translations of leading monographs in constitutional theory that have originally been written in languages other than English.

ALSO AVAILABLE IN THE SERIES

Authoritarian Liberalism and the Transformation of Modern Europe
Michael A. Wilkinson

Constitutionalism and the Paradox of Principles and Rules
Between the Hydra and Hercules
Marcelo Neves

Constituent Power in the European Union
Markus Patberg

Religion, Law, and Democracy
Selected Writings
Ernst-Wolfgang Böckenförde
Edited by Mirjam Künkler and Tine Stein

Constituent Power and the Law
Joel Colón-Ríos

Law and Revolution
Legitimacy and Constitutionalism after the Arab Spring
Nimer Sultany

After Public Law
Edited by Cormac Mac Amhlaigh, Claudio Michelon, and Neil Walker

Europe's Functional Constitution
A Theory of Constitutionalism Beyond the State
Turkuler Isiksel

Unconstitutional Constitutional Amendments
The Limits of Amendment Powers
Yaniv Roznai

Constitutionalism
Past, Present, and Future
Dieter Grimm

Euroconstitutionalism and its Discontents
Oliver Gerstenberg

Popular Sovereignty in Early Modern Constitutional Thought
Daniel Lee

Beyond the People
Social Imaginary and Constituent Imagination
Zoran Oklopcic

The Metaethics of Constitutional Adjudication
Bosko Tripkovic

Legitimation by Constitution

A Dialogue on Political Liberalism

ALESSANDRO FERRARA
University of Rome Tor Vergata

FRANK I. MICHELMAN
Harvard University

OXFORD
UNIVERSITY PRESS

OXFORD
UNIVERSITY PRESS

Great Clarendon Street, Oxford, OX2 6DP,
United Kingdom

Oxford University Press is a department of the University of Oxford.
It furthers the University's objective of excellence in research, scholarship,
and education by publishing worldwide. Oxford is a registered trade mark of
Oxford University Press in the UK and in certain other countries

First Edition published in 2021

Impression: 3

Published in the United States of America by Oxford University Press
198 Madison Avenue, New York, NY 10016, United States of America

British Library Cataloguing in Publication Data

Data available

Library of Congress Control Number: 2021941259

ISBN 978–0–19–285512–1

DOI: 10.1093/oso/9780192855121.001.0001

Printed and bound by
CPI Group (UK) Ltd, Croydon, CR0 4YY

In this year of the centennial of his birth, in tribute to his pathbreaking quest for a political conception committed to the freedom and equality of persons and to avoidance of oppression across constituencies deeply divided by clashes of values and pursuits, we dedicate this book to the inspiration and memory of John Rawls.

Acknowledgements

As noted more specifically in the chapters to follow, some passages in this book have been drawn by us from previously published articles and book chapters. A list of those sources can be found below. Credits for assistance in their preparation appear in the original publications.

Here we especially want to thank some friends and associates who helped to shape and guide the evolution of this book as a whole. It starts with Marek Hrubec, our friend and associate over the years in the Conference on Philosophy and Social Science ('the Conference', a.k.a. 'Prague' as we refer to it again soon below). Marek's idea, now some twenty years past, of collecting essays of ours into a book-length exchange in Czech translation was the first seed of this project. The resulting volume[1] still stands as the anchoring text for the extended series of exchanges over the years contained in this book.

At the nearer end of the line lies a special contribution from two friends, Vlad Perju and Johan van der Walt. Vlad and Johan each read carefully through our entire text as it was drawing toward a finish and responded with fine observations and suggestions that helped us greatly (as also, later, did comments from OUP's editorial advisers and anonymous readers) in reaching closure.

In between, over the stretch of time between start and finish, lies 'the Conference', lies 'Prague'. The Conference has a long history.[2] Every spring since 1993 (and only suspended by force of pandemic in 2020), the Conference—with wonderful hospitality from the Czech Academy of Science—has convened in Prague as a cross-disciplinary, intellectually diverse, globe-spanning congregation of scholars older and younger, for days of intensive exchange in panels and lectures on a range of topics including those treated in this book. This book could not exist but for Prague. Prague is what brought us two together and connected us in the first place. Over the years we each have made multiple presentations there of developing work touching on these topics. We are two among countless beneficiaries of the incomparable quality and tone

[1] Frank I. Michelman and Alessandro Ferrara, *Polemika o ústave* (Prague: CAS, Institute of Philosophy, 2006).

[2] See Alessandro Ferrara, 'Prague, or Critical Theory in the 21st Century' (2017) 43 Philosophy & Social Criticism 235.

of the critical discussions that ensued. We despair of trying to name all whose help we have thus received.

Finally, we owe gratitude to Italian artist Domingo Notaro for having offered his 1993 painting *Chaos-Chance-Thing* as a cover image. Its combination of energy-like, unshaped chromatic forms passing through and yet exceeding the neat geometrical frame inscribed in the overall pictorial space immediately moved the imagination of two advocates of 'legitimation by constitution'.

Some of the papers listed below were first prepared for live conferences or symposia, and we stand indebted for those occasions to organizers, commentators, and others in attendance. 'How Can the People Ever Make the Laws?' was presented at the Second Robert J. Henle Conference, St Louis University, April 1996, organized by James Bohman and William Rehg. 'Morality, Identity, and Constitutional Patriotism' came out of discussions at a panel of the Annual Meeting of the Society for Phenomenology and Existential Philosophy, Denver University, 1999. 'A Constitutional Horizon' appeared as part of a print symposium on Ferrara's *The Democratic Horizon* organized for *Philosophy and Social Criticism* by that journal's editor (and our constant friend and kibitzer over the years), David Rasmussen. 'Israel's Constitutional Revolution' was prepared for a conference on 'Judicial Review—Law and Politics' at the Tel Aviv University Faculty of Law on 4–5 June 2017, organized by the Cegla Center for Interdisciplinary Research of the Law and its Director Sharon Hannes. 'Political Liberalism's Constitutional Horizon: Some Further Thoughts' was presented at a seminar at the Luiss Guido Carli University in Rome, 7 April 2016, hosted by Antonio Punzi and organized with the major assistance of Michele Mangini. We are indebted for comments from the organizers and from Rainer Forst and Mario Ricciardi, who also took part in the discussion.

The materials in Part III of this book are for the most part published for the first time. They originate from a workshop on 'The Legitimacy of Transnational Orders: Discussing the Idea of a World State,' 12–13 April 2018, organized by the Clough Center for the Study of Constitutional Democracy at Boston College and its Director Vlad Perju. As worked through for publication here, these chapters bear the influence of papers or remarks from Vlad and from Cristina Lafont, Mattias Kumm, David Rasmussen, and William Scheuermann.

Previously published work from which Michelman has recalled ideas and some passages in the chapters below are as follows:

INTRODUCTION AND CHAPTER ONE

'Israel's "Constitutional Revolution": A Thought from Political Liberalism' (2018) 19 Theoretical Inquiries in Law 745.

‘Human Rights and the Limits of Constitutional Theory’ (2000) 13 Ratio Juris 63.

‘How Can the People Ever Make the Laws? A Critique of Deliberative Democracy’, in James Bohman and William Rehg (eds), *Deliberative Democracy* (MIT Press 1997) 145 (This paper also appeared in substantially similar form in (1997) 74 The Modern Schoolman 311.)

‘Can Constitutional Democrats Be Legal Positivists? Or, Why Constitutionalism?’ (1996) 2 Constellations 293.

‘Always Under Law?’ (1995) 12 Constitutional Commentary 227.

CHAPTER THREE

‘Morality, Identity, and “Constitutional Patriotism”’ (1999) 76 Denver University Law Review 1009 (This paper was later also published in (2001) 14 Ratio Juris 253.)

CHAPTER FIVE

‘A Constitutional Horizon?’ (2016) 42 Phil. & Soc. Crit. 240

CHAPTER SEVEN

‘Political Liberalism’s Constitutional Horizon: Some Further Thoughts’ (2017) 4 Rivista internazionale di filosofia del diritto 607.

Previously published works from which Ferrara has drawn ideas and some passages are listed below:

CHAPTER SIX

‘Judicial Review and Its Discontents: A Reply to Frank Michelman’ (2017) 4 Rivista Internazionale di Filosofia del Diritto 615.

CHAPTER EIGHT

‘Judicial Review and Its Discontents: A Reply to Frank Michelman’ (2017) 4 Rivista Internazionale di Filosofia del Diritto 615.

Alessandro Ferrara
Rome
Frank I. Michelman
Lexington, Mass.
April 2021

Contents

‘Legitimation by Constitution’: An Introduction

Alessandro Ferrara and Frank I. Michelman

The Ferrara–Michelman dialogue (singular, not plural) assembled in this book in fact transpired in stages over a span of two decades. Successive episodes seemed at first, as they came along, to be touching on rather a mixed bag of topics: the mysteries of a democratic constituent power; the tensions, post-Enlightenment, between government by the people and government by consent; the challenges thus posed to concretization by judicial authorities of national constitutional law; and then finally (the stage at which the unifying thread in our exchanges decided to dawn on us), a magnification of those mysteries, tensions, and challenges under the lens of ambition towards transnational legal ordering.

The dialogue commenced as a friendly exchange spurred in part by Ferrara’s 1999 study of contrasting models of the faculty of judgement in recent liberal-minded political philosophy, in which Michelman’s work had come in for discussion.[1] Its latest round is an upshot from a 2018 cross-disciplinary colloquium on prospects for transnational political orders.[2] Only in hindsight have we detected a focal interest inhabiting the exchanges throughout. What binds them together—we may now almost say as a progression—is an attraction we two have shared over these years (like moths drawn to a flame?) to the political-theoretic idea of democracy as ‘dualist’ (in the coinage of Bruce Ackerman) or (more commonly) ‘constitutional.’ But not just to that idea in general; more particularly, our shared attraction has been to that idea as offered in answer to a challenge especially thrown up by a recent turn in liberal thought, which we connect to work by both John Rawls and Jürgen Habermas. We mean the quest

[1] See Alessandro Ferrara, *Justice and Judgment: The Rise and the Prospect of the Judgment Model in Contemporary Political Philosophy* (Sage Publications 1999) 133–149, 174–177 (taking up for sympathetically critical examination then-recent work by Michelman) (hereafter Ferrara, *Justice and Judgment*).

[2] See below Part III, Chapters 9–12.

Legitimation by Constitution. Alessandro Ferrara and Frank I. Michelman, Oxford University Press. DOI: 10.1093/oso/9780192855121.003.0001

for the institutional conditions of political and legal validity (as Habermas would say) among citizens free and equal, in a post-Enlightenment age where 'consensus on issues of political justice can no longer be based on a settled traditional ethos that encompasses the whole of society'.[3] As posed by Rawls, the search is one for the possible terms of a just and stable pact of political cooperation among citizens free, equal, and divided by reasonable though incompatible religious, philosophical, and moral doctrines—the condition named by Rawls as that of a 'reasonable pluralism of comprehensive views'.[4] Axiomatic for both Rawls and Habermas has been the liberal mantra of the freedom and equality of persons as citizens. Sought by both Rawls and Habermas has been an institutional conception sufficiently broad and supple to be realistically pursuable in sundry differing locales at our time in history. For both, the idea of dualist democracy has come to the fore as a first-line response to that search.[5]

Along the way in our exchanges, we found ourselves giving a name to this liberal-theoretic idea of reliance on constitutionalism—the subjection of ground-level democratic lawmaking to the constraints of a higher-law constitution that all citizens supposedly could find reasonably acceptable—as a response to the problem of just and stable liberal government in visionary pluralist conditions. We called it the idea of 'legitimation by constitution', sometimes hereinafter written as 'legitimation-by-constitution' to mark it as a term of art. (In some earlier writings of Michelman—recollected in Chapter 1, below—the same idea appears as 'justification by constitution').

Among contemporaneous, liberal-minded political theorists, an instinct towards legitimation by constitution has not been unique to the thought of John Rawls. (Along with Ackerman and Habermas, already mentioned, we will soon below find Ronald Dworkin also serving as an exemplar.) Rawls undoubtedly, though, has been the leading philosophical expositor of the dualist-democratic implications of political liberalism. It is his encapsulation of them in a proposed 'liberal principle of legitimacy' that has centrally inspired our exchanges.

The exchanges proceed, as we now understand, from a shared sympathetic identification with the political-liberal statement of the problem for which legitimation-by-constitution is advanced as a solution. They address some

[3] Jürgen Habermas, '"Reasonable" versus "True", or the Morality of Worldviews', in Habermas, *The Inclusion of Other: Studies in Political Theory*, ed. Ciaran Cronin and Pablo De Greiff (MIT Press 1998) 75, 78 (hereafter Habermas, 'Reasonable versus True').

[4] John Rawls, *Political Liberalism* (Expanded edn, Columbia U. Press 2005) xx, 216–217. The main text of *Political Liberalism* was first published in 1993. Throughout this book, we refer to this text as Rawls, *PL*.

[5] See ibid. 231–232; Jürgen Habermas, *Between Facts and Norms: Contributions to a Discourse Theory of Law and Democracy*, tr. William Rehg (MIT Press 1996) 30 (hereafter Habermas, *Facts and Norms*).

perceived difficulties arguably standing in the way of that proposal's fulfilment on terms consistent with political liberalism's own defining ideas about political justification (as, for example, assembled by us in this book's Chapters 9 and 10). Our debates are in that sense internal to political-liberal thought.

1. A Constitution-Centred 'Liberal Principle of Legitimacy'

Near the start of *PL*, Rawls poses the question that his work in that book is to address.[6] 'How is it possible'—Rawls thus states his leading question—'that there may exist over time a stable and just society of free and equal citizens profoundly divided by reasonable though incompatible religious, philosophical, and moral doctrines?'[7] Rawls calls that 'the problem of political liberalism'.[8] He then immediately follows on with what he sees as the same question 'put another way'. How is it possible, he now inquires, 'that deeply opposed though reasonable [religious, philosophical, and moral] doctrines may live together and all affirm the political conception of a constitutional regime?'[9] Or take this formulation from a later work: 'By what ideals and principles are citizens who share equally in ultimate political power to exercise the power so that each can reasonably justify his or her political decisions to everyone?'[10]

In order fully to feel the force of Rawls's query, we need to have also before us his distinctly liberal-tinted understanding of democracy. Rawls, as liberal, conceives democracy as the vesting of political power—the power of rule—in citizens severally free and equal, acting consciously in concert.[11] Political power, 'which is always coercive power', is in a democracy a power by which citizens as a body 'impose on themselves and one another as free and equal'.[12] But thence springs a question:

[6] This section and some of the next are drawn from Michelman's pending draft for a book-length treatment (tentatively titled 'Constitutional Essentials: On the Constitutional Theory of Political Liberalism') of the rise, workings, and transformations, within Rawls's political philosophy, of ideas of the constitution and constitutional law.

[7] Rawls, *PL* xx.

[8] Ibid.

[9] Ibid.

[10] John Rawls, 'The Idea of Public Reason Revisited' (1997) 64 University of Chicago Law Review 765, 770.

[11] 'In a democratic regime', Rawls writes, 'political power is regarded as the power of free and equal citizens as a collective body.' John Rawls, *Justice as Fairness: A Restatement*, ed. Erin Kelly (Harvard U. Press 2001) 40 (hereafter Rawls, *Justice as Fairness*).

[12] Ibid.

> [I]f the fact of reasonable pluralism always characterizes democratic societies and if political power is indeed the power of free and equal citizens, in the light of what reasons and values . . . can citizens legitimately exercise that coercive power over one another?[13]

It is specifically in answer to that question that Rawls offers, in *PL*, the idea of a higher-normative pact—a 'constitution'—whose terms for the regulation of all subsequent political actions in that country any citizen might reasonably call upon all fellow citizens to accept, even as all would understand that some outcomes allowed by those terms will certainly turn out repugnant—and far from trivially so—to some fraction of the citizens. To a question cast initially in terms of a putative convergence on 'reasons and values', Rawls thus offers in response an institutional idea, that of the constitution as a table of terms for a procedural deflection of substantive political disagreements. Subject to variations of wording that do not reach to our concerns in this book, the principle reads as follows:

> Our exercise of political power is proper and hence justifiable [among citizens free and equal] only when it is exercised in accordance with a constitution the essentials of which all citizens may reasonably be expected to endorse in the light of principles and ideals acceptable to them as reasonable and rational. This is the liberal principle of legitimacy.[14]

The LPL (as we shall familiarly call it) presents us with an institutional object-class 'constitution', of which some members do and some do not, in certain essential respects, meet a test of hypothetical reasonable acceptability spelled out (more or less) by the LPL. The LPL then lets justification ride on the back of an actual constitution that meets the test. By hypothesis, in a well-ordered society, the constitution actually now in force in the country does meet the test. Majorities justify to protesting dissenters their exertions of political power by pointing to that constitution, with which those exertions can be seen to comply. Citizens severally engaged with their shares in this power—through, say, their votes on ballot questions and in partisan elections—thus claim to be acting with that constitution in view. A supreme court acts as institutional protector of that extant constitutional pact, to which officials and

[13] Ibid. 41.
[14] Rawls, *PL* 217; see ibid. 237; Rawls, *Justice as Fairness* (n. 11) 41.

citizens point by way of justification for their votes and other political actions.[15] We have, in sum, the political practice we call in this book by the name of legitimation-by-constitution.

2. Some Related Ideas: Ackerman, Dworkin, Habermas

Ideas of a key role for a higher-law constitution in the justification of coercive legislation among free and equal political associates have of course not been confined to John Rawls. Here we briefly locate the Rawlsian conception in relation to a few other prominent examples in the field.

In his move to place political-justificatory weight on a country's body of constitutional law, Rawls expressly took a cue from Bruce Ackerman's depiction of a constitutional democracy's legal order as dual in structure, comprising both an 'ordinary' law of legislative bodies and a 'higher' law of the people.[16] Rawls's point, though, in adopting this depiction, was a different one from Ackerman's. For Ackerman, the aim initially was explanation of how subjection of everyone to a mix of laws enacted by small handfuls of elected representatives, sprinkled with vetoes imposed by a minuscule handful of non-elected judges, could count as self-government by the people.[17] For Rawls, it was explanation of how subjection of dissenters to laws favoured by majorities could possibly still be legitimate. Democracy, for Ackerman, means authorship by the people of the laws they live under. So does it for Rawls. But *legitimacy*, for Rawls, means the justifiability among free and equal fellow citizens of the force of popularly legislated laws with which some fraction quite fundamentally disagree; it means the nearest possible approach, in such conditions, to the liberal grail of government by consent. The two quests start out from different places. For Rawls, while rule by current majorities would no doubt have to occupy a major part of the policy space in any democratically legitimate regime, it could not occupy all of it. Rather to the contrary, the question for him was how majoritarian forms of rule might *also* be or become legitimate.[18] Our exchanges below in

[15] See Rawls, *PL* 233.

[16] See ibid.

[17] See Bruce Ackerman, *We the People: Foundations* (Harvard U. Press, 1991) 6–7; 42–44 (hereafter Ackerman, *Foundations*); Bruce Ackerman, 'The Storrs Lectures: Discovering the Constitution' (1984) 93 Yale Law Journal 1013, 1044–1050, 1070–1071.

[18] This difference in leading concerns finds expression also in a difference over limits to the amending power in a constitutional-democratic regime. Where for Ackerman the people's self-government trumps any idea of such a limit, see Ackerman, *Foundations* (n. 17) 13–14, for Rawls the pursuit of legitimacy precludes reversal by an incumbent government or electorate of protection for basic rights endorsed by long historical practice, see Rawls, *PL* 239.

this book, in Chapters 5 and 6, will engage us directly with this duality of motivations for dualist (constitution-bound) democracy.

Ronald Dworkin saw his political philosophy as opposed in a fundamental respect to that of Rawls. Dworkin's objection ran to a receptiveness to moral scepticism that he thought must be lurking in Rawlsian 'political-constructivist' declarations like the following:

> The idea of approximating to moral truth has no place in a constructivist doctrine. The parties to [a fair framework political agreement] do not recognize any principle of justice as true or correct and so as antecedently given; their aim is simply to select the conception most rational for them, given their circumstances.[19]

Included in these circumstances would be any historically anchored political tradition in which the parties might find their society embedded in real political time. Dworkin apparently took exception to what he saw as a move by Rawls thus to detach from truth-claiming the basic-structural justice conception to which a country's citizenry (in their political engagements) would reciprocally appeal as a criterion of common consent. Even, insisted Dworkin, the very thesis that 'an acceptable theory of justice must be drawn from a plausible interpretation of the traditions of the community' would have to rest 'on controversial moral theories.'[20] He doubted the severability, in the end, of 'publicly reasoned' or 'political' argument from ethical argument at large, and accordingly rooted his own treatment of the topic of justice in a highly abstract, comprehensive conception of human dignity.[21]

Below, most particularly in Part III, you will find us wrestling with this sort of anti-anti-perfectionist resistance to the political-liberal ambition to drive a wedge between political fairness and moral truth. Our point for now, though, is that the resistance does not rule out convergence on a dualist conception of democracy sourced in a quest for a liberal-minded justification of democratic politics. As proof we can offer Dworkin's own extended reflection on the constitutional-interpretive work of courts of law.

[19] John Rawls, 'Kantian Constructivism in Moral Theory', in Samuel Freeman (ed.), *John Rawls: Collected Papers* (Harvard U. Press 1999) 303, 346, quoted by Dworkin in his *Justice for Hedgehogs* (Harvard U. Press 2011) 65.

[20] Ibid. 66.

[21] See Ronald Dworkin, *Is Democracy Possible Here? Principles for a New Political Debate* (Princeton U. Press 2006) 9–10.

That work, Dworkin maintained, can only proceed from the judicial interpreter's attribution to the constitution's authors of a conception of the 'upshot or point' of enacting a higher-law constitution in the first place.[22] A Rawlsian-minded judge might find that the historically embedded upshot or point of the constitutional-legal project of her country has been to provide justification—not just on the day the text is written but over some future course of political time while that text remains in place—for calls among fellow citizens for willing submission to laws with which some of them may disagree profoundly. We are imagining that judge as conversant with works of John Rawls, but you might equally imagine her (having never heard of John Rawls) as conversant with works of Ronald Dworkin. Dworkin, after all, quite explicitly proposed, as a crucial service of constitutional law to the fulfilment of a liberal political ethic, the establishment of background conditions for imbuing all citizens with a warranted sense of full 'moral membership' in the collectively self-governing political community, by which each can 'treat himself as bound together with others in a joint effort to resolve [political] question, even when his views lose'.[23] Dworkin thus pointed straight at what we are calling here a justificatory function for the constitutional law of a democracy.

John Rawls and Jürgen Habermas have famously disputed over conceptions of democracy and proceduralism.[24] Again, though, we find convergence on resort to higher-law constitutionalism for justification of democratic rule among free and equal citizens in visionary pluralist conditions. In the world of the post-Enlightenment, where 'consensus on issues of political justice can no longer be based on a settled traditional ethos that encompasses the whole of society', the sole remaining ground of law's legitimacy lies—so concludes Jürgen Habermas—in 'the democratic procedure for the production of law'.[25] We may take Habermas there to mean, by legitimacy, not a raw social fact of a population's high average submission to the force of a rule, but rather the

[22] Ronald Dworkin, *A Matter of Principle* (Harvard U. Press 1985) 35–36; see Frank I. Michelman, 'Israel's "Constitutional Revolution": A Thought from Political Liberalism' (2018) 19 Theoretical Inquiries in Law 745, 760–761. Dworkin soon thereafter would generalize the point beyond its application to 'constitutional practice' to the larger social practice known as 'law'. See Ronald Dworkin, *Law's Empire* (Harvard U. Press 1986) 66 (hereafter Dworkin, *Law's Empire*) ('[T]here must be an interpretive stage at which the interpreter settles on some general justification for the practice.... This will consist of an argument about why a practice of that general shape is worth pursuing').

[23] Ronald Dworkin, *Freedom's Law: The Moral Reading of the American Constitution* (Harvard U. Press 1996) 24–26.

[24] See Jürgen Habermas, 'Reconciliation through the Public Use of Reason' (1995) 92 Journal of Philosophy 109 (hereafter Habermas, 'Reconciliation'); John Rawls, 'Reply to Habermas' (1995) 92 Journal of Philosophy 132 (hereafter Rawls, 'Reply'); James Gordon Finlayson, *The Habermas-Rawls Debate* (Columbia U. Press 2019).

[25] Habermas, *Facts and Norms* (n. 5) 448; Habermas, 'Reasonable versus True' (n. 3) 75, 78.

virtue perceived in the rule—say, that it comes to pass through 'a rational legislative process'—by which it extends to addressees an invitation to follow the rule 'out of respect for the law'.[26] Legitimacy thus figures (as with Rawls) as *justification*—as what is aptly said in response to moral complaint—for the force of democratic law among disagreeing, free and equal citizens. Only a system whose legislative procedures measure up to a certain democratic conception, says Habermas, can provide to modern citizens a warrant which they all could have reason to accept for the deservingness of respect of their system's legislative outputs.

Habermas thus traces a presumptive respect-worthiness in the laws to the democratic character of the legislative process.[27] Along with Ackerman, Dworkin, and Rawls, he embraces a dualist differentiation between a state's ordinary laws—the ones that issue from the constituted authorities and that regulate, either directly or through lawfully established administration, people's conduct of their social and business lives—and its constitutional laws, the ones that regulate the production and implementation of the ordinaries. In response to concerns about legitimacy in ordinary laws, the Habermasian dictum passes buck to the constitutional ones. It says the ordinary laws will be observable out of respect for them as long, and only as long, as the constitution is democratic.

But if Habermas thus seems a companion-in-arms with Rawls when it comes to legitimation-by-constitution, still there is an issue between the two. Or so, at any rate, does Habermas maintain.[28] That issue comes with the problem of the need for a prior specification—at least initiatory and provisional if not final and complete—of what is to count as the democratic procedure or rational process that will ground justification for the further laws that issue therefrom. In the sight of Habermas, Rawls confronting this problem took flight to a philosophically excogitated, foundational conception ('principles of justice'); whereas Habermas, in keeping with the precept that only a democratic procedure can decide for a modern people the ground of validation for their further legislation, would offer an account to meet that demand in the form of a thesis, as he called it, on a 'co-originality' of public and private autonomy.[29] As with the issues between Rawls and Ackerman, and between Rawls and Dworkin, this one between Rawls and Habermas will figure in the exchanges: in Part I where

[26] Habermas, *Facts and Norms* (n. 5) 30–31. For further consideration of where to place Habermas in a sorting of political-legitimacy conceptions between 'sociological' and 'moral', see Frank I. Michelman, 'Legitimacy and Moral Support' (2019) 17 International Journal of Constitutional Law 1059.

[27] See Habermas, *Facts and Norms* (n. 5) 30.

[28] See Habermas, 'Reconciliation' (n. 24) 109.

[29] See e.g. Habermas, *Facts and Norms* (n. 5) 128–131 (addressing a seeming paradox of 'the emergence of legitimacy from legality').

we try together to figure out how the Habermasian co-originality thesis can possibly hold together in concept, and where Ferrara puts the foundationalist critique of Rawls to the test, finds it wanting, and finds further that, as between our two philosophers, Rawls has the superior account of a democratic grounding for a normative conception of democracy.

3. Plan of the Book

Take it, then, that ideas of legitimation-by-constitution and hence of democracy as dualist—ideas of a deflection of ground-level divisions among free and equal citizens to a higher-normative framework on which they all supposedly can find agreement—are widespread among democratic theorists of our times. We see further, though, that claims still can differ over the grounds of agreement and thus over other ends also to be met by the constitutional side of constitutional democracy. In the result, we find constitutions and constitutional law being saddled with a multiplicity of justificatory burdens. It is, in part, a confrontation with that multiplicity that has led us two, over the years, into the series of discussions recalled and extended in this book. Our puzzles have been several and our exchanges, accordingly, have passed through several iterations. While each has had its own distinct stimulus and preoccupation, we can see now how, at each stage, we were together testing the dualist-democracy idea for resilience under demand for institutional arrangements for political justice and stability in an age of irrepressible visionary plurality.

Each of the book's three Parts has its own focus. Part I centres on the enduring tension, inherent in Rawls's no less than in other accounts of democratic legitimacy, between the sovereignty of a constitution-making democratic will and the normativity of liberal rights. In its own way echoing Rawls's recollection of Locke's notion of constituent power,[30] Michelman, in a chapter assembled from work of the late 1990s, conceives of that power as always operating 'under law'. Exactly which type of normativity that recedingly abstract 'law' should be taken to instantiate—barring a recourse to natural law and rights or any other non-'political' notion—became the topic of our first round of discussion. With an eye to avoiding an infinite regress of higher and higher normative foundations, we debated the merits of a more Habermasian intimation of a discursively vindicated, 'unconditionally obligatory' reciprocity among the

[30] See Rawls, *PL* 231–232. See also Rawls, *Justice as Fairness* (n. 11) § 13.5, and 'Reply' (n. 24) 158.

consociates, on one hand, and a more Rawlsian anchoring of an equally irrecusable normativity in a standard of the 'most reasonable for us', on the other.

Part II centres on what might seem a disparate topic, that of the implications of political liberalism for judicial constitutional review. Under scrutiny is a conflict, alleged by Michelman, of two conceptions of the mandate of the highest judicial interpreter of the constitution. He says we want the court *both* to respect and confirm democratic authorship of the constitution *and* to uphold the constitution's continuing credibility as a framework for majoritarian politics that all can accept as reasonable. Michelman finds an irreconcilable tension between those two assignments. Ferrara offers to ease the tension, if not dissolve it entirely, by distinguishing between the constitution's binding normative directives and their underlying non-binding epistemic presuppositions. Michelman, sceptical about the analytical merits of that move, suggests that more promise lies in showing how the constitution's fixture as a prescriptive instrument must be presupposed by reliance on it as a procedural pact among citizens in a pluralist democracy. Finally, judicial review is revisited against the backdrop of the changing relation between the author and the interpreter of the constitution.

Part III revolves around difficulties connected with a transposition of the basics of political liberalism, including legitimation by constitution, from the domestic level to the transnational. In the opening chapter, Michelman charts six commitments that it seems must underlie any political-liberal idealization of constitution-making for a government domestic or beyond. Drawing a page from Rawls, he then considers the implications of those commitments for the basic regulation of a 'society of peoples' encompassing both liberal and some non-liberal states. Ferrara, responding, lists difficulties incurred by applications of political liberalism beyond the domestic scale, starting with the question of the status to be assigned to the basic charter for a society of peoples. Are we looking there at worldwide true principles of justice, or at a set of essentials sufficient to the legitimate exercise of powers by the society? Ascribing to Rawls the latter of those stances, Ferrara points to the ensuing need for an equivalent of the 'political conception' of justice (from which Rawls draws the domestic constitutional essentials) to fit the case of a transnational political formation encompassing non-liberal peoples. He suggests that a normative notion of humanity's flourishing, linked with a 'political conception of humanity', could fill that need. But then, says Michelman in rejoinder, we see that a Rawlsian conception for a law of peoples has a further need, and that is for a political conception of *a people*, to fill the place of the 'political conception of the person' in the domestic case. Michelman proposes a way to fulfil that need and traces some consequences. In the closing exchange, he and Ferrara debate the merits of envisaging a political formation comprising liberal and decent peoples along the lines of a 'chequerboard' or a 'multivariate' polity.

Some of this book's argumentative content (by no means all of it) could be read elsewhere if you knew where to look, in articles and book chapters we cite below. Expansions of some parts of it will, we hope, soon be readable in book-length treatments of political-liberal constitutional thought we each separately have near completion. This book, we hope, may have independent interest: as disclosure of a churn of earlier thoughts leading into more refined treatments and as exhibition of a conversation of minds in mutual and complementary engagement.

We remarked above on how we now, in retrospect, can see that at each stage of these exchanges we were together testing the dualist-democracy idea for resilience under demand for institutional arrangements for political justice and stability in an age of irrepressible visionary plurality. Typically, as we also now can see, it has been Michelman first raising doubts or questions, then Ferrara reaching for solutions into a richer philosophical toolkit than Michelman is set up to supply on his own, and then again (sometimes), Michelman not so sure that the worries have been fully put to rest. Whether this positioning in any way correlates to Michelman's primary professional location as (American) legal scholar, and Ferrara's as (European) political philosopher, we do not presume to say. We are anyway each here cheerfully trenching on the other's primary professional location.

We do not offer this book as a comprehensive treatise on legitimation-by-constitution and its problems. To the contrary, as you will see from our separate concluding reflections, the exchanges recollected here stop short of what either of us would consider resolutions of the issues at hand. We each have been separately conducting our own critical engagements with legitimation-by-constitution, and this book is offered as a testimony to the stimulations we mutually have gained from these exchanges, reflected (as we believe) in our separate works as those have developed over time.

PART I
POPULAR SOVEREIGNTY VERSUS HIGHER (AND HIGHER) LAW?

As the world heads towards the third decade of the twenty-first century, a recent upsurge of populist movements confronts constitutional-democratic regimes with claims from leaders, legislatures, cabinets, and parties to represent directly and authentically the will of the people. Even where formally unchallenged, democratic institutions then often operate in a political climate of impatience with procedural checks and other regulatory functions of constitutions. In academic circles, the constitutionalist idea of the subjection of legislation and administration to higher-legal control comes under suspicion as a device of the privileged to deflect or impede the people's will as expressed in fair elections. Thus has become most acutely visible the tension locked in the heart of constitutional democracy, between popular sovereignty as the touchstone of the legitimacy of political rule, and the notion that any true sovereignty, or any legitimate one, must operate within normative tracks that constrain it.

It is with all of that on our minds that we now recall the earliest round in the exchanges composing this book. It was seeded by a cluster of Michelman's writings from the late 1990s.[1] Parts of it appeared in print in 2006 in book form, in Czech translation.[2] The chapters in this Part I draw heavily from our respective contributions to that volume, aiming to recapture the substance of our exchange as it stood as of that time. We have done some rewriting with a view to

[1] Frank I. Michelman, 'Human Rights and the Limits of Constitutional Theory' (2000) 12 Ratio Juris 63; Frank I. Michelman, 'Morality, Identity, and Constitutional Patriotism' (1999) 76 Denver University Law Review 1009 (hereafter Michelman, 'Constitutional Patriotism'); Frank I. Michelman, 'How Can the People Ever Make the Laws? A Critique of Deliberative Democracy', in James Bohman and William Rehg (eds), *Deliberative Democracy* (MIT Press 1997) 145 (hereafter Michelman, 'How Can the People'); Frank I. Michelman, 'Review of *Between Facts and Norms*' (1996) 93 J. Phil. 307–315; Frank I. Michelman, 'Can Constitutional Democrats Be Legal Positivists? Or, Why Constitutionalism?' (1996) 2 Constellations 293; Frank I. Michelman, 'Always Under Law?' (1995) 12 Constitutional Commentary 227 (hereafter Michelman, 'Always Under Law').

[2] See Frank I. Michelman and Alessandro Ferrara, *Polemika o ústave* (CAS, Institute of Philosophy 2006).

focus and clarity, but have not tried to update or correct our thoughts from that time so as to bring them into line with exactly what we might rather say today.

Michelman had proposed that, in constitutional-democratic thought, all acts of lawmaking—emphatically *not* excluding the production of a country's nominal highest ranking positive law, its constitution—were necessarily to be understood as implementations of some still higher law already in place. Michelman called that 'the judgment view' of constitutional or higher lawmaking. Reflecting on the judgment view's connection to liberal-theoretic hopes for legitimation-by-constitution (see this book's Introduction), Michelman concluded that the view is not directly compelled by the hopes, but rather follows only when to the judgment view is coupled a democracy-based commitment to popular sovereignty, and thence to popular-political authorship of a country's constitution or basic law.

Michelman then went on, though, to find in this combination of assignments to the constitution—to serve as both a platform for political justification and a supposed expression of a particular people's higher-legislative will—a problem of mutual compatibility. He further suggested that a rising interest at that time in conceptions of political democracy as both 'deliberative' and 'deep'—of deliberative democracy going (as we might say) 'all the way down [or up]' in the hierarchy of laws—could be read as an intended, if itself problematic, solution to the compatibility problem.

Chapter 1 now following draws from Michelman's writings of that period—1995–2000—in order to present to the reader Michelman's thoughts as of that time regarding (i) the liberal attraction to legitimation-by-constitution, (ii) an apparent tension between that attraction and a democratic attraction to popular sovereignty understood as a particular people's own ultimate authorship of the highest laws of their country, and (iii) an inability of ideas of deep, deliberative democracy to resolve that tension without a resulting problematic implication of a regress of ever-and-ever higher laws. It was these writings that drew Ferrara's responsive commentary in *Justice and Judgment* (1999), later restated by him for our joint book of 2006, the substance of which comes below in section 2 of Chapter 2.

Feeling himself committed (democratically) to the credible authorship of even the very highest laws of a country by that country's people, and (liberally) to legitimation-by-constitution, Ferrara draws in Chapter 2 from two sources—a classical differentiation between ideas of a people qua 'ethnos' and qua 'demos', and a modern philosophical-constructivist account of the 'singular laws' entailed in judgements of aesthetic validity—in order to meet two challenges presented by Michelman. Ferrara aims thereby both to chart an avenue of relief of deep, deliberative democracy from the regress baggage with which Michelman had saddled it, and also to explain how a democracy possibly could claim justification for its laws, among free and equal citizens in conditions of reasonable pluralism, without appeal to some trans-political ('modern universalist') postulation of the basics of political right and wrong. In Chapter 3, Michelman then recalls his own reading (*circa* 1999) of some work by Jürgen Habermas, as a path of mediation between democracy's call for a politically immanent basic law and the contrary-seeming universalist implications of ideas of political justification among citizens in conflict over the most basic rights and wrongs of politics.

That response by Michelman in fact comprised the concluding chapter of our volume of 2006. In Chapter 4 below, newly written for this book, Ferrara now points out how the political constructivism of John Rawls, with its ideas of the politically reasonable and most reasonable 'for us', might have served equally with Habermas (if not in preference to Habermas) as our guide at that time towards a solution to that dilemma. Chapter 4 thus opens the way towards the subsequent exchanges comprising Parts II and III of the present book

1

'Always Under Law?'

Frank I. Michelman

1. 'Always Under Law?' A Question of How in Fact we Think

By the expression 'popular sovereignty', we generally mean the special prerogative of a country's people to make the laws of their country be whatever in fact the people from time to time decide by due and fair deliberation, no further questions asked.[1] I will suggest, however, that this notion's deeper signification, for liberal-minded adherents to democracy of the constitutional kind, is of a wish to believe something like the opposite: that whoever at any time actually does lay down higher law to the country does so in a spirit of answering to some prior established, popularly generated, limiting conception of rightness in politics. I claim that adherents to constitutional democracy always and necessarily conceive higher lawmaking to be itself, in that sense, 'under law', problematic as such a conception must be. Problematic, because if even the highest politics of a country have necessarily to be understood as an application of *a given people's own* antecedent law, then what becomes of liberal hopes for justification through that higher law of expectations of willing compliance, by deeply dissenting free and equal citizens, with ground-level laws issued by democratic majorities, in conditions of reasonable pluralism?

[1] The material in this chapter is newly arranged from publications by Michelman in the period 1995–2000, see articles cited in n. 2. I have selected and combined the material so as to make an orderly and unified presentation of the lines of thought that would later be attracting Ferrara's attention, omitting portions extraneous to the topics of ensuing exchanges and avoiding redundancies across the articles. Using mainly passages drawn straight from the articles (sometimes amended for clarity, brevity, or consistency of expression), I have aimed to present my grasp, as of that time, of the ideas of 'legitimation-by-constitution' and of the 'judgment view' of higher lawmaking, and then my claims regarding

- the judgment view's necessary implication from popular sovereignty,
- a tension of that implication (and hence of popular sovereignty) with legitimation-by-constitution,
- a resulting resort to ideas of deep deliberative democracy, and
- that resort's problem of a seeming infinite regress of high (and higher) laws.

Legitimation by Constitution. Alessandro Ferrara and Frank I. Michelman, Oxford University Press. © Alessandro Ferrara and Frank I. Michelman 2021. DOI: 10.1093/oso/9780192855121.003.0002

Constitutional democrats find themselves in this delicate position insomuch as we think that only through a constitution both popularly given and politically transcendent can our scheme of government be justified. By 'our scheme', here, I mean nothing more specific than what (say) John Rawls means by 'constitutional democracy'—that is, our familiar broad model of a governmental order based on majority rule, representative government, and higher-law limitation. My aim here [that is, in these writings of 1995–2000] is to catch hold of, to look into, habitual thoughtways and conceptualizations that enter quietly and unselfconsciously, if also perhaps sometimes problematically, into people's intuitive convictions that constitutional democracy thus understood is an apt broad model for schemes of government for a society of beings conditioned and situated as we every-daily think we are.

2. 'Justification by Constitution'

A Division of Justificatory Labour (The Constitution as Justificatory Platform)

Somehow or other, sooner or later, liberal democrats have to justify expectations for normal compliance by free and equal dissenting citizens with mandatory edicts issued by political majorities. To those who affirm the existential primacy of individuals and the surpassing value or dignity attached to the rational agency of each, justification seemingly must mean, at the very least, a finding of approvability in principle by everyone affected by a law. It must mean that all of the persons subject to the range of the governmental force in question should be able to see that they severally have what are actually, for them as individuals, good enough reasons to consent to exertions of that force.

Perhaps, though, we needn't demand such a showing for every single law as it comes along. Perhaps, for most such enactments, it suffices to show that they have followed properly from the terms of a prior, government-chartering political act that itself supposedly can claim everyone's agreement. A division of political acts into the higher constitutive and the ground-level ordinary thus may allow for concentration of liberal demands for universal reasonable acceptability on the former, while allowing ground-level acts then to be justified derivatively, by showing how they issued from a universally acceptable set of basic organizing requirements.

Such a division of justificatory labour into higher/constitutional and ordinary caters for liberal striving, in the face of inauspicious social conditions—societal immensity, complexity, and anonymity combined with irreducible plurality and conflict of considered political opinions—to preserve a sense of the consensually justified character of political government. These conditions evidently preclude the possibility of country-wide agreement on the moral and other merits of the sundry, compromised legal-policy choices that day-to-day government must make. By positing a higher tier of relatively abstract, regulative rules and standards for the conduct of that daily government, we may hope to have opened the possibility of country-wide agreement or agreement-in-principle—or something like that or approaching it or standing in for it—on the political merit, including the fairly arguable consonance with everyone's interests, of at least this basic charter for government.[2]

The Requisite Character as 'Law' of the Higher-Regulatory Platform

What stands, in this picture, to be justified (or not) is not simply the idea in general of coercive government. It is also, necessarily, something relatively more concrete, a specifically identifiable practice of government here and now in place. It is for *this practice* that there is to be observably in force a determinately correspondent scheme of authorizing constitutional directives that supposedly, in their turn, can merit everyone's agreement. But then the putative holders of reasons for consent to *this* authorizing scheme must themselves, with the same sort of relative concreteness, be envisaged as members of the population of the country in question. Political justification *to them* must then entail the establishment of reasons why *this* people (these people)—in their conditions as they make them out given their ways of understanding self, freedom, society, and value—can reasonably and rationally see that they and all their fellows have for submitting to *this* constitutive scheme observably in force over them.

Along with this requisite, relative concreteness of political-justificatory reason goes the demand for *a law* for government to be under, insofar as we mean by 'law' a sensibly unified and consistent set of public, durable, antecedently binding principles to govern all determinations of matters coming within their scope of application. These demands for unity, publicity, durability, and antecedence of the regulatory higher norms are there because to

[2] Michelman in later work would highlight the 'procedural' character of this idea. See e.g. Frank I. Michelman, '"Constitution (Written or Unwritten)": Legitimacy and Legality in the Thought of John Rawls' (2018) 31 Ratio Juris 379. He did not do so, though, in the writings of 1995–2000.

permit power-wielding officials or popular majorities to resolve or modify them on the fly (so to speak) would be, in effect, to set loose the exercise of governmental power from any higher-constitutive scheme whose actual establishment in the here and now an actual people could supposedly cite to each other as a sufficient ground for supporting in general the acts of government that issue from it. In order to serve in such a role, the constitutional justificatory platform must be fixed, as a law is fixed, into the country's institutional firmament.

That conclusion does not yet answer, though, the question of whether this kind of law—the country's government-chartering law, whose justified character is to be inheritable by specific acts of government that issue from it—must itself be under law.

Why 'Always Under Law'?

I have already briefly described the 'always under law' thesis. In order more fully to set it forth, I need to stipulate a pair of definitions. Let us, therefore, understand 'constitutional essentials' (I draw the term from John Rawls) to mean higher-legal provisions for the structure and process of government—votes and elections, allocations of powers among branches and offices, and so forth—and also for limits and constraints upon government as a whole, including basic 'rights and liberties that [government] is to respect'.[3] It is on the putative wide acceptability of the country's scheme of constitutional essentials that liberal hopes for legitimation-by-constitution are to rest. The term 'higher lawmaking' will refer, then, in the first place to (i) events of legislation of a country's scheme of constitutional essentials. But not to these events only: also to whatever events we may envisage of (ii) legislation of standards to govern type (i) lawmaking, or (iii) legislation of standards to govern type (ii) lawmaking, or (iv) ... etc. *ad inf.* (So type $n + 1$ lawmaking is always 'higher' than type n.) Then the 'always under law' thesis is this: constitutional-democratic thought is always taking for granted that whoever is engaged in higher lawmaking for a country (and I don't care how high up the n's you want to go) is, in that engagement, answering to some still higher law that is already there, in place; for every $n + m$ there is an $n + m + 1$.

Does this seemingly paradoxical taking-for-granted (where does the regress end?) follow inexorably from the hope for legitimation-by-constitution?

[3] Rawls, *PL* 227.

It does not. In the bare idea of the constitution as platform for justification of controversial ground-level legislation, there is nothing yet to support this deduction of a regress of higher and higher laws. The bare idea fits neatly to those classical forms of liberal constitutional thought that posit, from the start, a foundational set of universal, human ('natural') substantive rights, to which any and every justified government must, by stipulation, conform. Yes, those posited anchoring rights may themselves include a right of persons (say) to equal political enfranchisement. But then that right would itself be coming out of some prior stage of foundational reasoning about political rightness. At that foundational stage, whenever we reach it, any regress would stop.[4]

So it is not—at any rate, it is not solely—the constitutional (liberal) side of the complex idea of constitutional democracy from which flows the pressure for the regress of 'always under law'. That pressure must rather be traceable to the democratic side. In the following section, we trace it to popular sovereignty.

3. Popular Sovereignty

Popular sovereignty signifies government not only for the people but by the people, the condition of a populace living under a regime of laws that they themselves collectively make or adopt. Popular sovereignty, accordingly, conceives of higher lawmaking events as deliberate acts of a capital-P People legislating. What is more, the idea envisions a People legislating not only to the official agents—parliaments, presidents, courts—whom they license by their higher lawmaking acts, but to themselves as the selfsame (self-governing) People as those who legislate.

A People legislating a constitution legislate to themselves, qua People. They do so at least insomuch as every constitution (worthy of the name) is a law containing a special binding rule about how itself—starting with this special rule for revision—may be revised. Apparent, then, is a dimension of

[4] Perhaps a look-alike thesis to 'always under law' can be formulated for the classical foundational view. The nominal ledger of universal natural rights—so the thought would run—must be kept underdeterminative for any given country's constitution, because the concrete particulars for a constitution to fulfil these rights must vary according to local historical, cultural, etc. conditions. If we then fall back on some intermediately abstract (say, regionally differentiated) set of semi-concrete standards to govern the ultimately concrete formations of constitutional schemes, we will again face the same need. At higher and higher levels, these increasingly abstract-universal sets of standards (to govern selection among lower-level sets of standards) will approach asymptotically, without ever reaching, the ultimate abstract-universal—the at-the-last ineffably abstract and universal—ledger of natural rights. (We will approach the point, say, of 'a right to justification', see Rainer Forst, *The Right to Justification*, tr. Jeffrey Flynn (Columbia U. Press 2012).

political freedom that we both attribute to the chartering People and deny to the People as thus chartered—that is, the freedom to set procedures of higher lawmaking. The charterers ('We the people of the United States') thus seem to stand on a different plane of authority from the chartered ('our posterity'), as creators to creatures. How is it possible to construe such an event as one of self-government?

For a People to be self-governing means for them to legislate to themselves as the self-same People as those who legislate. This means that the lawmaking act emanates from a People whose collective character or political identity continues through the process of enactment undissolved and self-identical but also, by the same token, pre-exists the process.[5] We need to say, then, what it is we think confers political identities on empirical human aggregates, identities of a sort that allows us to check for the sameness of the identities of the People who lay down constitutional law and the People to whom it is laid down. What do we think this people-constituting, identity-fixing factor could possibly be? Must it not finally come down to an attitude of expectation or commitment shared by constituent members of the putative capital-P People? Of expectation of the presence among them of some substantially contentful normative like-mindedness, or at the very least of commitment to searching out the possibility of this? An expectation of, or commitment to, some cultural or dispositional or experiential commonality from which they can together try to distil some substantially contentful idea of political reason or right?

Think, now, about how matters look from the standpoint of the People on the downstream side of an event of higher lawmaking. As a self-governing people, *they* cannot accept law from anyone save themselves. But it seems they can know themselves as themselves—can know themselves as, so to speak, a collective political self—only by knowing themselves as a group of sharers, joint participants in some already present, contentful idea, or proto-idea, of political reason or right. This means they can know their lawgivers as legitimate—as sharing political identity with them—only through the lawgivers' perceived or supposed participation in some political-regulative idea that's sufficiently distinct to be identifiable—identifiable, that is, as the same one as theirs. A population's conception of itself as self-governing, as legislating law to itself, depends on its sense of its members as, in their higher lawmaking acts,

[5] Compare Bruce Ackerman, *We the People: Foundations* (Harvard U. Press 1991) 204 (hereafter Ackerman, *Foundations*). Ackerman writes, it seems to me paradoxically, of 'an entire People . . . break[ing] with its past and construct[ing] a new political identity for itself'.

commonly and continuously inspired by and aspiring to some distinct regulative idea of political justice and right—*but always, too, an idea that itself has sprung from the politics of the selfsame self-governing People.*

Whoever, as constitutional democrat, attributes higher (and higher) lawmaking to a country's 'People themselves'[6] is thus barred from a view of higher-legal events as total-revolutionary or as writing on a clean slate. Higher law for constitutional democrats must always be a product of a political process or event that itself is framed by some already present idea of political reason or right, which itself is likewise such a product. When the higher lawmakers are conceived to be the people themselves, the law that even the highest politics is under must itself be understood as an application of that people's own antecedent law. But—and here is where the trouble starts—by *that* conclusion we may seem to be dashing liberal hopes for justification, through some politically transcendent higher law, of expectations of compliance by free and equal citizens with laws issued by democratic majorities over steadfast minority dissent.

4. Democracy in Depth

A Problem of Deliberative Democracy

To that trouble comes as possible relief the procedural ideal of democratic deliberation or public reasoning. Deliberative democracy, as advanced by thinkers such as Jürgen Habermas, is 'deep' democracy in the following twofold sense. First, it conditions a legislative product's approvability by everyone not just on its verifiable compliance with whatever set of higher-law directives may then be in force (which we may assume will include requirements for the formally democratic character of the ground-level lawmaking regime), but on manifest reasonability in the course of production itself. The call is for lawmaking whose combined organizational, motivational, and discursive attributes are such, we judge, as to qualify or help qualify its legislative product as approvable in the right way by all who stand to be affected. Second, deep deliberative democracy seeks its ultimate authorization not from political-moral axioms that we start out by accrediting as right, or from political-moral authority that we start out by accrediting as warranted, but rather on the basis that the deliberative democratic

[6] See *The Federalist* No. 40; Ackerman, *Foundations* (n. 5) 177–178, 192.

procedure is itself a validity condition for political-moral reasoning or authority in the first place. *No* reasoning in this field is accreditable as sound, and *no* authority is accreditable as warranted, that does not itself already show deliberative-democratic provenance or credentials.

The good news, then, from the deliberative-democracy side is that *as long as* (say) a set of constitutional essentials *can* be seen to have come out of a procedure we can recognize as deliberative-democratic, that quasi-procedural fact will give everyone reason to accept the result and, along with it, ground-level legislation that conforms to its terms. In that way, deliberative democracy offers itself as an answer to the puzzle of how a constitution sprung from popular political authorship can possibly serve as a platform of justification to all free and equal citizens for the force of ground-level laws. It also, though, by the same token, adds its own bite to the impossibility concerns that gnaw at the root of this chapter.

There is something in this regulative idea of deep deliberative democracy that apparently renders the practical pursuit of it impossible. By that, I do not mean merely that the motivational and discursive demands of deliberative democracy, once we have them more fully specified, will prove to be such that we must realistically expect to see them often failing to be met in practice. What I rather have in mind is that this idea is so framed as to set going a regress of imperatives such that no programme could be devised for its pursuit that we could ever possibly set going. If, say, someone told you to write a book whose every chapter begins with the terminal sentence of an immediately preceding chapter, your problem wouldn't be one of inability to carry the task through to completion, but rather one of inability to begin it.

Again (as with the 'always under law' thesis), I point out that what sets this regress going is *not* the political-liberal proposal for legitimation-by-constitution. *That* proposal may doubtless be read to allow that only a constitution *for* a democracy could possibly claim assent from all citizens reasonable and rational. It does not, however, say that only a constitution *itself democratically produced* can hope to meet that test. It contains, in itself, no explanation for why a constitution excogitated by a Solon, a Lycurgus, or a John Rawls could not meet that standard, in what Rawls would call a wide and general reflective equilibrium spread among citizens of a given country at a given time. In order, then, to complete our construction of the deep-democratic view of political rightness, we need still to find out what prompts that view's resistance to a *non*-deep-democratic—sometimes called a 'rights-foundationalist'—idea of political rightness.

Sourcing the Problem: The Claim for Deep Democracy

Jürgen Habermas declares that 'the democratic procedure for the production of law evidently forms the only postmetaphysical source of legitimacy'.[7] On his account, the legitimacy-conferring characteristic of a constitutional law—the characteristic in virtue of which the law exerts upon all within range of its force a claim to rational acceptability—is and can only be a procedurally constructed characteristic: only those fundamental laws are legitimate that might claim the agreement of all citizens in a discursive process equally open to all. Now, *that* claimable agreement may be hypothetical or in-principle, a matter subject to judgement by you or by me. In the view of Habermas, however a *valid* judgement that all do indeed have reason to agree can arise only against the background of an *actual* democratic-discursive forum to which the question is at all times submissible. Only such constant submissibility to actual democratic-discursive re-examination can sustain a 'presumption' of fair results.[8]

That does carry us to the verge of an explanation for the deep-democracy demand, even from within a liberal-minded view of political rightness to which a rights-foundationalist position initially seems so congenial. The crucial proposition is that no political philosopher or lawgiver, unaided by actual live dialogic encounter with the full range of affected others, can reliably presume to see and appraise a set of proposed fundamental laws as all those others will reasonably and justifiably see and appraise them. No unaided internal effort of empathy can suffice to answer the question of universal reasonable approvability of the fundamental laws, reliably enough to pass the test of legitimacy on which depends the rightness of a coercion-backed political regime.[9] '[I]ndividual private rights,' Habermas writes in one exemplary passage,

[7] Jürgen Habermas, *Between Facts and Norms: Contributions to a Discourse Theory of Law and Democracy*, tr. William Rehg (MIT Press 1996) 448 (hereafter Habermas, *Facts and Norms*). This section and the one following incorporate passages from Michelman, 'How Can the people' (n. 1) 160–162 and 165–166, included here with the kind permission of the MIT Press. These sections recapitulate a debate that was later described in detail, ably and critically, by Ciaran Cronin, 'On the Possibility of a Democratic Constitutional Founding: Habermas and Michelman in Dialogue' (2006) 19 Ratio Juris 342 (hereafter Cronin, 'Dialogue').

[8] Habermas, *Facts and Norms* (n. 7) 32, 147.

[9] Cronin reports the view of Habermas as follows:

> [U]nless citizens have a say in the process by which their rights are translated into law, and especially in how their needs and interests are defined in descriptions of social 'problems' in need of regulation, they can have no assurance that their liberties will in fact be protected. Thus, processes of legislation and policy-making can inspire confidence in the legitimacy of the resulting laws and regulations in their addressees, including outvoted minorities, only on the condition that they are based on public discussion and debate which is conducted in such a way that it fosters informed and balanced opinions on matters of public interest. And, conversely, citizens can only develop and freely exercise the rational capacities which enable them to make informed judgments on matters of public concern when they enjoy the freedom from manipulation, coercion, constraint, and violence which can only be secured

> cannot even be adequately formulated, let alone politically implemented, if those affected have not first engaged in public discussions to clarify which features are relevant in treating typical cases as alike or different, and then mobilized communicative power for the consideration of their newly interpreted needs.[10]

Only by actual democratic discourses, Habermas apparently means, can we attend to possibilities of the sort described by Nancy Fraser:

> that biases might become apparent in even what have been thought to be relatively neutral forms of discourse; that such forms could themselves become stakes in political deliberation; that subordinated groups could contest such forms and propose alternatives, and thereby gain a measure of collective control over the means of interpretation and communication.[11]

These possibilities explain why Habermas thinks that, as a condition of political legitimacy, 'consociates under law must be able to *examine* whether a contested norm could meet with the agreement of all those possibly affected'[12]—why only *an actual* available process of deeply democratic scrutiny can begin to justify a presumption of fair results.

We would have before us, then, what we may call a strong normative version of an epistemic theory of democracy. By an epistemic theory, I mean a theory that cites, as one reason for favouring democratic procedures, a supposed tendency in such procedures to reach outcomes approximating to procedure-independent standards of political rightness or justice.[13] An epistemic-democracy theory is a 'strong normative' one when it goes beyond offering the claimed epistemic virtues of democratic-discursive procedures as a functional argument in favour of their use, to the further point of asserting that a political system that omits them fails for that reason alone (never mind the consequences) to produce legitimate laws and fails, therefore, to be a morally defensible system. Strong normative-epistemic considerations are the only

> by the individual liberties. Thus, on a deliberative conception of democracy, neither the enjoyment of individual liberties nor the opportunity to participate in processes of political self-determination can claim priority; rather, each is a necessary precondition of the other. (Cronin, 'Dialogue' (n. 7) 347)

[10] Habermas, *Facts and Norms* (n. 7) 450.
[11] Nancy Fraser, 'Toward a Discourse Ethic of Solidarity' (1986) 5 Praxis International 425, 425–426.
[12] Habermas, *Facts and Norms* (n. 7) 104.
[13] So I wrote in 1997. For doubts about whether this applies to Habermas, see Cronin, 'Dialogue' (n. 7) 352–353.

motivation I have been able to find for our unlikely-seeming combination of an individualistically liberal view of political rightness with an unrestricted binding of political right reason to democratic process, 'all the way up' the hierarchy of legal norms.

A Residue of Regress

According to the strong-normative epistemic-democratic view, the moral justification of legal-systemic coercion requires that the most fundamental legal resolutions of the regime have been and remain visibly exposed to the test of an actual and proper democratic debate—one that has not only addressed itself to the right question (say, is this law one to which, hypothetically, all citizens might rationally be expected to agree in an ideally democratic discourse?) but that also is itself an instance of such a discourse, or at any rate is open to all in some normatively requisite sense.

But *whether* the basic-law resolutions have been and remain so exposed is itself the sort of basic-law question for which an answer is required already, in order to instil the procedure used to resolve *that question* with the very epistemic virtue that is supposed to make the resolution validity-conferring and hence morally mandatory. As Habermas himself arrestingly puts the matter, a validity-conferring procedure of democratic examination of the laws is one 'that is itself legally constituted'.[14] If so, if it takes a legally constituted democratic procedure to bring forth valid fundamental laws, then the (valid) laws that frame *this* lawmaking event must themselves be the product of a conceptually prior procedural event that itself was framed by (valid) laws that must, as such, have issued in their turn from a still prior (properly) legally constituted event. And so on, it would appear, without end: 'The idea of the rule of law sets in motion a spiraling self-application of law.'[15] 'The citizens themselves ... decide how they must fashion the rights that give the discourse principle legal shape as a principle of democracy.... They make an originary use of a civic autonomy that thereby constitutes itself in a performatively self-referential manner.'[16] But then the question must be: where in history can this 'originary' constitutive moment ever be anchored? Granting that it is necessary, how may it be possible?

[14] Habermas, *Facts and Norms* (n. 7), 110; see ibid. 454–455, 458.
[15] Ibid. 39; see ibid. 83 (on 'the paradoxical emergence of legitimacy out of legality').
[16] Ibid. 128.

5. Alleviations

First Ending: Luckily Thrown? *(In Medias Res)*

Here we already are, living under a set of fundamental laws (those of us who luckily are) that we as inhabitants of this very legal culture reasonably construe as an intentional, if always necessarily imperfect, approximation to the ideal of an endlessly cycling resubmission to the critical rigours of democratically constituted public discourses (themselves correspondingly evolving), of the very laws that for the sake of political rightness have to constitute those discourses as democratic (their constituents as free and equal, and so on).[17] Granting that no one could ever have held a democratic warrant for setting the project off on its first iteration, that truth wouldn't disable *us*, in our lucky situation, from doing our parts to carry the project on. We could not perfectly confidently pronounce our ongoing and evolving political practice to be issuing in just or legitimate results, because we would know that no acculturated denizen of *this* ostensibly deliberative-democratic practice could presume to know that the practice had not for some time been spiralling off in a wrong direction due to some bias of the kind that Nancy Fraser compellingly warns that no human flesh can ever surely evade. Might our doing our parts to uphold and advance the practice nevertheless be what rightness requires of liberals? Might liberal rightness in politics after all consist in our honest best bet on the justice-tending characteristics of an (arguably) extant fundamental lawmaking procedure?

Liberal conviction tells us that (i) we need a system of coercive laws, and (ii) there are such things as truly just and truly unjust laws and legal systems. Liberal modesty tells us that none of us knows certainly and fully what just and unjust laws and systems concretely are for our society here and now, and that we cannot look for agreement on what they are (even after casting out all the 'unreasonable' opinions), specifically enough to describe a workably concrete set of constitutive laws for our country. But we do (so might run the thought) have overlapping inklings of some general contours of just institutions, and what we already have going seems to us as likely to carry us in the right direction as anything else we are just now able realistically to propose. Perhaps we, as liberals, are fated to have to be ready, sometimes, to accept as morally binding—as a kind of 'political' but not 'comprehensive' truth—inherited fundamental-law resolutions that we can see to be in some material degree deviant from justice,

[17] Michelman's writings from the period in question seem to have issued in two alternative proposals for response to the possibility question. We present both of them here.

while seeing also that those resolutions are ensconced in a nest of historical events of politics that we judge to be reasonably defensible as justice-tending and justice-seeking.

We cannot here try to settle whether proceeding in that way truly is what anyone morally ought to do.

Second Ending: Sovereignty as Jurisdiction?

From to time to time, Americans hear proposals for an amendment to our Constitution to reverse our Supreme Court's currently standing interpretations of it to bar prosecutions for politically expressive burnings of American flags.[18] Suppose there were actually to occur a formal act of constitutional amendment to such an effect. Suppose further we would construe that act—as I have argued is the necessary implication of constitutional-democratic thought—to reflect a kind of legal-like judgment on the American people's part, a purported application by them of an American ultimate law or proto-law of which any extant 'Constitution of the United States' is but a currently standing implementation. Would it then necessarily follow that our courts of law might properly refuse to give effect to the formal act of amendment, on the ground (should such be the judicial judgment) that the act was legally erroneous, a misapplication of an ultimate American law?

That would not follow. To say that a question is one to be settled by application of a publicly established norm antecedently grounded in the politics of a country—that the question is in that sense 'under law'—is not to say that the application falls within the authoritative keeping of any particular tribunal. To the contrary, divisions and hierarchies of judicial jurisdiction are commonplace in our legal systems. Take again the flag-burning controversy in the United States. No lower-level bench of judges here can properly set aside our Supreme Court's interpretations of the extant Constitution to bar prosecutions for politically expressive flag-burnings. With full internal consistency, all the following could then also be true, according to the best conception of our constitutional democracy: (i) that the extant Constitution is the highest law within the Supreme Court's ken; but also (ii) that this law is itself 'under law', and (iii) that the law it is under is one to be construed and applied by, and only by, a different court: say, a court of the People themselves.

[18] See *United States v. Eichman*, 496 U.S. 310 (1990); *Texas v. Johnson*, 497 U.S. 397 (1989).

If a constitutional-democratic people saw fit to reserve certain applications and ministrations of higher-legal content away from the law courts and exclusively to a tribunal of the People, would it not, then, in the end be that jurisdictional reservation itself that finally seals the constitutional-democratic premise of popular sovereignty? Not 'sovereign is who decides the exception', but rather 'sovereign are they in whom jurisdiction in the higher matters reposes'. In the ambiguity that always must lurk at the boundary between acts of interpretation of higher-law norms and acts of origination of those norms—in the knowledge that secondary acts of interpretation cannot always be held securely distinct from originary acts of legislation—we see taking shape a reason for such a jurisdictional reservation by any would-be sovereign people.

As long as an appointed judiciary confines itself to applying higher-legal norms legislated by the People, popular self-government persists. Should higher norm-*origination*, however, itself ever fall into the hands of judicial appointees, popular self-government will to that extent have perished. Now, in constitutional-democratic thought, do-overs of higher-normative materials simply are not all readily and cleanly divisible between the categories of norm-application and norm-origination. Some of them may rather look like being both (or being equivocally the one or the other)—but both (or either) in such a way that criticism of them can be no proper business of an appointed judiciary. In the sight of American judicial officers, I am suggesting, a flag-desecration amendment should be received as the People's act of norm-origination—even as, in the sight of a citizenry always claiming self-government, it is to be construed as an interpretive act.

Such a splitting of the difference makes sense if and to the extent that we take what the People amending the Constitution to be ultimately engaged in interpreting is no less *themselves* than it is their law—themselves, that is, as a People who take themselves to be committed to the project of governing themselves by a law that they themselves have uttered. In such a light, we can see how adoption of a flag-desecration amendment can be regarded, from the standpoint of citizen action, as interpretive and secondary, an act of following what is already there, but from the standpoint of judicial officers as sovereignly originary and beyond criticism. *Self*-interpretation is something that no one but the subject can finally do. Of course, the subject can get it wrong. The validity of a people's self-interpretation is always open to criticism by historians, philosophers, and other social critics. Unless and until such interventions bring the people themselves around, however, there is no way a *legal* supervisor can credibly overrule the People's solemn declaration of self-understanding.

It hardly needs saying that we deal here with counterfactuals. Few believe that the American people considering a flag-desecration amendment will have been engaged in a morally backgrounded ethical discourse. Few claim much understanding of how 'the people' of such a huge, plural, diverse, divided country could ever possibly be so engaged—without, at any rate, a much deeper, richer, more considerate, more widely engaging background political culture, or political public sphere, than there is now any sign of in the United States.

But the counterfactuality of it does not mean that a certain vision of what higher lawmaking must be or consist in cannot in fact be sunk into constitutional-democratic political thought. In asking how people in fact think about government, we must leave open the possibility that they think about it in ways that are themselves counterfactual—idealizing, imaginative, utopian—much more so than they usually notice or admit. It is in that spirit that I suggest that the notion of popular sovereignty in our political thought, although usually taken to express the idea that the people have the right to make the law be whatever they in fact decide, is also, at the same time, an expression of a wish to believe something like the opposite.

2

On the Paradox of Deliberative Democracy

Alessandro Ferrara

Democracy in ancient times meant the rule of the people, the section of the population possessed of citizenship. The rule of the people was not tempered by rights. A sudden turn of the will of citizens could consign you to the fate of Socrates, or you might end up ostracized. Ever since the rise of the modern idea of rights, as inalienable prerogatives of individuals, and their codification in bills of rights and constitutions, democracy has had to sustain a tension between its aspect of rule by the will of the citizens and its aspect of rule by laws that constitute as citizens the persons on the scene.

Frank Michelman is among the constitutional theorists who have contributed most creatively to shed light on the central tension of constitutional democracy, between popular sovereignty and government under law, and to excogitate ways of allaying it. In this chapter, my aim is (a) to reconstruct Michelman's understanding of this tension; (b) to discuss some implications of his posit, as a necessary implication of popular sovereignty, of an identity of 'the People as charterers and the People as chartered'; (c) to probe further and rethink the meaning of that identity; and, finally, (d) to reconfigure Michelman's groundbreaking view of constituent power as 'always under law' in such a way as to defuse the infinite regress in which deliberative-democratic theorists may entangle themselves when they embrace the ideal of a democratic self-constitution of a People.

1. 'Legitimation by Constitution' and the Paradox of Deliberative Democracy

Michelman's theory of constitutional democracy focuses on a paradoxical problem of compatibility or 'possibility'. A democratic country's body of constitutional law is assigned to fulfil simultaneously two functions: (a) to serve as a public platform of justification for the force of majoritarian laws among free

Legitimation by Constitution. Alessandro Ferrara and Frank I. Michelman, Oxford University Press. © Alessandro Ferrara and Frank I. Michelman 2021. DOI: 10.1093/oso/9780192855121.003.0003

and equal citizens in deep disagreement over the morality and policy of those laws, and (b) to serve as a true warrant of popular sovereignty—namely, of government of the country by the people of that country. These two functions are at least in tension, if not in outright contradiction, with each other. Over the last quarter-century, as he further points out, a political-theoretic turn towards deliberative democracy has come to be considered a solution to such tension or paradox. Michelman's most groundbreaking contribution concerns that new theoretical turn towards what he calls 'deep democracy': the 'possibility problem' emerges in full force, in the form of deep democracy's projection of an infinite regress of higher and higher laws for which Michelman sees no way to ever be anchored in the actual history of any country. I follow and accept Michelman's argument all the way through to that final step, but then suggest that his theory of constituent power as 'always under law' offers a strategy for a sort of historical anchoring of justification-bearing constitutional laws that can rightly be attributed to the political will of the people.

Michelman and I start from the shared premise that any sensible view of constitutional democracy must incorporate not only Rawls's fact of reasonable pluralism, but also an account of the 'inauspicious conditions'—as Michelman has called them—that the classical liberal ideal of government by consent is bound to be affected by in contemporary society. More specifically, the idea of government by consent must meet four challenges: (a) the sheer extension of the body politic in complex societies, (b) the complexity of the institutional order, (c) the anonymous character of the processes of political will formation, and (d) the irreducibility of cultural pluralism.[1]

Just as the acceptance of the fact of reasonable pluralism consisted, for Rawls, in acknowledging that it is extremely unlikely, in free societies, that basic disagreements about the good life will ever cease to exist, so confrontation with the inauspicious conditions leads to the realization that it is extremely unlikely that legitimation might ever cover every institutional aspect of a political order and every political act accomplished by its officials. Given that understanding, then, any theory of democracy that wishes to remain faithful to the ideal of government by consent must renounce the unrealistic requirement that liberal institutions and specific policies be convincingly justifiable to anyone anytime and ought, instead, to reconcile itself with the sober acknowledgement that there will always be aspects of governmental policies, of the legislative activity

[1] Frank I. Michelman, 'How Can the People Ever Make the Laws? A Critique of Deliberative Democracy', in James Bohman and William Rehg (eds), *Deliberative Democracy* (MIT Press 1997) 154 (hereafter Michelman, 'How Can the People').

of parliaments, and of the adjudication process, that some citizens will experience as unjust: as deeply unfair to their own person or political convictions, or to those of the social group to which they belong, or to those of others—fellow citizens—living in the country and abiding by its laws.

The liberal ideal of government by consent can only survive if translated into a non-utopian ideal in touch with the historical conditions of contemporary complex societies. The dualist understanding of constitutional democracy developed by Ackerman and Rawls is designed precisely to restrict the applicability of *direct* justification—be it justification via a political conception of justice undergirding the constitutional essentials, via a Habermasian 'discourse', via Ackerman's 'constrained dialogue', or any other procedural scheme—to the higher level of law and institutional design, the level that possesses constitutional relevance. For all the lower levels of the legal and institutional order, including policies and administrative procedures, an *indirect* legitimation based on their compatibility with the provisions of higher law will suffice. As a quintessential rendition of such 'legitimation by constitution', Michelman offers Rawls's liberal principle of legitimacy: 'our exercise of political power is fully proper only when it is exercised in accordance with a constitution the essentials of which all citizens as free and equal may reasonably be expected to endorse in the light of principles and ideals acceptable to their common human reason'.[2]

Michelman's possibility problem presupposes acceptance of legitimation-by-constitution as a *necessary* response to the problem of realizing government by consent in pluralist conditions. Michelman then adds a further premise about popular sovereignty. Prevailing ideas of constitutional democracy, he points out, seek a rapprochement between the classical liberal emphasis on government by consent and the republican and democratic emphasis on government by the people. However, Michelman's concern is not only—as for Habermas and Rawls—with the classical opposition of Locke and Rousseau, but furthermore with certain intuitions embedded in American constitutional culture, and more specifically two ideas about political freedom that are in a reciprocal tension: namely, (a) the notion that insofar as a people is politically free, '*they* cannot accept law from anyone save ... themselves' and (b) the idea that a people's 'conception of itself as self-governing, as legislating law to *itself*, depends on its sense of its members as ... commonly and continuously inspired by and aspiring to some distinctive regulative idea of political justice

[2] Rawls, *PL* 137.

and right—but always, too, an idea that itself has sprung from the politics of the selfsame self-governing People'.[3]

The tension between these two ideas derives from the fact that the first refers mainly to the exercise of a *sovereign* will and the second to *limits* to that exercise. Even if the limits, in the form of rights, can be understood as flowing from the sovereign will, as *self-imposed* limits and not as limits deriving from natural rights, there is still room for tension. For example, the limitations self-imposed at one time by the people may become unbearable constraints a few generations later. Michelman suggests that constitutional-democratic thought is motivated to allay this tension because it also embeds the background supposition that higher-law always originates from 'a political event that it itself is framed by some already present idea of political reason or right, itself politically grounded'.[4] Again, as with legitimation-by-constitution, I accept Michelman's premise that higher-law is itself 'always under law'.

Furthermore, I share with Michelman a sympathy towards ideas of deliberative democracy as being *liberal* in the sense that 'only individuals, and not any supraindividual entity such as a people or a majority, figure as self-authenticating sources of claims in the view's derivations of rightness requirements for political regimes'.[5] In our assessment of the rightness, legitimacy or justness of institutions, political arrangements, policies, legislative initiatives and so on, the proper object of consideration is their impact on the life of citizens qua individuals. Such stance distinguishes deliberative democracy *with a liberal spirit* from majoritarian or populist democracy but, in keeping with Rawls's 'political' conception of the person, does not commit us to any substantive view of the individual—least of all to the atomistic view associated with classical liberalism. On the contrary, an intersubjective view of the individual as constituted by relations of reciprocal recognition can be combined with the notion that our social and political world is populated by 'individuals severally possessed of minds and lives of their own and severally possessed, furthermore, of worthwhile ... capacities for rational agency, for taking some substantial degree of conscious charge of their own minds and lives, making and pursuing their own judgments about what to do, what to strive for, what is good, and what is right'.[6] The priority of the individual is a priority of *concern*, not an ontological priority.[7]

[3] Chapter 1, p. 12.

[4] Ibid.

[5] Michelman, 'How Can the People?' (n. 1) 152.

[6] Ibid. 153.

[7] In 'The Subject of Liberalism', Michelman spells out further the conception of the individual embedded in his view of democracy. He starts out with illustrating five basic aspects of every liberal

Finally, I share with Michelman his description of theories of deliberative democracy as 'intrinsically process-bound'. By deliberative-democratic understanding, political philosophy cannot possibly generate by itself a blueprint for a legitimate system of higher law for a political community.

Interestingly, where a philosopher committed to deliberative democracy such as Habermas sees a solution to the tension between justification and sovereignty, Michelman detects a problem. In fact, an *infinite regress* threatens to undermine the deep-deliberative view of democracy by virtue of making the legitimate establishing of a democratic order a task practically impossible to achieve on account of its conceptual incoherence.

Deliberative constitutional democrats proceed from the assumption that

> deliberative democracy seeks its ultimate authorization not from political-moral axioms that we start out by accrediting as right, or from political-moral authority that we start out by accrediting as warranted, but rather on the basis that the democratic procedure is itself a validity condition for political-moral reasoning or authority in the first place.[8]

Actual discourses and deliberations are needed, if the promise of government by the governed is to be fulfilled. Even Habermas, notes Michelman, cannot go so far as to say that from the rationally accessible idea of a fair democratic procedure, understood as dialogue under idealized conditions, one could deduce 'a set of fundamental laws for a given country in given times'. Quoting Habermas to the effect that 'the democratic procedure for the production of law forms the only postmetaphysical source of legitimacy',[9] Michelman reports (in his own words) that according to Habermas valid judgements as to the legitimacy of higher law 'arise only against the background of an *actual*

conception of the individual. First, individuals are assumed to be *ethically several*, i.e. each capable of leading 'a life of its own that is conceptually distinct from the lives of other subjects' and that constitutes a 'distinct field of value', 'The Subject of Liberalism' (1994) 46 Stanford Law Review 1812. Second, individuals are assumed to be *interest-bearing*, i.e. to be 'differentially affected for better or worse by various events'. Third, individuals are assumed to be *self-activating*, a synonym of 'autonomous', namely to possess the ability to contemplate their interests, reflect on their implications and to initiate modifications of their own internal state or of the external world. Fourth, individuals are assumed to be *communicative*, in the sense of being 'capable of intentionally affecting other subjects' perceptions of reasons for action' and of being 'intentionally affected by others'. Fifth, individuals do possess a property of *reflectiveness* understood as an awareness of oneself as an 'ethically several, interest bearing, self-activating and communicative' subject (ibid.).

[8] Chapter 1, pp. 23–24.

[9] Jürgen Habermas, *Between Facts and Norms: Contributions to a Discourse Theory of Law and Democracy*, tr. William Rehg (MIT Press 1996) 30 (hereafter Habermas, *Facts and Norms*), 448.

democratic-discursive forum to which the question is at all times submissible',[10] that no 'unaided internal effort of empathy' will by itself suffice to ground the legitimacy of higher law arrangements which result in legitimate coercion, and so (here quoting Habermas) that 'consociates under law must be able to *examine* whether a contested norm could meet with the agreement of all those possibly affected'[11] and that only an '*actual* process of deeply democratic scrutiny' can do that job.

Now, the impasse originates precisely in the requirement that the rightness of a legal order, i.e. its deserving to be 'approved by all citizens in a democratic discourse', be linked conceptually (a) with the law's passing successfully the test of an actual democratic discussion and (b) with understanding the democratic character of such discussion in *legal* terms.[12] How can the framing of a constitution ever amount to a democratic jurisgenerative process, if the *democratic* quality of the discussion which supposedly should ground the rightness of the constitution can only be defined in terms of an already existing law? The political task of establishing a deliberative democracy, from this perspective, appears as hopelessly unfeasible as the enterprise of writing a novel in which the opening sentence of each chapter should be identical with the closing one of the preceding chapter. The problem 'wouldn't be one of inability to carry the task through to completion, but rather one of inability to begin it'.[13]

It is worth emphasizing that, as Michelman points out, Rawls's liberal principle of legitimation is *not* entangled in this conundrum. The programme of 'legitimacy by constitution', according to Michelman,

> may doubtless be read to say that only a constitution *for* a democracy could possibly claim assent from all citizens reasonable and rational. It does not, however, say that only a constitution *itself democratically produced* can hope to meet that test. It contains, in itself, no explanation for why a constitution excogitated by a Solon, a Lycurgus, or a John Rawls could not meet that standard, in what Rawls would call a wide reflective equilibrium among citizens of a given country at a given time. In order, then, to complete our construction of the deep-democratic view of political rightness, we need still to find out what prompts that view's resistance to a *non*-deep-democratic—sometimes called a 'rights-foundationalist'—idea of political rightness.[14]

[10] Chapter 1, p. 25.
[11] Habermas, *Facts and Norms* (n. 9) 104.
[12] See Frank Michelman, 'Review of Jürgen Habermas's *Between Facts and Norms*' (1996) 93 JP 310–312.
[13] Chapter 1, p. 24.
[14] Ibid. p. 24

Habermas's solution to the impossibility of grounding a democratic regime democratically amounts to what Michelman calls a *strong* epistemic theory of democracy. A strong epistemic theory of democracy posits democratic-discursive procedures as a necessary condition for claiming that a political system produces legitimate laws, 'all the way up' through the whole hierarchy of higher and higher laws. This posit, Michelman argues, provides the only reconciliation, of which he is aware, 'of an individualistically liberal view of political rightness with an unrestricted binding of political right reason to democratic process'.[15]

Having said all this, however, the spectre of infinite regress continues to loom large even within Habermas's solution. If actual and legally constituted democratic discussions are what validates fundamental laws and their coercive force as legitimate, then the normativity that establishes and grounds this practice of legitimate lawmaking must 'be the product of a conceptually prior procedural event that itself was framed by (valid) laws that must, as such, have issued in their turn from a still prior (properly) legally constituted event'.[16] In the words of Habermas, a 'spiraling self-application of the law' is thus set in endless motion. Following Habermas, Michelman wonders where in history can one find an 'originary' constitutive moment that would stop the regress, and how that moment could be conceived.

In sum, it seems that we will have in the end to renounce one of two claims: either the idea of a prior legal authorization for every lawmaking stage (i.e. government under law) or the requirement of a 'prior democratic authorization for every institutionalization of democracy' (i.e. popular sovereignty).

How does Michelman respond to this paradoxical predicament? He outlines *two* distinct paths of escape, but then he leaves us readers with the challenge of assessing the merits of these two paths. The first path—which he, ironically gesturing at Heidegger's jargon, calls the path of *lucky thrownness*—is the one closest to the Rawlsian project of political liberalism and to Rawls's casting of the ultimate normative credentials for a political conception of justice—'justice as fairness', for example—in terms of its being the conception *most reasonable for us*.[17] Typical of this path is the renunciation to provide 'a democratic warrant for setting the project off on its first iteration'[18] and the concomitant claim that in spite of its unwarranted beginnings, and lack of safeguard from

[15] Ibid. pp. 26–27.
[16] Ibid. p. 27
[17] See John Rawls, 'Kantian Constructivism in Moral Theory' (1980) 88 Journal of Philosophy 519, and *PL* 28.
[18] Chapter 1, p. 28.

embedded injustice or bias, the present liberal-democratic constitutional arrangements can be understood as the most justice-tending arrangements known to, and reasonable for, us. If we follow this path, we will let the sleeping dog of infinite regress lie, will take refuge in a kind of 'political', not 'comprehensive' understanding of truth and political rightness, and will then confidently endorse 'fundamental-law resolutions that we can see to be in some material degree deviant from justice, while seeing also that those resolutions are ensconced in a nest of historical events of politics that we judge to be reasonably defensible as justice-tending and justice-seeking'.[19]

The second path is more ambitious. It leads back to Michelman's 'always under law' thesis,[20] here recast as 'sovereignty as jurisdiction'. The idea is that the practice, in almost all constitutional legal orders, of amending the existent constitution according to certain provisions (and sometimes beyond the purview of these provisions), can be taken as evidence that the highest law can itself be judged inadequate or in need for correction—as the rules of a game may arguably be in need of correction—and this act of judgement (entrusted to some separated powers or directly to the people or both) can be understood as 'an interpretation of the community's ultimate law or proto-law of which the from-time-to-time enacted and amended and interpreted Constitution is to be understood as a series of representations and applications'.[21] Legal cultures differ over whether a supreme or constitutional court should be allowed to pass judgment on the substantive appropriateness of amendments duly enacted according to the existing formal provisions.[22] But whether it is a court on behalf of the people or the electorate through a referendum, or other means, that assesses the acceptability of a proposed constitutional alteration, this judgment in any case can be construed as an act of application of a pre-existent higher law. A 'jurisdictional' reservation of this judgment for the people, Michelman

[19] Ibid. pp. 28–29.

[20] See Frank Michelman, 'Always Under Law?' (1995) 12, 2 Constitutional Commentary 227 (hereafter Michelman, 'Always Under Law?').

[21] F.I. Michelman, 'Can Constitutional Democrats Be Legal Positivists? Or, Why Constitutionalism?' (1996) 2 Constellations 293, 303.

[22] Some constitutional regimes admit as legitimate only amendments that strictly conform with the amendment provisions found in the Constitution (Canada, Switzerland, Australia); other constitutional regimes allow significant modifications of currently standing constitutional practice or understanding that do not conform with the formal amendment provisions (the United States, where the Supreme Court's function of judicial review is neither written in the Constitution nor the object of a formal Amendment, and the New Deal and Civil Rights legislation never took the form of formal amendments); a third group of constitutional regimes allows a constitutional court to pass final judgment on the substantive conformity of formally approved amendments with the 'basic structure' or the fundamental principles of the Constitution (Germany, India, South Africa). For an interesting comparative reconstruction of the diverse approaches to the legitimacy of constitutional amendments, see Richard Albert, 'Nonconstitutional Amendments' (2009) 22, 1 Canadian Journal of Law & Jurisprudence 5–47.

concludes, might then be compatible with both the 'always under law' thesis and the thesis of popular sovereignty. Schmitt's famous dictum 'Sovereign is who decides the exception' is ingeniously recast by Michelman along constitutional-democratic lines as: 'sovereign are they in whom jurisdiction in the higher matters reposes'.[23]

However, one problem remains unsolved. How to ground such a division of jurisdiction between a court, as judicial agent of 'the people' qua author of the constitution, and 'the people themselves'? Michelman's solution unfolds in three steps. First, he introduces the distinction between *norm-origination* and *norm-interpretation*. As long as the highest judicial interpreter of the constitution 'confines itself to *applying* norms legislated by the People . . . popular self-government persists', but 'should norm-*origination* . . . itself ever fall into the hands of judicial appointees, popular self-government will to that extent have perished'.[24]

However, and this is the second step, constitutional amendments of the constitution 'are not all readily and cleanly divisible between the categories of norm-application and norm-origination'.[25] Against the backdrop of recent US constitutional history, for example, a hypothetical 'flag-desecration amendment', aimed at reversing past opinions of the Supreme Court that held unconstitutional legislation and prosecutions targeting politically expressive flag-burning, could quite plausibly count as falling into either category, or both. Thus, it could possibly be the case that 'in the sight of American judicial officers . . . a flag-desecration amendment should be taken as the People's act of norm-origination—even as, in the sight of a citizenry always claiming self-government, it must . . . be construed as an interpretive act'.[26]

The third and final step consists of a suggested reason for thus reserving to the people some matters of higher-normative interpretation, namely, that 'what the People amending the Constitution are in the first instance called on to interpret is . . . *themselves*. [italics AF] Themselves, that is, as a People who take themselves to be committed to the project of governing themselves by logos, reason, a text that they themselves have uttered.'[27] Thus, a flag-desecration amendment takes the appearance of an interpretive act when considered from the angle of the sovereign citizens, an act 'of following what is already there', but

[23] Chapter 1, p. 30.
[24] Ibid.p. 30.
[25] Ibid.
[26] Ibid.
[27] Ibid. p. 30.

for a supreme judicial interpreter of the Constitution it takes the semblance of a sovereign pronouncement.

To sum up, Michelman's suggestion is that to revise, and a fortiori to frame, a constitution is an act that presupposes at some point something like *self-interpretation*—an answer to the question of who are we and do we want to be—and, in line with theories of self-constitution, Michelman posits that '*self-interpretation* is something that no one but the subject can finally do'.[28] Contrary with what many theorists of self-constitution seem to hold, Michelman allows that an individual or in our case a collective subject is not necessarily always the best interpreter of itself, but may sometimes stand subject to correction by historians, social and cultural critics, or philosophers professionally reflecting on the merit of these self-interpretations. However—Michelman claims—'unless and until such interventions bring the people themselves around ... there is no way a *legal* supervisor can credibly *overrule* the People's solemn declaration of self-understanding'.[29] A Rousseauian legislator may have deeper insights into the People's potentials, best interest, understanding of justice than the multitude he addresses, yet he still has to obtain consent and cannot *overrule*, at least legitimately, what the multitude thinks, if the latter is to remain *sovereign*.

To be sure, Michelman concludes, 'we deal here with counterfactuals'. No one thinks that a population, or the subset thereof that counts as 'the People', appoints itself as a court to deliberate over its identity and how to best inscribe it in a constitution or over how to revise an existent constitution in the light of new turns in that identity's narrative. All classical contract theorists—Hobbes, Locke, Rousseau—admitted this fact, and it comes as no surprise that we should do likewise. In that counterfactual spirit, the subject called 'the People' might think of its political existence in more 'idealizing, imaginative, utopian' ways than those embedded in daily political routines and in that modality might endorse the notion that popular sovereignty, 'usually taken to express the idea that the people have the right to make the law be whatever they in fact decide', on the other hand also presupposes 'a wish to believe something like the opposite'.[30]

[28] Ibid.

[29] Ibid. Are the powers to frame and revise a constitution really on an equal footing? For a stimulating argument to the contrary, and for a *three-track* (as opposed to *dualist*) theory of constitutional democracy, which allows for judicial review of both the procedural and substantive aspects of amendments enacted by 'secondary constituent power' (i.e. a power superior to constituted and separated powers, but still subordinate to primary constituent power), see Yaniv Roznai, *Unconstitutional Constitutional Amendments: The Limits of Amendment Power* (OUP 2017) 105–175 (hereafter Roznai, *Unconstitutional Constitutional Amendments*).

[30] Chapter 1, p. 31.

2. On the People as Charterers Being the Same as the People as Chartered

The most interesting aspect of the conception of deliberative constitutional democracy developed by Michelman is to be found, from my perspective, in the notion of normative validity that implicitly underlies it. He is primarily interested not so much in an abstract scheme of justice or normative rightness, but in the normative validity of occurrences and processes of higher lawmaking, the area of law having as its object what Rawls called 'constitutional essentials' or, in other words, the standards by which all other, lower-order acts of lawmaking are to be evaluated. Just like Habermas, Dworkin, Rawls—and differently from those who have understood constituent power as *legibus solutus*—Michelman conceives of higher lawmaking as being always an application of a prior normative posit. Yet, differently than for Habermas, Dworkin, and the earlier Rawls of *A Theory of Justice*, for Michelman the prior norm that the constitution is under is itself *a law* in the political sense of that term; it is a *politically immanent* creation, not something that proceeds from a principle of discursive generalization, an overarching value of equality specified in certain rights, or a deliberation of rational actors under a veil of ignorance. It remains to be clarified how it is possible for the will of the people to be sovereign while at the same time remaining responsive to a normative framework more comprehensive than any of its single political acts, including the framing of a constitution, and yet *not external to it*.

Notice the close analogy that exists here with the problem of accounting for aesthetic value. To account for an exemplary aesthetic experience means to show how the artistic intent or formative will of the artist can be 'sovereign' and, at the same time, responsive to a kind of framework of sorts, more comprehensive than any of the manifestations of the artist's will but at the same time immanent within and not external to those manifestations. In both cases, the philosophical challenge is to account for the possibility of a practice to respond to an *individual law* in Simmel's sense.[31]

Then, how exactly are we to understand the pre-existent idea of political rightness, of which the original constitution is supposedly an interpretation and an application? One avenue that seems to remain open, barring the invocation of transcendent standards, is to understand the broader idea of political reason and right as equivalent to 'the constitution as the People intended it' as

[31] Georg Simmel, 'Das individuelle Gesetz' (1913), in Georg Simmel, *Das Individuelle Gesetz: Philosophische Exkurse* (Suhrkamp 1987).

opposed to 'the constitution as it was actually worded' owing to the contingencies of the debate in the constitutional convention or assembly, to contextual limitations of the vocabulary available to the framers, and so on—much like the work of art as planned by the artist (to the extent that we can extrapolate it from various sources) can be compared with its actual realization.[32] This way of answering the question, however, would entangle us in the dubious exercise of recovering the 'original intent' of artists and constitution-framers acting in the name of the People, with all the paradoxes pointed out by Dworkin[33] and the difficulties incurred by 'originalism' as an approach to constitutionalism.

A different and more promising way to identify the 'law' that supposedly the constitution is under could start by examining more closely one implicit assumption that undergirds Michelman's requisite, posited as a condition for the unabated persistence over time of real popular sovereignty, of the self-sameness of *the People* as *charterers* and as *chartered*. The need for closer scrutiny rests on a problematic facet of that requisite best illustrated by paraphrasing one of Rousseau's famous lines as follows: 'A people can give itself a constitution: then a people is a people before it gives itself a constitution. Consequently, before examining the act by which a people gives itself a constitution, it would be proper to examine the act by which a people becomes a people.'[34] When is a human population entitled to call itself a people? Only after that prior question is answered can we then address Michelman's question, now reformulated: how can a population constitute itself *democratically* as a People, if democracy properly speaking begins with a democratic constitution?

The prior, Rousseauian question is so impervious to answer that both classical contract theorists (Hobbes, Locke, Rousseau) and contemporary theorists of deliberative democracy (Rawls and Habermas) have all premised their discussion of the legitimacy of a polity on the assumption that a People already exists and, in the somewhat strange company of Burke and Schmitt, have exempted that mere historical fact from all kinds of normative inquiry. If the People is the source of legitimacy, the formation of the People has to be considered beyond the scope of any inquiry into its legitimacy.[35]

[32] The same opposition will be surface again below, in a slightly different context, in Chapters 5 and 6.

[33] See Ronald Dworkin, *Law's Empire* (Harvard U. Press 1986) 318–324.

[34] See Jean Jacques Rousseau, *The Social Contract*, in *The Social Contract and the Discourse on the Origin of Inequality* (first published 1762), ed. L. G. Crocker (Simon and Schuster 1967), I, 5, 16 (hereafter Rousseau, *Social Contract*).

[35] On this point a very interesting analysis can be found in Sophia Näsström, 'The Legitimacy of the People' (2007) 35, 5 Political Theory 624.

On this prior question concerning the legitimacy of constituting a People—a question unaddressed also by Michelman—let me offer three considerations, which in the end should also cast further light on the 'always under law' thesis.

The People as *Demos* and as *Ethnos*

First, 'people' is an ambiguous term in English, French, Italian, and Spanish. Just like 'nation'—which had greater diffusion in the Neo-Latin linguistic areas (in the German-speaking world a similar role is played by the term *Volk* and in the Russian and Slavic one by the term *Narod*)—'the people' covers a very broad semantic field, which can be fruitfully differentiated, for our purposes, by using the two Greek terms *ethnos* and *demos*. Both designate aggregates of individuals. In the case of an *ethnos*, individuals are thought to be related on the basis of non-political characteristics—for instance, but not exclusively, the use of a language, patterns of conduct, lifestyles, shared codes of politeness and civility, umdietary habits, historical memories. About 7,079 distinct idioms are documented to exist.[36] Some of these languages are spoken by no more than a few hundreds persons, and 3,000 of them are expected to undergo extinction during the twenty-first century. Considering only those spoken by thousands of speakers, about 700 to 800 languages can be counted and to each of them corresponds *at least* one *ethnos*—strong and widespread languages such as English, Spanish, Arabic, etc., being obviously spoken by more than one *ethnos*.

A *demos* is an *ethnos* about which it can defensibly be stated, by any member or external observer, that at a certain point in time it has taken the form of a body-politic or of a political order, and that thereafter its members have been living within commonly accepted structures of authority, democratic or non-democratic. Both the conflation of *demos* and *nation*—the ultimate legacy of Jacobinism and the seed of all sorts of nationalism—and the conflation of *ethnos* and *nation* have to be avoided. It is between 1748, when Montesquieu introduced the term 'general spirit of a nation', and a few decades later, when Herder theorized about *Volksgeist*, that the idea took hold that an *ethnos* sort of naturally has a 'national' magnitude. In the ancient world, the Middle Ages and early modernity many *ethnoi* have existed on a more local scale: the so-called *nationes* of Roman antiquity, the aboriginal nations of Canada, United States, and Australia, and city-states as *demoi* premised on a sub-national scale.

[36] See David M. Eberhard, Gary F. Simons, and Charles D. Fennig (eds), *Ethnologue: Languages of the World*, 23rd edn (SIL International 2020). Online version: <http://www.ethnologue.com>.

From the standpoint of Anthropocene, time, processes of merging, assimilation, and conquest have brought the *ethnoi* to coalesce in ever broader and inclusive *demoi*: it has been calculated that 5,000 years ago about 600,000 human settlements existed, each with its structure of authority, sorts of *proto-demoi* as it were.[37] Today the officially recognized *demoi* are 195 sovereign states, within which a few hundreds of *ethnoi* exist.

Thus a *demos* originates in an *ethnos* or a plurality of *ethnoi*: as in an iceberg, it constitutes the politically visible tip of it or them. Not every *ethnos* gives rise to a *demos*, but all *demoi* are also *ethnoi* (or aggregates of *ethnoi*). This does not mean, however, that in the post-Westphalian global world each structure of authority should correspond to a *demos* (and to one or more *ethnoi*). The EU notoriously lacks a unitary *demos* and even more a unitary *ethnos*, though it regulates the life of half a billion individuals who are citizens of a plurality of *demoi*. Institutions such as IMF, World Bank, WTO, and of course the Security Council of the United Nations do exert regulatory functions, which ultimately display effects on individuals and collectives, but their relation to actual *demoi* and *ethnoi* is even more tenuous.

The Making of a *Demos*: A 'Commitment to Make Commitments' and the Constitution

Second, written constitutions are a recent phenomenon. Neither Hobbes nor Locke had ever seen a proper constitution, but only their glorious forerunners—the Magna Charta (1215) and the Bill of Rights (1689)—and Rousseau outlined only the Constitution for Corsica, in 1768. While in the late eighteenth century constitutions were the exception, in the nineteenth and to an even greater extent in the twentieth codified and collated written constitutions became the paradigmatic political act through which a *demos*, not an *ethnos*, came into being.[38] By no means a necessary condition, as the cases of the United Kingdom and several countries of the Commonwealth attest, a population's observable and ongoing adherence to a set of conventional rules

[37] Alexander Wendt, 'Why a World State is Democratically Necessary?', transcript of a presentation given by Alexander Wendt at Hiram College, 2 July 2015, <http://wgresearch.org/why-a-world-state-is-democratically-necessary/> accessed 17.3.2018.

[38] Of all the states formed after the French Revolution, 85 per cent enacted a Constitution within their first two years of life, and 95 per cent within the first five years. Including all the states that have meanwhile been terminated, and those which adopted more than one Constitution during their existence, about 900 written Constitutions exist. See Tom Ginsburg, 'Written Constitutions Around the World' (2015) 15 IL&S 4.

of the political game—its collective 'constitutional willingness', understood, to paraphrase Arendt, as a 'commitment to share joint commitments'—is doubtless a sufficient condition for transforming an *ethnos*, or a collection thereof, into a *demos*. An *ethnos* becomes a *demos*—it takes on a recognizable *political* identity—through the dual process of (directly or indirectly) creating a political unity through a pact and accepting a constitution. Having said this, Rousseau's dictum—'before examining the act by which a nation (*un peuple*) elects a king, it would be proper to examine the act by which a nation (*un peuple*) becomes a nation (*un peuple*)'[39]—can be rephrased in the following way: before examining the act by which a people 'elects a king' or, more generally, adopts a scheme of government, it would be proper to examine the act by which an *ethnos* turns into a *demos*. This reformulation allows us to see under a different light the neglect of the legitimacy of people-formation on the part of classical and contemporary normative theorists.

The coming into being of an *ethnos* is a factual process, best explained from an anthropological, sociological, or historical point of view. To argue about the legitimacy of the coming into being of an *ethnos* makes no more sense than to debate the legitimacy of the formation of Mount Everest or the modification of the riverbed of the Danube. Only the transformation of an *ethnos* into a *demos* can be sensibly assessed as legitimate (or valid) or not, insofar as it amounts to a voluntary action retrospectively imputed to a collective subject (Kelsen) or to a preliminary step towards establishing a new rule of law (Schmitt).

In 1580, Montaigne, in his autobiographical *Essays*, wrote a groundbreaking and wonderfully concise sentence: 'I have made this book to no greater extent than this book has made me.'[40] The theories of self-constitution propounded by Korsgaard, Frankfurt, and Larmore[41] remind us that even without questionably postulating an internal essence that realizes itself in and through our actions (knowing which, even if we were possessed of it, would be as impossible as for the eye to see itself), nonetheless we achieve self-unity through the commitments we make and the defining actions that we perform.[42] To put it with

[39] Rousseau, *Social Contract* (n. 34) I, 5, 16.

[40] 'Je n'ay pas plus faict mon livre que mon livre m'a faict', Montaigne, *Essais* (first published 1580) (Garnier-Flammarion 1969) II, 326.

[41] See Charles Larmore, *Les pratiques du moi* (PUF 2004); Christine Korsgaard, *The Sources of Normativity* (CUP 1996) Christine Korsgaard, *Self-Constitution* (OUP 2009) (hereafter Korsgaard, *Self-Constitution*); Harry Frankfurt, *The Importance of What We Care About: Philosophical Essays* (first published 1988) (CUP 2007). For a discussion of what Rousseau's implicit theory of the authenticity of the self can teach these theorists, see Alessandro Ferrara, *Rousseau and Critical Theory* (Brill 2017) 34–45.

[42] The term 'commitment' is used here as a common denominator standing for what Korsgaard calls 'reflexive endorsement', Larmore calls 'engagement', and Frankfurt calls 'wholehearted identification'. Significantly, Korsgaard reformulates in terms of individual self-constitution the same paradox

Montaigne, the commitments we undertake, the actions we accomplish, *make us no less than we make them.*

The 'Sameness of the Charterers and the Chartered' Reconsidered

Third, it is then inaccurate to imagine that a pre-existing *demos*—for example, the Italian *demos*—used to ground interaction among its members on a principle of the priority of labour over property and then, after a change of regime, in 1948, decided to found its republican life 'on labour'.[43] Rather, regime-change resulted in a democratically elected constitutional assembly which in turn produced a new constitutional charter premised, among other principles, on the priority of labour over property. That priority, expressed through Article 1 of the Constitution of Italy, is then posited as a principle inspiring the common political life of a republican community, and through this act it gives shape to a *demos* distinct from others also, *inter alia*, because it affirms such principle. Likewise, it is inaccurate to state that if 'a people elects a king' such people exists in the same form prior to that act. To be sure, it pre-exists as an *ethnos*, and perhaps even as some kind of *demos*. However, only at the moment, say, of the Glorious Revolution, when the two Houses of Westminster, meeting in a Convention Parliament in January 1689, decided to ask William and Mary of Orange to reign no longer by divine right but on the basis of the consent of the ruled, only then was the form of a limited, no longer absolute monarchy created, and simultaneously a self-governing *demos* came into being, constituted by that decision.

In sum, the political identity of a people-qua-*demos*, differently from its identity-qua- *ethnos*, emerges not *prior to* but *from* the constitutional principles through which the people decides to regulate its political life. Following Montaigne, constitutions, through the commitments they embed—for example 'to remove those obstacles of an economic or social nature which constrain the freedom and equality of citizens, thereby impeding the full development of the human person',[44] or to reject war[45]—make a *demos* no less than a *demos* makes a constitution.

highlighted by Rousseau in *The Social Contract*: 'How can you constitute yourself, create yourself, unless you are already there?', *Self-Constitution* (n. 41) 1.

[43] 'Italy is a democratic Republic founded on labour', Constitution of Italy (1948), art. 1.
[44] Ibid. art. 3.
[45] Ibid. art. 11.

That consideration gives us a new insight into the 'sameness' that democracy demands (in Michelman's terms) of 'the charterers' with 'the chartered'. That sameness exists not *outside* the purported act of self-chartering (which Michelman sets up as paradoxical) but *within* that act, as a product of it. Such act *simultaneously brings the charterers and the chartered into existence*. This interpretation frees us from the difficulty of conceiving the charterers as being left unchanged by their action: in the most banal sense, as an agent they have now acquired a new experience. The sameness of charterers and chartered must then be understood along cultural and historical lines. Among the ingredients of such 'sameness', Michelman mentions 'some substantially contentful normative like-mindedness' or a 'cultural or dispositional or experiential commonality'.[46] But how to define that core identity to which the framing of the constitution stands as an act of interpretation in such a way as not to make a collectivity endowed with a *political* identity stand to the same collectivity, now considered under the aspect of its *cultural* identity, as an attribute stands to an essence? As Michelman points out, the core of the people's identity can't be conceived as an ethical core, otherwise our view of constitutional democracy would not be consistent with the fact of pluralism. A different candidate is a commonality of historical experiences, including experiences of conflicts and divisions, from which a perceived commonality of destiny flows. But it is part of the notion of public or political autonomy that the constitution cannot 'derive' from things factually true about the People.

At this juncture, the family of analytic theories of self-constitution mentioned above proves helpful. If the relation of a subject, individual or collective, to itself is a *practical* relation—whereby the subject *makes itself* by way of choosing certain self-descriptions over other possible self-descriptions—then a constitution can be understood as the selective objectification of *one* among several *political* identities congruent with the People's history—namely, the variant freely chosen as a project by the People itself. The future-oriented moment inherent in this choice frees the notion of fit from a naturalistic understanding in terms of 'reflecting' certain given, factual identity components. Peoples, no less than individuals, can centre their identity upon projects of radical self-reform.[47] The 'political identity' created by a constitution can be part of the project whereby a collectivity, hitherto endowed with a cultural

[46] Chapter 1, p. 22.

[47] Constitutions that emerge from regime-change all involve this more or less radical 'self-reforming' transformation of the identity of the constituting/constituted People. For a discussion of France, Italy, India, South Africa, Poland, Israel, and Iran as (at least partially) successful cases, see Bruce Ackerman, *Revolutionary Constitutions: Charismatic Leadership and the Rule of Law* (Harvard U. Press 2019).

identity alone, seeks a transformative emancipation from certain undesired, or no longer desired, aspects of its own identity. The cases of the German *Grundgesetz* (1949) and, to some extent, of the Constitution of Italy (1948), both born from regime changes after the Second World War, exemplify processes of constitution-making that, through firm commitment to democratic principles and fundamental rights (safeguarded through judicial review), were meant more to clear away the dark shadows of the recent past than to carve in marble the bright achievements of the historical People. In order to allow for the possibility of conceiving constitution-making as not just expressive, but also *corrective*, of certain aspects of the People's identity, we need to operate with a version of this notion that goes beyond Montesquieu's 'general spirit of a nation' or Herder's *Volksgeist* (two notions that either remain factual or become 'essentialistic' if understood as normative). Such a new version must include a stronger emphasis on the project-like, future-oriented component of identity which functions as the focal point of the practical relation of the collective with itself.

Finally, the metaphor of the work of art also helps us to elucidate a crucial distinction between two distinct layers of higher lawmaking. In 'Always Under Law?', Michelman refers to a 'lower layer' and an 'upper layer' of higher lawmaking and connects them with the jurisdiction of the Supreme Court and the jurisdiction of what he calls the 'People's Court',[48] or the People's political and legal prerogative to intervene directly at any time in the process of higher lawmaking via the established procedures for constitutional amendment.[49] The criterion for attributing legal subject matters to one or the other jurisdiction cannot simply be that *norm-origination* pertains to the People and *norm-interpretation* or the *application* of norms pertains to the judiciary. For, Michelman argues, also the 'People's higher-law ministrations are *always interpretive*, never originary',[50] even the framing of the constitution being a (self-)interpretive act addressing the political identity of the People. Thus *another* criterion must ground the distinction.

Again, the aesthetic analogy becomes relevant.[51] The *lower-level* 'higher-law ministrations', entrusted to a Supreme or Constitutional Court concern

[48] Michelman, 'Always Under Law?' (n. 20) 246–247.

[49] These upper and lower levels of higher lawmaking correspond to what Yaniv Roznai calls respectively 'secondary constituent power' (still supposed to operate with the formal and substantive tracks provided by the original framers of the Constitution) and constituted judicial power (in its highest version, as a Supreme or Constitutional Court). See Roznai, *Unconstitutional Constitutional Amendments* (n. 29) 113–123.

[50] Michelman, 'Always Under Law?' (n. 20) 247.

[51] For a more detailed discussion of the aesthetic analogy see Alessandro Ferrara, *Justice and Judgment: The Rise and the Prospect of the Judgment Model in Contemporary Political Philosophy* (Sage 1999) 197–201.

the best way of *understanding* the project embedded in the constitution. The *upper-level* 'higher-law ministrations', meant to remain the prerogative of the People, include questions that call for a *reassessment* of the project and as such are (potentially, not necessarily) transformative.[52] The distinction remains then fully consistent with the attribution of an interpretive character to *both* kinds of questions. In the case of *lower-level* 'higher-law ministrations' what needs to be duly interpreted is the constitution as a sedimented reflection of the identity of the People qua collectivity endowed with a *political* identity. In the case of *upper-level* 'higher-law ministrations' what needs to be interpreted is the alignment of the political identity reflected in the constitution with the broader *cultural* and *historical* identity of the People.

Under liberal premises, however, the People in this latter capacity, or the *ethnos*, cannot be the subject of any political decision, except for the enactment of a constitution, which brings into being the People's *political* identity. This is why, at subsequent historical junctures, it is incumbent on the already constituted-*demos* to act as a fully authorized trustee and interpreter of the *ethnos*—a prerogative which includes the reassessment of the political project embedded in the constitution—just as the Supreme Court or an equivalent institution can legitimately act as a trustee of the *demos* and as an interpreter of the constitutional project as it unfolds in the history of the political community.

The distinction between an upper and lower level of higher lawmaking does not imply a relapse into the positivist view according to which the People is the sole and final arbiter of the normative legitimacy of constitutional amendments. This consequence can be avoided if one understands Michelman's distinction as allowing also for *criticism* of the self-interpretation eventually adopted by the People. Legal philosophers, political philosophers, historians of law, social critics, and judges can all conceivably argue in a public space about why a certain self-understanding of the People is dubious or flawed. The 'People's court' is thus the final one only in a *legal* sense. Above it stands a *still higher-order* judgment on the congruity of the People's self-understanding with the People itself—a judgment that, as with individual identities or the symbolic identities of works of art, can be rendered by participants and observers alike. Such a higher 'History's Court' or 'Judgment's Court' must be presupposed if Michelman's idea of a 'People's Court', standing above the Supreme Court, is

[52] The distinction between interpreting and transforming, as prerogatives respectively of the highest judicial interpreter of the constitution and of its author, will be addressed again below, in the context of a different discussion. See Chapters 5 and 6.

not to reintroduce an element of legal positivism in the form of the unquestionability of the will of the People.

An example from the constitutional history of the United States illustrates the interplay of these levels of higher lawmaking: the Eighteenth Amendment on prohibition. To introduce the prohibition of the 'manufacture, sale, transportation and importation' of 'intoxicating liquors' was perceived as something that exceeded the mere interpretation of the Constitution and the proper jurisdiction of the Supreme Court. Such a prohibition was made higher law in 1919 by amending the Constitution, via the procedure outlined in Article Five.[53] Yet in 1933, merely fourteen years thereafter, the amendment was repealed through the same process. Unless one finds it appealing to account for this process as an instance of the People changing its mind on the basis of purely arbitrary preference—a preference oriented in one direction in 1919 and in the opposite direction in 1933—our account here must be that the interpretive judgment rendered by the People in 1919 was soon thereafter found erroneous by it and the mistake corrected. This account need not be retrospective. A judgment-based conception of higher lawmaking allows for the possibility that a judgement on the adequacy of the People's judgement be formulated by legal philosophers or other concerned persons at any time, even prior to the recognition of the mistake on the part of the People. Only the *legal* cogency of that judgement would have to wait for a pronouncement of the People.

3. Defusing the Problem of Infinite Regress

If we understand the sameness of the charterers and the chartered (required by democracy) along these lines, we can address the difficulties raised by Michelman's 'sovereignty-as-jurisdiction' path for reconciling the idea of a 'prior legal authorization for every lawmaking stage' and the requirement of a 'prior democratic authorization for every institutionalization of democracy'.

For Michelman, higher lawmaking, no matter whether we are considering the framing or the amendment of a constitution, is always an interpretation 'of the community's ultimate law or proto-law of which the from-time-to-time enacted and amended Constitution is to be understood as a series of representations and interpretations'.[54]

[53] See Herbert Ashbury, *Great Illusion: An Informal History of Prohibition* (Greenwood Press 1968) and Richard F. Hamm, *Shaping the Eighteenth Amendment: Temperance, Reform, Legal Culture and the Polity (1880–1920)* (U. of North Carolina Press 1995).

[54] Frank Michelman, 'Can Constitutional Democrats Be Legal Positivists?' (1996) 2 Constellations 303.

The legal Big Bang fathomed by classic contract theory—the creation of the commonwealth or the sovereign *ex nihilo*—is here replaced by a *continuum*, a gradual transformation of a human group, initially thrown together as an *ethnos* by contingency, which subsequently, in the course of intragroup and external interaction, comes to acquire a communal identity, understood as a self-conscious representation of shared characteristics and circumstances. There soon grows a representation of the communal way of regulating relations among members—perhaps, as Herbert Spencer has suggested, there first emerges a way of regulating the relation between those in charge and the governed.[55] There emerges also a shared will to make joint commitments, where previously only the convergence of individual action existed, and to articulate these commitments in a charter that all can endorse. The framing of a constitution then appears to be an act of *interpretation* in the sense that it brings to expression a normative content which previously was only *implicit* in the ethnical identity of the People. Just as, in political liberalism, the ultimate normative credentials of 'justice as fairness' qua political conception of justice consist of its being *the most reasonable conception for us*, groundbreaking in Michelman's argument is the idea that we never get out of the circle of the 'for us'. We are not 'we' without expressing that notion of a certain proper way of living together politically. An *exemplary* notion of normativity undergirds the 'Always Under Law?' strategy for addressing infinite regress.

Against the objection that this is a 'relativist' view of validity, we could contend that precisely the optimal and exemplary congruence between who we are and the constitutional essentials that we converge on—between who we are as an *ethnos* and who we are as a *demos*—may make our constitutional essentials inspiring also to other peoples. If we adopt this line of thought, then we defuse the problem of infinite regress and at the same time are able to retain a normative understanding of validity, albeit an *exemplary* normative one. The constitutive act that inaugurates a democratic order can be qualified as *democratic* on the basis of the consuetudinary proto-law which, according to the principle *ubi societas, ibi jus*, is part of the *ethnos* with which the resulting *demos* stands in a relation of continuity and interpretation.

Michelman's 'Always Under Law?' model not only defuses the infinite regress of a democratic foundation of the democratic order, which haunts Habermas's co-originality thesis, but also frees our understanding of democratic legitimacy

[55] See Herbert Spencer, 'Progress: Its Law and Cause' (1857), in *Herbert Spencer on Social Evolution*, ed. and introd. J. D. Y. Peel (U. of Chicago Press 1972) 42.

from the strictures of the long-prevailing Kelsen versus Schmitt binary to which it has remained hostage for a long time. According to Schmitt,

> A constitution is legitimate ... when the power and authority of the constitution-making power, on whose decision it rests, is acknowledged. The political decision reached regarding the type and form of state existence, which constitutes the substance of the constitution, is valid because the political unity whose constitution is at issue exists ... The decision requires no justification via an ethical or juristic norm. Instead, it makes sense in terms of political existence. A norm would not at all be in a position to justify anything here. The special type of political existence need not and cannot legitimate itself.[56]

On this view, constituent power is beyond normativity, being the source of it: constituent power simply exists, and that is all there is to it. Michelman's 'always under law' model, instead, allows us to question the facticity of constituent power, insofar as constituent power may fail to properly interpret the community's ultimate law or proto-law. Michelman's view also allows us, on the other hand, to take distance from Kelsen's formalism. Kelsen rejects the notion that a democratic constitution presupposes a concrete act performed by a collective entity called a people. Only retrospectively, and only if the enactment of a constitution has been successful, do the citizens—contends Kelsen—attribute to one another a consummated exercise of constituent power. Within Kelsen's model of legitimacy, the *demos* exists only as a series of self-attributive acts: by way of exercising their constitutional rights, the citizens retrospectively take on, or presuppose, the perspective of a 'we' that in the past has enacted a constitution and has done so in accordance with a *basic norm*, which likewise can only be presupposed.[57]

In the footsteps of theorists of self-constitution, Hans Lindahl has aptly suggested that 'the paradox of constituent power indicates that self-constitution

[56] Carl Schmitt, *Constitutional Theory* (first published 1928), tr. and ed. J. Seitzer, foreword by E. Kennedy (Duke U. Press 2008) 136.

[57] If the legitimacy of a constitution rests on an antecedent *Grundnorm*, in turn 'the basic norm is not created in a legal procedure by a law-creating organ. It is not—as a positive legal norm—valid because it is created in a certain way by a legal act, but it is valid because it is *presupposed* to be valid; and it is presupposed to be valid because without this presupposition no human act could be interpreted as a legal, especially norm-creating, act.' Hans Kelsen, *General Theory of Law and State* (Harvard U. Press 1949) 116, my italics. For an interesting vindication of Kelsen's view as most consistent with the liberal ideal of a law that, by renouncing all appeal to a unified, reconciled and undivided social life, can best serve the regulatory needs of a plural, divided world, see Johan van der Walt, *The Concept of Liberal Democratic Law* (Routledge 2020) 198–204 and 243, and *The Horizontal Effect: Revolution and the Question of Sovereignty* (De Gruyter 2014) 315–323.

begins as the constitution *of* a political unity *through* a legal order, not as the constitution of a legal order *by* a political unity'.[58]

This idea offers yet another perspective from which the groundbreaking quality of Michelman's view of constituent power as 'always under law' can be grasped: free from all risk of infinite regress, that view suggests that an *ethnos*, which is not yet a *demos*, forms a commitment to set under way a constitutional project in the terms that history contingently makes available to it. Through that constituent process it reflexively grows aware of its political identity and by finally enacting a constitution turns into a demos. This process may be called *democratic* in the sense that what was only *implicit*—a *democratic colouring* of the shared ethos—has now become *explicit* as a commitment positivized in the form of constitutional law.

[58] Hans Lindahl, 'Constituent Power and Reflexive Identity: Towards an Ontology of Collective Selfhood', in Martin Loughlin and Neil Walker (eds), *The Paradox of Constitutionalism* (OUP 2007) 22.

3

The Challenge of 'Most Reasonable for Us'

Frank I. Michelman

Government by consent of free and equal persons taken severally is one idea, government by mandate of a country's people 'as a collective body' is another.[1] As premised by us both in this exchange, the historical mission of liberal constitutional democracy has been to knit together these two ideas—'government by consent', 'government by the people'—in a unified practice of politics. But these are two analytically distinct ideas whose mutual compatibility is not a priori guaranteed, and our exchange has accordingly been concerned with how best to explain the possibility, in concept and in practice, of a true coupling of individual to collective self-rule.

From the democracy side (government by the people), we two have agreed, there follows the proposition of 'always under law'—at least if we leave sufficiently open, for now, exactly what we will mean by 'law'. If a country's highest lawmakers are conceived to be a particular people acting as a body—so runs that proposition—the law that even that country's highest politics is under must itself be understood as an application of *that people's* own antecedent law—or, as I have taken care to allow in Chapter 1, its antecedent 'proto-law' whatever that might mean. But then, given further a fact of reasonable pluralism, an apparent dilemma takes shape. If it is all and only by virtue of due implementation of a given people's antecedent law or proto-law that every latest utterance of constitutional essentials claims democratic validity, then what has become of liberal hopes for legitimation-by-constitution—our hopes, that is, for dependence on a higher-law constitution to support a mutuality of expectations, among free and equal citizens, of everyone's willing compliance with laws issued by democratic majorities over minority dissent. We seem to be caught between embrace and rejection of the idea of a trans-historically

[1] See John Rawls, *Justice as Fairness: A Restatement*, ed. Erin Kelly (Harvard U. Press 2001) 40 ('in a democratic regime political power is regarded as the power of free and equal citizens as a collective body').

Legitimation by Constitution. Alessandro Ferrara and Frank I. Michelman, Oxford University Press. © Alessandro Ferrara and Frank I. Michelman 2021. DOI: 10.1093/oso/9780192855121.003.0004

reasonable conception of rightness in politics, sufficiently robust in content to work persuasively as a test of justification.

In Chapter 2, Alessandro Ferrara offers a possibility of reconciliation through the idea of a people's historical emergence over time from a state or aspect of *ethnos* (a people with a cultural identity) to a state or aspect of *demos* (a people with a political identity), gauged in something like the way we gauge an artwork's success in fulfilling the singular law to which, as art, we hold it accountable. The *ethnos*-to-*demos* construction opens the way for Ferrara's illuminating comparison of the politico-legal act of application of a background-level, normative-directive text to the aesthetic-critical act of judgement of the merit of an artwork. 'The framing of a constitution', he writes,

> then appears to be an act of *interpretation* in the sense that it brings to expression a normative content which previously was only *implicit* in the ethnical identity of the People. Just as, in political liberalism, the ultimate normative credentials of 'justice as fairness' qua political conception of justice consist of its being *the most reasonable conception for us*, groundbreaking in Michelman's argument is the idea that we never get out of the circle of the 'for us'. We are not 'we' without expressing that notion of a certain proper way of living together politically. An *exemplary* notion of normativity undergirds the 'Always Under Law?' strategy for addressing infinite regress.[2]

In that way, as Ferrara has elsewhere suggested, we can purge from a liberal people's ultimate standard of rightness or fitness for politics all traces of 'modern universalism', or of 'externality' to that people.[3] That would hold, of course, for us heirs of the tradition of constitutional democracy, with our aboriginal, irrecusable proclivity (here I stand; I can do no other) for reciprocal recognition of each other as persons free and equal and hence for government by consent—meaning, upon due reflection, government under certain broadly-speaking liberal constitutional essentials.

It is that suggestion from Ferrara, of a liberal escape from modern universalism, to which I want to give some further consideration here. To that end, I draw now from an essay of mine from 1999,[4] responding to a paper by Jürgen

[2] Chapter 2, p. 52.

[3] See Alessandro Ferrara, *Justice and Judgment: The Rise and the Prospect of the Judgment Model in Contemporary Political Philosophy* (Sage Publications 1999) 174–177.

[4] See Frank I. Michelman, 'Morality, Identity, and 'Constitutional Patriotism' (1999) 76 Denver University Law Review 1009. The following paragraphs, until further notice, are taken from that publication and are included here with the kind permission of the Denver Law Review.

Habermas on 'Hermeneutic and Analytic Philosophy: Two Complementary Versions of the Linguistic Turn'.[5]

Habermas is here concerned with the philosophical aftermath of an early nineteenth century turn in metaphysics and epistemology, which he traces to works of Wilhelm von Humboldt. As Habermas sees matters, the linguistic turn has required all of social theory ever since to cope with the idea that language 'constitutes the world'. According to this world-constructing view of language, its 'lexicon and syntax'

> shape the totality of concepts and ways of apprehension by which first a conceptual space is articulated for everything the members of the community may come upon in the world. [... Each] language articulates a certain 'view' of the world as a whole. Thus the formula of language being the 'formative organ of thought' may be understood in the transcendental sense of spontaneous world-constitution. Through this linguistic pre-understanding of the world, a language simultaneously structures the form of life of the community.... Language is no longer primarily seen as a [transparent medium for] representing objects or facts, but as the medium for shaping a people's spirit.[6]

Thus language, by pre-inscribing the grid of conceptual possibilities on which facts can be spread, is said to assume a priority over the representation of the world, whether by oneself to oneself or by oneself to others. And language then further takes priority over intention, by limiting what it is possible to think or say regarding the categories—objectives, purposes, motives, values, sensations, sentiments, beliefs, attractions and aversions, hopes, and fears—by which one represents to oneself and to others the conative state of one's own mind.

At no point does Habermas offer denial of this transcendental position of language, meaning its decisive, irresistible, and limiting control over the construction of all possible objects and categories of experience and observation. But he does have a problem with it. Every natural language is both a historically contingent matter and an indissolubly social one. If a people's language decisively shapes and limits both the spirit of that people and the ways in which it is possible for that people to perceive and to judge, then there are in the history of the world, and on our planet today, an indefinite but certainly plural number of mutually non-translatable, indissolubly collective spirits and ways of seeing

[5] Jürgen Habermas, 'Hermeneutic and Analytic Philosophy: Two Complementary Versions of the Linguistic Turn' (1999) in Habermas, *Truth and Justification*, tr. Barbara Fultner (MIT Press 2003) 51.
[6] Ibid.

and judging, a plurality of 'semantically closed universes'[7] from which any possible escape could only—since no one has conscious experience at all outside of language and society—be tantamount to immediate entry into another, comparably limiting worldview.

The linguistic turn thus calls into question the notions of moral experience and moral obligation, as Habermas and many others would understand those terms. It does so by seeming to preclude the possibility of there being any transculturally accessible concepts, any concepts that remain the same, invariant, in the eyes of beholders from different 'comprehensive views', as John Rawls might call them, of the world and of the good. Any such preclusion must, it seems, extend to motivational sorts of concepts, such as values, reasons, maxims, norms, and obligations. But if a value, reason, maxim, norm, or obligation cannot retain its identity under regard by persons speaking different languages, how can it be one that is unconditionally binding on every individual human agent, just as human? If the answer is that it cannot, then an apparent result of the linguistic turn has been to preclude there being anything to which Habermas would concede the title of a moral value, reason, maxim, norm, or obligation. (Thus, reverting for a moment to terms of Ferrara, 'modern universalism' (and with it any possible 'externality' of a higher-law norm to a particular *ethnos/demos*?) would apparently be precluded from post-'turn' discourses of political justification.)

Or so it might seem. In fact, Habermas believes that an experience of the universal and unconditional bindingness of the class of maxims and reasons for action we call moral can be salvaged from the linguistic turn. He aims to retrieve 'universalistic tendencies'[8] from the linguistic turn as rendered by Humboldt, and his 'Linguistic Turn' paper is in considerable part the story of a salvage operation in which his own philosophy has played a major part, although he gives others a generous share of the credit.

Those universalist tendencies, Habermas explains in his paper, lie in the 'communicative' function that Humboldt was the first to attribute to language, along with its informative and expressive functions. They lie in the perception that when parties to a disagreement or misunderstanding enter into verbal exchange about it, both parties—as Habermas puts the matter—'must, from their own point of view, share the assumption of a point of convergence.'[9] That is, neither can make sense of what they are doing together, absent a working

[7] Ibid.
[8] Ibid.
[9] See ibid.

assumption in the mind of each of there being a single object at hand, of which the parties are giving competing accounts. That alone can explain the parties' expenditures of effort to 'learn to understand' each other's reports (descriptions, analyses, assessments) of the object.[10]

Thus does Habermas recover from the seeming devastation of the linguistic turn the possibility of the experience of objectivity, and thus of moral reasons and moral experience. But the recovery, as we now go on to notice, is not a completely clean one.

Habermas finds in Humboldt the idea that a conviction of the standpoint-independent, identical reality of objects under discussion—a reality that it's worth getting truly to know—is what keeps disagreeing observers committed to the work of coming to understand one another. But notice a circularity of motivation here. The parties' sense of there being some single object they are all perceiving, the truth about which they are trying to resolve, is supposed to support their loyalty to their shared or public enterprise of dialogue. But then what would have instilled in them this sense of objectivity? We could say that it arises out of the experience of the discursive engagement itself. But then we would have to ask what in the first place could have drawn the parties into the engagement, or made the engagement seem possible to them; what possibly, except an antecedently existing expectation, among the parties to the conversation, of each feeling a pressure to strive for a successful result? But then what in their world and in their lives could prompt and sustain such an expectation? Only, it would seem (if we accept the linguistic turn), a *language*. Specifically, it would be a language in which the categories exist for recognition of the freedom and equality of persons and of resulting reciprocal obligations of persons to treat each other as such.

Must *every* human language necessarily be like that? If so—if there are categories that a human language necessarily must have—what is really left of the linguistic turn? But if not, then what Habermas has done is something rather beyond a simple retrieval from the linguistic turn of the possibility of moral experience and moral obligation. What he has done is to show how human beings can, and some of us do, maintain in our lives the category of the unconditionally obligatory (the moral), even as we, accepting the linguistic turn, know that moral reasons and experience are reasons and experience into which we must always enter not in entire forgetfulness but trailing clouds of consciousness from our particular linguistic home. In other words, what Habermas has done (at least it seems so to me) is to make clear how there can be a wholly valid

[10] Ibid.

experience of the unconditionally obligatory that is not necessarily accessible from within every human form of life.[11]

'Proto-liberal' (as we might say) is the form of life that is home to that experience. We find at its core a radical, normative-individualist inspiration, an insistence on the normative primacy—that is, as objects of moral concern—of notionally free and equal individuals. For purposes of a liberal theory of democracy, what issues from this inspiration is a demand for the consonance of the constitutional essentials to the reasons of each (not 'all', in some collectivized sense of 'all') of countless persons among whom rational (and reasonable) conflicts of interests and vision abound. It is to this extent and in this sense that individualism remains political liberalism's quintessential premise. It is in this light that the 'irrecusable' liberal commitment to self-government has to be understood. The commitment, ultimately is and must be to the self-government of persons, not of groups.

In what sense 'must'? In this sense: from within the proto-liberal form of life, one simply *notices* that there is no other way but reciprocity to go about the conduct of one's life in society, without a betrayal of one's ineluctable sense of oneself as a free being—whose own freedom is unthinkable without positing and honouring the equal freedom of others with whom one is bound in society. It will simply be a question of what choice one has, seeing what one sees and knowing what one knows.

With the aid of philosophers like Habermas and Ferrara, we may learn to take a detached, reflective view of this experience of universal necessitation constraining in some ways—and so (as thus reflectively apprehended) external to—our pursuit of our own (otherwise) deepest convictions of right and wrong in politics. We may learn thus to see it as itself a contingency of ethnic particularity and so not a universal law of human nature, even as our internal experience—the liberalizing experience—of universal necessitation nevertheless remains unshaken.

That is what I drew from Habermas in 1999 (and again in 2006). How does it stack up against the Rawlsian political-liberal test of 'most reasonable for us' for approval of a set of justification-bearing constitutional essentials? That question will be fraught with consequence for subsequent exchanges between us two.

[11] Wordsworthians may see in what I just wrote an implicit equation of language with God, but isn't that, after all, one way of describing the linguistic turn? In the beginning was ... *We have now reached the end of the extract from my 1999 paper on Habermas and the linguistic turn. The rest of this chapter is loosely drawn from Chapter 3 of our joint work of 2006.*

4

The 'Most Reasonable for Us', or 'Irrecusability' as Preserving Authenticity

Alessandro Ferrara

While I am in total agreement with the reconstruction of my position offered by Frank Michelman in Chapter 3, on one specific point I believe that it could be useful to push the discussion further. How to understand the meaning of what Michelman has called 'our', that is to say our 'pre-*demos*' 'irrecusable proclivity' for 'reciprocal recognition of each other as free and equal and hence for government by consent'?[1] Why is this liberal ideal of a legitimate polity 'irrecusable' for us, where 'irrecusable' stands for a succinct, adjectival rendition of Luther's famous phrase 'Here I stand; I can do no other'?

Michelman reconstructs the normative force underlying that sense of 'irrecusability' by approvingly drawing on Habermas's account of the change of philosophical horizon known as 'the linguistic turn'.[2] According to Habermas, the linguistic turn is a drama in three acts. The first opens up with Humboldt's philosophy of language. Then two complementary and reductive versions of the twentieth-century linguistic revolution follow up—Wittgenstein's analytic philosophy and Heidegger's ontological hermeneutics. Finally, the universalistic insights of Humboldt's vision are vindicated in the programme of a 'universal formal pragmatics'. At stake in this drama is a proper grasp of the *cognitive* and *representational* function of language within a fully-fledged reconstruction of the relation of language to mind and world.

[1] See Chapter 3, p. 56.

[2] See Habermas, 'Hermeneutics and Analytic Philosophy: Two Complementary Versions of the Linguistic Turn?' (first published 1999), in Jürgen Habermas, *Truth and Justification*, tr. Barbara Fultner (MIT Press 2003) 61 (hereafter Habermas, 'Two Complementary Versions').

Legitimation by Constitution. Alessandro Ferrara and Frank I. Michelman, Oxford University Press. © Alessandro Ferrara and Frank I. Michelman 2021. DOI: 10.1093/oso/9780192855121.003.0005

1. Habermas's Reconstruction of Two Flawed Versions of the Linguistic Turn

How is it possible to hold on to the formative function of language and at the same time escape relativism? It is possible, according to Habermas, because Humboldt avoids conflating the *cognitive-representational* function of language—the only one which for Habermas contains a context-transcending potential—with the *semantics* of linguistic forms. Rather, Humboldt assumes that the representational function is exerted in the context of linguistic *interaction* or *dialogue.* If understood along merely *semantic* lines, the formative role of language becomes a prison for subjectivity: the peculiarities of our languages become the peculiarities of our worlds, and we end up entrapped in both without escape. However, by postulating an additional *pragmatic* dimension, in the sense that the shaping or disclosing of worlds always unfolds within a process of communication whereby differently located participants try to reach an understanding *about* the world, then we recover a universalistic potential without falling into the trap of semantic relativism.[3]

Humboldt, in other words, had the merit of highlighting 'the pragmatic interplay of the cognitive and the communicative functions of language' and to show how the partiality of worlds constituted by locally dominant languages could be overcome not *by stepping out of language* but, on the contrary, by way of relativizing each of the 'local worlds' in the process of confronting the inhabitants of other worlds. The limit of Humboldt's account, in Habermas's opinion, lies in the fact that fruitful as his view of language might be for explaining how differently constituted perspectives may come to overlap in the process of intercultural communication, his pragmatic approach in the end fails to explain 'how we can grasp facts in the vertical dimension of reference to the objective world, and how controversy about statements of fact can yield knowledge'.[4] The inadequacy of this account of the representational function of language will pass on to the subsequent hermeneutic tradition. In the twentieth century, a somewhat similar distribution of strengths and weaknesses is reflected in two versions of the linguistic turn. According to Habermas, the *analytic* strand, inaugurated by Frege and reaching its most complete articulation in Wittgenstein's *Tractatus*, focuses on the *semantic* relation of language

[3] Habermas's understanding of the universalist potential inherent in the pragmatic dimension of language is reconstructed along similar lines also by Michelman, see Chapter 3, pp. 56–60.
[4] Habermas, 'Two Complementary Versions' (n. 2) 61.

to the world and highlights how language can represent something outside language. The *hermeneutic* strand, championed by Heidegger, focuses on the *world-disclosing* function of language and highlights how linguistic forms can create a world within which we can *then, subsequently*, talk about facts. In establishing a priority of 'alétheia' over 'adaequatio', of the 'happening of truth' over the 'truth of predicative sentences', Heidegger 'simply does not allow for the possibility that the meaning of a vocabulary is affected by the results of learning processes within the world'.[5] Further ahead along this road, we lose all possibility of distinguishing the *validity* of an utterance from its *social acceptance*. The source of these symmetrical weaknesses lies, according to Habermas, in a common characteristic underlying both the analytic and the hermeneutic versions of the linguistic turn: despite their approaching language from opposite starting points, both confine themselves to the *semantics* of language and neither of them expects 'the structural features of speech to make an essential contribution to the rationality of communication'.[6] How can these difficulties be addressed? One line of response simply radicalizes the *priority-of-'alétheia'-over-'adaequatio'* stance common to Wittgenstein and Heidegger: this line is adopted by the post-empiricist philosophy of science, neopragmatist linguistic philosophy, and the post-structuralist critique of reason. The other line follows in the tracks of Russell's and Carnap's analysis of language and develops 'a merely methodological understanding of the linguistic turn, a strand that has gained worldwide acceptance through the work of Quine and Davidson'.[7]

2. Habermas's 'Pragmatic' Third Way

Habermas suggests a third line of response, for which he modestly credits Putnam, Dummett, and Apel, leaving his own name aside. These authors 'take seriously the linguistic turn in the sense of a paradigm shift, without paying the price of the culturalist assimilation of being true to taking to be true'.[8]

The recovery of the cognitive-representational function of language—as the key to restoring its universalistic dimension of validity via pragmatics—is operated by Habermas in three steps. First, Habermas links meaning and validity by defining 'understanding a sentence' as 'knowing how to justify its

[5] Ibid. 62.
[6] Ibid. 69.
[7] Ibid. 69.
[8] Ibid. 69.

truth' and 'knowing what obligations follow from one's accepting it as true'. Second, communication aimed at agreement focuses on the certainties of the life-world and questions them in a 'discourse'; third, the ability of discursively reached insights to transcend the boundaries of locally prevailing interpretive frameworks 'is explained by the discursive processing of action-related experiences.... Experiences that indicate the collapse of routine practices can initiate a revision of assumptions and normative expectations and, ultimately, even affect linguistic knowledge itself'.[9] In the context of this last step, the cognitive function of language supposedly operates independently of world-disclosure, by generating a tension between the formative power of world-disclosing frames of meaning and the recalcitrant aspects of reality highlighted in the course of learning processes.

What remains unclear is how the cognitive-representational function of language—manifested to us by 'experiences that indicate the collapse of routine practices'—can really bridge the gap opened by the clash of competing language games, paradigms, traditions, conceptual schemes, or world-disclosing frames. If we take seriously the world-constituting function of language, why should disagreement over forms of world-disclosure not generate disagreement over the 'collapse of routine practices'? Or, to paraphrase Kant: how are cross-paradigmatic experiences of the collapse of routines possible at all? By assuming that they *are* possible, Habermas commits himself to either (a) asserting that (at least) the disappointing quality of experiences and consequent collapse of routine practices are independent of the world-disclosing schemes—in which case the relativism of the Wittgenstein–Heidegger conception has not been responded to, but has simply been wished away—or (b) conceding that the clash between distinct forms of world-disclosure inevitably results also in a different assessment of the routine-disrupting quality of our experiences.

The problem with the project of a formal-pragmatic completion of the linguistic turn is that the universalist aspect of the use of language continues to be unduly conflated with the *cognitive* or *representational* function, as though this function, now harnessed to the *pragmatic* aspect of language, could work *independently* of the world-disclosing moment. This problematic quality of his pragmatic (and formerly 'procedural') solution to the problems raised by the linguistic turn continues to affect Habermas's thought even in his latest major philosophical work, *Auch eine Geschichte der Philosophie*.[10]

[9] Ibid. 78.
[10] Jürgen Habermas, *Auch eine Geschichte der Philosophie* (Suhrkamp 2019), vol. 2, chapter 9.

No detailed discussion can be found of Wittgenstein's theses. Habermas's fully de-transcendentalized, 'embodied post-metaphysical reason'—the ultimate evolutionary outcome of the differentiation of philosophy from theology, metaphysics, and modern science—seems to rest on the reconstruction of the presuppositions of a language-game that is primarily a philosophical creature, a procedural meta-language-game assumed to undergird all local language-games no less than the Kantian transcendental categories used to deprive cultural and historical differences of all significance for the constitution of experience. To put it in the language of our two post-metaphysical heroes, even Habermas's latest philosophical effort fails to clarify what should ground the expectation that 'the uncoercive force of the better argument' will quell what Rawls calls 'the burdens of judgment'. Unfortunately, both our heroes can't be right on this point. If the better argument can prevail over the burdens of judgement, no 'fact of reasonable pluralism' holds, but we revert to the old understanding of pluralism as the temporary product of unfortunate conditions—in this case, the imperfect realization of the 'ideal conditions of communication'. In addition, then, we have no real use for the idea of something 'most reasonable for us', and indeed Habermas consistently urged Rawls to anchor more firmly 'the reasonable' in the 'morally right', showing no appreciation of the distinct normative status of public reason, the reasonable, and 'the most reasonable':

> The notion of reasonableness is either so etiolated that it is too weak to characterize the mode of validity of an intersubjectively recognized conception of political justice, or it is defined in sufficiently strong terms, in which case what is practically reasonable is indistinguishable from what is morally right.[11]

If, on the contrary, the burdens of judgement are taken to prevail over the unifying force of the better argument, then the 'most reasonable for us', as distinct from the pragmatic anticipation of a cognitive convergence on a 'truth-to-come', is all we can have at our disposal for coping with a fact of reasonable pluralism which can never be assumed to fade away.

[11] Habermas, '"Reasonable" versus "True", or the Morality of Worldviews', in Ciaran Cronin and Pablo De Greiff (eds), *The Inclusion of Other: Studies in Political Theory* (MIT Press 1998) 77 (hereafter Habermas, '"Reasonable" versus "True"').

3. Michelman's Interpretation of Habermas on the Linguistic Turn

Michelman finds his own share of flaws in Habermas's argument, including a circularity of explanation. The sense that, underneath epistemic or practical disputes, a unique and selfsame object exists 'the truth about which' is under contention, comes literally from nowhere. It cannot come from the *practice* of language use, because such practice if anything reinforces our perception that language shapes our world. We could point then to a more specific practice, namely our engagements in truth-seeking dialogues—including dialogues about the validity of the assumption of the 'freedom and equality of each citizen' at the centre of liberalism. But then, Michelman continues, 'we would have to ask what in the first place could have drawn the parties into the engagement, or made the engagement seem possible to them'[12]. It obviously must be some kind of inner-felt 'pressure to strive for a successful result'. What could 'prompt and sustain such an expectation?'[13] Habermas's reconstruction of the linguistic turn seems to lead us to look at some feature of language for an answer. If under dispute is the liberal assumption of freedom and equality, then we would have to look at linguistic presuppositions that support the presumption of such an obligation to treat each other as 'free and equal'. At this juncture, as Michelman points out, the suspicion of circularity arises: if 'there are categories that a human language necessarily must have'—in our case the freedom and equality of all participants in a truth-seeking dialogical practice—'what is really left of the linguistic turn?'[14] However, very charitably he credits Habermas with having escaped circularity and having persuasively shown how we can 'maintain in our lives the category of the unconditionally obligatory (the moral), even as we, accepting the linguistic turn, know that moral reasons and experiences are reasons and experiences into which we must always enter not in entire forgetfulness but trailing clouds of consciousness from our particular linguistic home'.[15] This Habermasian restatement of the normative clarifies, for Michelman, 'how there can be a wholly valid experience of the unconditionally obligatory that is not necessarily accessible from within every human form of life'.[16]

[12] Chapter 3, p. 59.
[13] Ibid..
[14] Ibid. pp. 59–60.
[15] Ibid..
[16] Ibid.

In our case, a 'proto-liberal' form of life is the 'home' of an 'irrecusable' commitment to what 'is and must be' a self-government of persons, not of groups. From within such a linguistically mediated proto-liberal lifeform, one 'simply *notices*' that there is no way to ground *our* communal political life other than on the premise of freedom and equality for everyone, 'without a betrayal of one's ineluctable sense of oneself as a free being'.[17]

I find Habermas's account of the linguistic turn less helpful than Michelman suggests, for answering our question. It remains anchored to a *cognitive* view of context-transcending, and simply tries to shift the anchor-point from the semantics to the pragmatics of language, with all the difficulties already highlighted above, some of which in the end reverberate also on Michelman's account. In fact, if the cognitive-representational inflection of 'necessity' is not relinquished, then how can the irrecusability of freedom and equality project cogency beyond the circle of 'us', the members of an already *liberal ethnos* or proto-*demos*? If no such context-transcending of any sort takes place, how is this account different from a mere *description* of our ways?

4. Another Solution: Rethinking 'Irrecusability' as Preserving Authenticity

These difficulties can be solved by adopting Rawls's way of rethinking normativity after the linguistic turn, overlooked in Michelman's take on Habermas and modern universalism. The most innovative aspect of the legacy of Rawls is certainly the invention of *political* liberalism, in complete dissonance with the dubious linkage of previous forms of liberalism with 'modern universalism'. The 'reasonable', in fact, entirely breaks free of the imaginary of the cognitive-representational. That radical break—far more radical than Habermas's relocating the context-transcending potential of language, *still harnessed to its representational function*, from the semantic to the pragmatic aspects—is signalled by Rawls's famous capturing of the normative credentials of 'justice as fairness', qua political conception of justice, no longer as 'its being true to an order antecedent to and given to us' but as connected with 'its congruence with our deeper understanding of ourselves and our aspirations' – ultimately, 'given our history and the traditions embedded in our public life', with its being '*the most reasonable doctrine for us*'.[18]

[17] Ibid. p. 60.

[18] John Rawls, 'Kantian Constructivism in Moral Theory' (1980) 88 Journal of Philosophy 519. A similar point is made in *PL*, 28.

Rawls's formulation breaks free of two myths. The first is the myth, originating from Plato's Allegory of the Cave, that the cogency of something normatively binding on us should originate from the truth of some statement about the world, an epistemic treasure whose latest reincarnation is to be found in Habermas's faith in language's capacity to express disappointing experiences and the breakdown of routine practices across paradigmatic divides.[19] The second myth consists of the belief that short of anchoring the reasonable in cross-paradigmatic epistemic truth, we are doomed to conflate the validity of a statement or a norm with the social acceptance of its validity.[20] Radical contextualists such as Rorty rightly criticize external epistemic standpoints, Archimedean points, and 'the view from nowhere', but then they offer no way to make sense of how one 'vocabulary' could be preferable over another. By contrast, Rawls's uncoupling of normativity from cognition or representation, through his concept of reasonableness, enables him to explain how one normative notion—be it 'justice as fairness' or 'government by consent among free and equal citizens'—can be judged as 'more reasonable' than a competing one or as being the 'most reasonable' *for someone*.

How to account, then, for the sense of 'necessitation' that we may experience in recognizing government by consent, premised on the freedom and equality of citizens, as most reasonable for us? Again, that sense of 'necessitation', of being unable to choose differently, can be understood from Rawls's perspective neither as linked with the recognition of some truth external to us nor as the expression of a collective preference. It is best understood along practical, as opposed to cognitive-representational lines, as reflecting a commitment that cannot be disavowed without forfeiting the possibility, on the part of the *ethnos*-about-to-turn-*demos*, of conceiving of itself, in the eyes of its members, as the selfsame subject.

This is how I interpret Michelman's reconstruction of the irrecusability of government by consent as a kind of *simply noticing*, on the part of the members of a people, that 'there is no other way but reciprocity to go about the conduct of one's life in society, without a betrayal of one's ineluctable sense of oneself as a free being bound in society'.[21]

[19] For a reconstruction, against the backdrop of Plato's Allegory of the Cave, of Rawls's radically innovative understanding of pluralism and of the standard of 'the most reasonable for us', see Alessandro Ferrara, 'Sideways at the Entrance of the Cave: A Pluralist Footnote to Plato', in Volker Kaul and Ingrid Salvatore (eds), *What is Pluralism?* (Routledge 2020) 81–98.

[20] See Habermas, '"Reasonable" versus "True"' (n. 11) 99–100.

[21] See Chapter 3, p. 60.

At this point, however, a possible misunderstanding must be cleared away. *Ethnos*—i.e. the term introduced above to designate the pre-political forerunner of a *demos*—does not mean *any ethnos*. We cannot possibly claim, consistently with a rejection of all ethnocentric foundationalism, that any *ethnos* on the planet is bound to find the liberal ideal of government by consent irrecusable. Rather, the cultural identity of *a modern, pluralistic ethnos*, at a point in time when it still has to decide to constitute itself as a *democratic demos* with a constitution, is the starting point of my argument. This modern, pluralistic *ethnos* is the same as the 'proto-demos' assumed by Habermas when raising his co-originality question 'what rights must citizens mutually grant one another if they decide to constitute themselves as a voluntary association of legal consociates and legitimately to regulate their living together by means of positive law?'[22] Such a proto-*demos* is not yet a democratic *demos*, strictly speaking, because it is photographed conceptually at a point in time when the constitution doesn't yet exist and no rights have yet been granted. Any Western-modern *proto-demos* (for those who feel aversion to the word *ethnos*) is then a collection of individuals who, given their history (punctuated among other things by religious intolerance and religious wars), cannot but orient themselves to equal respect and reciprocity. What makes of this collection of individuals a 'modern' *ethnos* or *proto-demos* is their sharing a postconventional ethos centred on the premise that no one can legitimately be bound other than by laws to which one has autonomously consented. What makes of these individuals a 'democratic' *ethnos* or *proto-demos* is the *substance* of the principle underlying their communal bond—i.e. the principle of consent among free and equals. On my own view of liberal justification, then, respect for pluralism is there from the beginning, even before the *demos* comes into being, because of the specific historical identity of the individuals who set the constitutional-democratic process in motion. There is nothing else than the *authenticity* of these prospective citizens' reflexive endorsement[23] of freedom, reciprocity, and equal respect that grounds the irrecusability of 'government by consent'.

Now, to expand further on how this irrecusability is to be understood, the judgement and exemplarity approach to the justification of government by consent rests on the distinction between (a) understanding a certain normative provision as resulting from a preference that a people happens to share (e.g. freedom to strike is protected as part of freedom of association in the United

[22] Jürgen Habermas, 'Postscript to *Faktizität und Geltung*' (1994) 20(4) Philosophy & Social Criticism 140.

[23] See Chapter 2, n. 42, above.

States, but is protected as a separate right in the Italian, Spanish, Portuguese and Greek Constitutions)[24] and (b) understanding a certain normative provision (e.g. such constitutional essentials as freedom of speech or religious freedom) as so ingrained in what the principles called 'equal respect' and 'government by consent' require, so bound up with the way a group of individuals have come to constitute themselves as a people, that they cannot renounce such provision without feeling that they have thereby turned themselves into a different, and alien, political subject.

This interpretation of 'irrecusability', as aimed at preserving authenticity, is corroborated by one difficulty incurred by the competing, more cognitive-representational, interpretation. Should we understand Michelman's view of the irrecusability of a principle of reciprocity as anchored 'in one's simply *noticing* that there is no other way but reciprocity to go about the conduct of one's life in society' along the cognitive-representational lines suggested by Habermas's response to the linguistic turn, then we would run into the implausibility of holding the standpoint of reciprocity as irrecusably true for *any* and *every* society. That understanding would lead us to explain the fact that not all of the 195 states of the world are constitutional democracies—by the latest 2020 count, no more than 83 are[25]—in terms of a cognitive deficit: namely, the individuals who have lived and live in these non-democratic states miss on some kind of self-evident truth, they 'fail to notice' some normative necessity, which instead the citizens of 3 states (and among them only 2 or 3 came to this insight on their own, without external political influence) did notice, grasp and build their political order on. By the standard of political liberalism, shared by Michelman and me, would such a view of the irrecusability of government by consent, then, not instantly forfeit its 'political' character and become just another comprehensive doctrine?

If belief in the irrecusability of government by consent cannot be defensibly ascribed to all individuals in all societies, then the conclusion seems inescapable that such irrecusability must be understood as resting on *our* (severally) noticing that there is no other way *for us* to go about the conduct of our life in society, no other basis on which to build *our* relation with other fellow citizens compatibly with our remaining who *we*, we 'modern Westerners', are. Historical experiences then differ over the specific ways and timing of this

[24] See the Constitutions of Italy (Article 40), Spain (Section 28), Portugal (Article 57), and Greece (Article 23). In the United States a right to strike has been derived from the First Amendment, and at times from other provisions, but no specific one mentions it.

[25] Freedom House Report 2020, at <https://freedomhouse.org/report/freedom-world> accessed 20 April 2020.

'noticing'. The individuals composing the British, American, and French *demoi* somehow 'noticed' first—which is why the word 'revolution' is usually associated with their historical experiences—while other sets of individuals, such as those composing the Italian, the German, and many other *demoi*, took full notice only after 1945. But, speaking now for a larger set, all peoples that live in democratic regimes are at one in endorsing a principle of reciprocity to which their national constitutions stand in that sort of interpretive relation that Michelman so convincingly reconstructed in 'Always Under Law?' This version of the defence of the irrecusability (or 'reasonable non-rejectability')[26] of government by consent, consistent with the evidence at hand, then does away with the cognitive-representational way of elucidating 'necessitation'.

That the linkage of irrecusability and necessitation cannot be manufactured at the actor's will, by just bringing about a certain degree of social acceptance, can be illustrated by contrasting the irrecusability of government by consent with the putative irrecusability of other political ideals. Consider, for example, the welfare state. Millions of people in all democracies worldwide believe that equal respect also means that the dignity of citizens must be protected against certain dynamics of the market: that it would be unacceptable to let anyone starve to death, remain medically untreated or uneducated as a result of market processes. Other millions of people, however, think the opposite and want to dismantle the welfare state provisions thus far in place.

What is then the difference between belief in the irrecusability of the ideal of government by consent on one hand and the widely, though not universally, shared belief in the irrecusability of certain basic welfare state provisions? The difference cannot be that some transcendent normative structure or objective moral truth 'from out of the cave' enjoins us to support government by consent but not the welfare state. Nor can the difference be that empirically more individuals agree on, or happen to prefer to have, government by consent than there are individuals who agree on the irrecusability of the welfare state. Our (correct, in my opinion) perception of a different 'degree of irrecusability' originates in a (reflective) judgement about the salience of the ideal of government by consent, as an ideal based on the principle of equal respect, to our sense of who we are. In other words, we would not be *we* without government by consent and equal respect, whereas we can still, by and large, be *we* with a welfare state rolled back, though of course many individuals, including Michelman and myself, would like to see the day when government by consent and the welfare state will be equally irrecusable. But

[26] See Thomas M. Scanlon, *What We Owe to Each Other* (Harvard U. Press 1998) 191–197.

they are *not* equally irrecusable for the time being, regardless whether this circumstance is to our liking or not.

To sum up, it is hard to see how interpretation and judgement (which, as Kant's theory of reflective judgement shows, entail a claim to trans-contextual validity not found in merely empirical preferences) can be left out from our reconstruction of why something irrecusable is indeed irrecusable. Consequently, our 'noticing' the irrecusability of government by consent has to be construed as our noticing its irrecusability *for us*, lest we are prepared to turn liberalism into a comprehensive doctrine. To conclude, interpretation cannot be driven off the picture of irrecusability, as we may expect given the reflective nature of the judgement concerning the non-renounceable core of the people's political identity.

PART II
A DEMOCRATIC HORIZON

This book is a record of conversations between two liberal-minded subscribers to the problem (as John Rawls calls it) of political liberalism—the problem, that is, in postmetaphysical societies, of the justification, among free and equal citizens, of the force of laws enacted by democratic majorities over grave opposition and dissent. Our exchanges all have in view a proposal from Rawls to meet the problem with a programme for dualist democracy and legitimation-by-constitution. The exchanges in Part I—the first round—looked into certain doubts about that programme's actual or possible approximation by actual events in historical time, and even about its coherence in concept; and then into how best to restate or explain the programme in terms to meet those doubts. The four chapters of Part I thus compose a conversation on conceptual and practical possibility.

The conversations in Parts II and III can be described as 'bracketing' the possibility questions of Part I. We do not, in these exchanges next to come, assume those doubts resolved. We rather proceed on the basis that contemporary constitutional democracies do in fact rely on two-track democracy for response to the problem of political liberalism. (To Rawls's presumed social facts of reasonable pluralism and oppression, we add—you might say—a presumed political-cultural fact of legitimation-by-constitution.) In Part II, you will find us conversing about one piece of evidence (Michelman would say) for that third fact's existence—to wit: the inextinguishable debates, within and across our countries, over the aims and methods of judicial constitutional review and related debates over judicial restraint. In Part III, the focus turns to limits of legitimation-by-constitution in conditions (as we might call them) of *un*reasonable pluralism, and the possibilities of somehow still salvaging, for our societies and the world, the moral cores of freedom and equality, reciprocity and tolerance, in the project of political liberalism.

These two conversations—on the constitutional role of the judiciary, and on limits of liberal tolerance—both stem initially from commentary by Michelman, published in 2016, on Ferrara's book of 2014, *The Democratic*

Horizon.[1] Some account of the aims and terrain of that book is accordingly in order here.

In *The Democratic Horizon*, Ferrara proposes to amend the Rawlsian paradigm of political liberalism at four specific junctures, so as better to fit it to contexts outside the United States and better to meet the challenge posed by *hyperpluralism*—the challenge, that is, to bridge across visionary gaps more drastic than, say, the rift in the constitutional-democratic tradition over the relative primacies, in a well-ordered society, of the 'liberties of the moderns' and 'liberties of the ancients', which Rawls mentions as exemplary of the divisions to which his philosophy is addressed.[2]

First, as their response to hyperpluralist conditions, some liberal-minded theorists suggest that political justification simply should rest with a more modest aim than establishing the acceptability of liberal principles and constitutional essentials to all the diverse constituencies found within our societies. Rather, the aim would be to show 'what kind of arguments, if any, citizens *already committed* to certain basic liberal norms can legitimately offer to one another'.[3] Ferrara rejects that sort of restriction of the addressees of liberal political justification, as paving the way to a 'liberal oppression' of potentially large constituencies (not just isolated law-breakers) by pressures to submit to principles they don't endorse. The opening and fundamental question set by Rawls in *Political Liberalism* is that of the possibility of a society in pluralist conditions (not restricted to liberals) that is just and stable both. The corresponding principle of legitimacy accordingly links the proper exercise of political power to compliance with a constitution endorsable by all citizens in the light of principles and ideals acceptable 'to them' as reasonable and rational.[4]

A liberal society, Ferrara maintains, cannot consistently ground the legitimacy of its institutions on a sort of normative gerrymandering that reduces the constituency of the reasonable, to be addressed by political justification, to those already fully committed to liberalism.[5] His preferred response to hyperpluralism is, first, to pick up the challenge of persuasively inviting citizens already partially reasonable by strict liberal lights—those who can endorse some but not all of the liberal constitutional essentials—across the line to full reasonability. For that purpose, however, Ferrara finds the idea of public

[1] Alessandro Ferrara, *The Democratic Horizon: Hyperpluralism and the Renewal of Political Liberalism* (CUP 2014) (hereafter Ferrara, *Democratic Horizon*).
[2] See John Rawls, *Justice as Fairness: A Restatement*, ed. Erin Kelly (Harvard U. Press 2001) 2.
[3] Jonathan Quong, *Liberalism Without Perfection* (OUP 2011) 5.
[4] Rawls, *PL* 217.
[5] Along similar lines, see also Erin Kelly and Lionel McPherson, 'On Tolerating the Unreasonable' (2001) 9 Journal of Political Philosophy 38.

reason of limited use. As a form of reasons-giving that enjoins participants to use only shared premises to support their conclusions, public reason idles if and when the stock of available shared premises runs short. A possible remedy consists then, Ferrara suggests, of supplementing public reason with *conjectural arguments* (mentioned by Rawls but not by him pursued in depth),[6] that offer to partially reasonable citizens reasons internal to their comprehensive conceptions for recognizing the burdens of judgement and acceding further, then, to the liberal constitutional essentials. This conjectural turn can generate a sort of *reflexive* pluralism: citizens reasoning from different comprehensive conceptions would embrace pluralism for diverse reasons.[7] To paraphrase Rawls, reflexive pluralism applies pluralism to itself, putting a stop to those comprehensive (and performatively contradictory) versions of it that would consider pluralism acceptable in most domains of political disagreement, but not in that of the justification of pluralism.

Now, there can be no guarantee that conjectural arguments, given their interpretive nature, will deliver the desired result. What to do when not *all* the citizens—as mandated by the liberal principle of legitimacy—can endorse all the constitutional essentials in the light of principles and ideals acceptable *to them* as reasonable and rational? Then the paradigm could be amended, Ferrara urges in *The Democratic Horizon*, by lifting the implicit, but unnecessary, assumption that the polity moves all of a piece, holistically, through the stages of moderation of political conflict: *modus vivendi*, constitutional consensus, and finally an overlapping moral consensus. In *The Law of Peoples*, Rawls outlines a hypothetical and desirable political condition of the world as what Ferrara now names as a 'multivariate' political entity, based on a mix of principled and prudential considerations. One larger component of the world would include liberal and decent peoples sharing a commitment to principles of justice in and for a 'Society of Peoples'.[8] Then these 'well-ordered' peoples, as members of the society of peoples, jointly relate to other types of peoples (those ruled through 'benevolent absolutism', 'burdened societies,' and 'outlaw states')[9] via a mix of differently weighted considerations of justice and prudence.

Thus, the lesson for the domestic case: when domestic hyperpluralism proves intractable not only to public reason, but also to conjectural arguments,

[6] Rawls, 'The Idea of Public Reason Revisited', in *PL* 465–466.

[7] For some proponents of this perspective, see Andrew March, *Islam and Liberal Citizenship: The Search for an Overlapping Consensus* (OUP 2009); Lucas Swaine, *The Liberal Conscience: Politics and Principle in a World of Religious Pluralism* (Columbia U. Press 2006).

[8] See John Rawls, *The Law of Peoples* (Harvard U. Press 1999) 63, 125 (hereafter Rawls, *Law of Peoples*).

[9] See ibid. 63, 81, 106.

a properly renewed political liberalism is not left resourceless. Drawing from *The Law of Peoples*, it can still offer the idea of a multivariate democratic polity, where most citizens embrace all the constitutional essentials in the light of principles agreeable to their comprehensive moral conceptions (as in the standard version), while other groups embrace some constitutional essentials in the light of principles and some only out of prudence, and a third group embraces all of the constitutional essentials out of prudence alone. The legitimation of authority then follows a differentiated pattern, but still remains true to a liberal aim of government by consent of all citizens.

The multivariate democratic polity should not, says Ferrara in *the Democratic Horizon*, be seen as a crass concession to political realism or a modus-vivendi type liberalism,[10] or as one initial step down the slippery slope to a balkanized society. Its aim is entirely normative: to extend the ideal of government by consent to democratic societies (e.g. the European Union) encountering epoch-making waves of incoming new and non-liberal constituencies, even as committed political liberals in those societies recoil from imposition of liberal views through legal coercion. The path to redemption of the liberal-democratic polity from liberal oppression then lies through a realistic allowance of endorsement out of prudence (thus, not outright rejection) as a second-best, provisional kind of consensus that still allows the exercise of political authority to meet with the citizens' consent. In hyperpluralism-affected societies, the final clause of Rawls's principle of liberal legitimacy, envisaging that the endorsement of constitutional essentials proceeds out of 'principles and ideals', is modified so as to accept also prudential reasons on the part of some of the citizens.

That solution makes normatively better sense, to Ferrara, than an inverse insistence that endorsement proceed solely out of reasons of principle, thus forcing admission that such endorsement does not anyway come from *all*, but only from a shrinking fraction of citizens. The multivariate solution carries instead, Ferrara says, a forward-looking, inclusive political dynamism that is missing from the alternative. It brings non-liberal, 'partially reasonable' citizens within the circle of the addressees of political justification and sets the stage for deeper forms of political inclusion. As Rawls pointed out when elucidating the transition from a modus vivendi to a constitutional consensus, if political institutions incorporate liberal principles and operate on the basis of

[10] See John Gray, *Two Faces of Liberalism* (Polity Press 2000) and John Horton, '*Modus vivendi* and Political Legitimacy', in J. Horton, M. Westphal, and U. Willems (eds), *The Political Theory of Modus Vivendi* (Springer 2018) 131–148. For a critical appraisal, see Alessandro Ferrara, 'How to Accommodate *Modus Vivendi* within Normative Political Theory' (2018) 53 Biblioteca della libertà 9.

public reason, trust among citizens increases over time.[11] There is no reason to suppose that such a positive cycle, which created liberal polities out of countries devastated by religious wars, could not operate in hyperpluralized societies, where historical developments pose a need to integrate citizens whose comprehensive conceptions only allow a prudential endorsement of the liberal principles.

As a third suggestion from Ferrara in *The Democratic Horizon*, political liberalism can benefit from rethinking the democratic ethos. The most insidious competitor of democracy today is 'elective oligarchy', a type of regime that can camouflage itself as democratic under the guise of elections, a perfunctory pluralism, and an ersatz freedom of the press. The pseudo-democratic form is best smoked out not so much in terms of procedures—always at risk of being paid lip service while being actually enervated—as by its evident lapse from the *public ethos* of a democracy worthy of the name. A two-centuries-old discussion, among the likes of Montesquieu, Rousseau, Tocqueville, Emerson, Thoreau, and others, delivers a list of democratic virtues that includes an orientation towards the common good, a passion for equality, a passion for individuality, and the dispositions towards toleration, reasonableness, and civility emphasized by Rawls.[12]

Is this consolidated picture of the democratic ethos fully adequate for democratic regimes immersed in the inhospitable conditions of the twenty-first century? Plausible additions to the list of democratic virtues come to mind. If we focus on hyperpluralism as a condition in which, for significant segments of the citizenry, one or another of the constitutional essentials is problematical in the light of their differing comprehensive conceptions of the good, then one of those supplementary virtues would be that of *openness*, understood as a political public's readiness to give serious consideration to unconventional or radical-seeming solutions for chronic problems, rooted in a culture of receptiveness to new possibilities for a life form, a historical horizon, a social configuration.[13] Openness addresses a set of concerns similar to those addressed by recent proposals from other authors for a variety of new democratic virtues. As do Charles Taylor's *agape*[14] and Jacques Derrida's

[11] Rawls, *PL* 159. More specifically, 'when citizens believe that political institutions and procedures are just (as these principles specify), they are ready to do their part in those arrangements when assured others will do theirs' and 'if other persons with evident intention do their part, people tend to develop trust in them' (ibid. 163).

[12] See ibid. 194.

[13] For a more detailed account and a genealogy of openness, see Ferrara, *Democratic Horizon* (n. 1) 48–54.

[14] *Agape* is an ethical disposition revolving around the theistic intuition of a 'divine affirmation of the human, more total than humans can ever attain', see Charles Taylor, *Sources of the Self: The Making of the*

hospitality,[15] *openness* issues a call to the public culture of a contemporary democracy for an accommodation of hyperpluralism without repression. Unlike those proposals, however, openness cohabits easily with rights and principles. The very idea is one demanding constant attention to dangers of excess or imbalance ('too much openness'), which the ideas of *agape* and *hospitality* would seem unable to do. Finally, whereas Stephen White's *presumptive generosity*[16] seems to focus primarily on the primal scene of welcoming others and preventing initial unfamiliarity from slipping into enmity, *openness* includes not only ethical receptivity towards the other, but also a kind of cognitive receptivity towards untried paths for the self, untried doctrines, untried theoretical developments.

Above all and finally, Ferrara says in *The Democratic Horizon*, when theorizing the democratic ethos we should avoid being trapped within Western-centric lines. Thus a *fourth* suggestion for rethinking political liberalism, inspired by studies on the Axial Age and 'multiple modernities', is to consider that democratic cultures anchored in diverse civilizational contexts might generate *multiple versions* of the just and stable society of free and equal citizens.

For example, several ideal-types of democratic ethos can be distinguished if we bracket the points of convergence, among major historical religions, concerning the values of the common good, of pluralism, of collegial deliberation, of the equality and individuality of persons, and focus instead on two points of dissonance: (a) the idea of the priority of rights over duties and (b) the role of political conflict within a democratic polity. The idea of a priority of subjective rights, as prerogatives of the single individual against the word and wish of communal authority, runs against the grain of the most typical religious approaches to communal life. The other point of friction concerns the role of contestation. Rights-centred democracies somehow institutionalize Machiavelli's reflections on the positive role of the conflict between nobility and common people in the Roman republic. Political cultures predominantly steeped in Catholic, Muslim, Confucian, Buddhist, Hindu religious backgrounds, even when they do prize pluralism, majority rule, the separation of

Modern Identity (Harvard U. Press 1989) 521. See also Charles Taylor, *A Secular Age* (Harvard U. Press 2007) 738.

15 Derrida's 'absolute' or 'unconditional' *hospitality* is understood as 'a law without imperative, without order and without duty. *A law without law, in short* [emphasis mine]', Jacques Derrida, *Of Hospitality: Anne Dufourmantelle Invites Jacques Derrida to Respond* (Stanford U. Press 2000) 83.

16 *Presumptive generosity* is meant as an 'initial gesture toward that thin bond of negative solidarity among creatures whose dignity and equality reside in their peculiar foreknowledge of mortality', Stephen K. White, *The Ethos of a Late-Modern Citizen* (Harvard U. Press 2009) 107.

powers, do so with an instinctive aversion to conflict and contestation. We have *consociationalist* democratic cultures and democratic cultures that incline towards *agonism*.

Provisionally, then, the pluralization of the democratic ethos could start from construing four versions of it. The combination of an agonistic and rights-centred view of the democratic process is just one type, most resonant with the Protestant and especially Puritan version of Christianity. However, agonism and contestation could be combined with a duty-centred political culture, premised on a preference for political confrontation and mediation over litigation in court for settling contested principles and rights, a stance found in all forms of strong republicanism: Athens, the Roman republic, Venice and the Florentine republic, the Puritan republic of Cromwell.

On the consociationalist side of the spectrum, 'pure consensualist' democratic cultures combine both aversion to conflict and the centrality of duties, as the case might be with the Islamic retributive understanding of rights, with the Confucian emphasis on harmony and with Buddhism. On the other hand, democratic regimes exist, in continental Europe, that formally endorse the priority of rights but do so with a strong aversion to democratic contestation: Italy's formerly Christian-Democratic-dominated polity, pluriconfessional Belgium and Switzerland, and Germany's practice of 'concertation'[17] perhaps belong in this area.

To conclude this summary of Ferrara's intervention in *The Democratic Horizon*: political liberalism has broken new ground. It has loosened the core of political normativity from the hold of first principles, self-evident truths, and transcendentally anchored laws. It has freed us from the epistocratic spell of Plato's cave without making us hostage to scepticism, as occurred in earlier attempts to rehabilitate the inside of the cave as the true locus of politics. It has offered instead, as a normative core, ideas of public reason and the reasonable. Its teaching is that the most cogent kind of normativity for those who inhabit a democratic horizon is the normativity of what is 'irrecusable' because *most reasonable for us*—where what is most reasonable for us cannot be determined independently of who we want to be, without thereby collapsing public reason into some form of theoretical or practical reason. Ferrara's four proposed

[17] In the Federal Republic of Germany of the late 1960s and beyond, 'concertation' designated a practice of social partnership and tripartite policy negotiation involving industrial employers' and employees' organizations and state institutions as mediators of these diverse interests. See Stefan Berger, 'Germany in Historical Perspective: Between Theory and Practice', in Stefan Berger and Hugh Compston (eds), *Policy Concertation and Social Partnership in Western Europe: Lessons for the 21st Century* (Berghahn 2002) 125–138.

reconsiderations—rethinking the ethos of democracy, de-Westernizing it, conjectural approaches to justification, multiple avenues of consent to meet the varied situations of citizens in hyperpluralized societies—are meant not as retreats from these advances, but rather as pointers to directions in which they can best be conserved amid newly challenging conditions.

5

Constitutional Interpretation: A Dualist Democrat's Dilemma

Frank I. Michelman

1. Constitutional Democracy Under Stress

The term 'democracy' commonly signifies the rule of a country by its people collectively.[1] So it does throughout this book; our questions always are about a coupling of democracy, thus understood, to an equally demanding liberal value we have named as government by consent.[2] Those also were leading questions in our past separate writings attracting each other's attentions. Thus Ferrara, in *The Democratic Horizon* (2014), used 'democracy' to mean the rule of the people collectively, yes, but that rule conducted in recognized constitutional-legal good order. Ferrara's democracy envisaged a subjection of daily rulership to basic laws themselves attributable to the people, at least in reason if perhaps not always quite provably in history. Included would be higher laws subjecting the whole apparatus of power to interdepartmental checks, to overarching fundamental rights, and to steering from a political public sphere itself screened off from administration but influentially connected to it by channels of election and representation. And what ultimately, then, gave the people their unity as such—and hence their capability as an agency of rule—would be their shared attachment to these very constitutional-democratic institutional forms and ideas.

Near the start of *The Democratic Horizon*, Ferrara recalls from prior work of mine a listing of oncoming social conditions deemed 'inhospitable' to constitutional-democratic self-understanding. Among them is a daily subjection of citizens in our countries to sundry regulatory regimes—some governmental, some privatized—of which they cannot plausibly see themselves as

[1] This chapter is extracted, with no substantive change, from a paper of 2016, written as part of a print symposium on *The Democratic Horizon*. See Frank I. Michelman, 'A Constitutional Horizon?' (2016) 42 Philosophy & Social Criticism 640.

[2] See Chapter 1, pp. 1, 5; Chapter 2, pp. 33–34.

Legitimation by Constitution. Alessandro Ferrara and Frank I. Michelman, Oxford University Press. © Alessandro Ferrara and Frank I. Michelman 2021. DOI: 10.1093/oso/9780192855121.003.0006

even remotely the authors. Ferrara then additionally brings front and centre, as a further inhospitable condition, an increasingly visible influx, into the countries of a professedly democratic West, of populations who do not at all or do not fully include themselves or their ways within the historical tradition we know as constitutional democracy, with resultant pressure on our countries to seek out 'a form of democracy that does not amount to a Westernization'.[3] That condition Ferrara neatly names as 'hyperpluralism', by way of contradistinction to John Rawls's posited social fact of reasonable pluralism.

Ferrara's book is a confrontation, then, with threats apparently posed by a fusion of two historically recent attritions in constitutional-democratic self-confidence: an attrition in the felt reality of popular-political regulatory mastery in the social-transactional space, and an attrition in the felt reality (and even of any remote semblance?) of social consensus on even the most fundamental aims and goods of political ordering. Call the first of those a concern about *occlusion of authorship*, the second a concern about *shortfall of agreement*. *The Democratic Horizon* records a search for philosophical breakthroughs from these two threats by an extension or updating—a 'renewal', Ferrara calls it—of the body of thought bequeathed to us, by John Rawls and others, under the name of political liberalism.

Now, somewhere near the crux of Ferrara's hopeful reconsideration of that thought stands the class of institutional fixtures we know as 'constitutions'—using that word to name a country's scriptural basic law, its publicly cognizable corpus of canonically worded sentences ordaining the country's basic institutional framework. It is thus no less tellingly a 'constitutional' than a 'democratic' horizon that Ferrara's work, in conjunction with Rawls's, shows us to be facing.

2. Two Kinds of Inhospitable Conditions: Three Texts On Legitimacy

'Occlusion of authorship' means the daily subjection of citizens to sundry coercive regimes of which they cannot readily see themselves as authors, owing to forces of globalization, marketization, and pressures for extensively delegated modes of public regulatory authority. 'Shortfall of agreement' means the increasingly insistent presence in countries of the constitutional-democratic

[3] Ferrara, *The Democratic Horizon: Hyperpluralism and the Renewal of Political Liberalism* (CUP 2014) 17 (hereafter Ferrara, *Democratic Horizon*).

West of populations who do not at all or do not fully include themselves or their ways within the (broadly speaking) liberal political culture and tradition.

These two kinds of inhospitable conditions, 'occlusion' and 'shortfall', are neither the same nor are they interchangeable. Each could exist without the other. Citizens who, as a body, exercise full and direct control over the laws they all will have to obey could perfectly well confront, in doing so, a shortfall of agreement amongst them over what those laws should be. Citizen bodies in full and perfect agreement about those laws could nevertheless confront an occlusion of authorship of them—say, by imperial rule from overseas. When a theorist says he writes in response to threats to democracy from inhospitable conditions, it may sometimes be important to clarify which kind of condition—occlusion or shortfall—he has in view.

In the case of Ferrara writing in *The Democratic Horizon*, the answer would be 'both'. Consider three texts:

a. ***A. Ferrara:*** *We can rethink democracy by replacing the idea that the citizens are ultimately the authors of the laws immediately demanding obedience from them with the idea that citizens are ultimately the free and equal subscribers of a constitutional pact that in turn imposes legal limits on all subordinate legislative and administrative action, and thereby serves also as a benchmark for the legitimacy of such action that may then follow different, more technicized channels as long as they comport with those limits and directives.*[4]
b. ***A. Ferrara:*** *Structures and methods of governance . . . do not [detract from democracy] if and only if (a) they take place within the boundaries of 'constitutional essentials' that meet with the consent of free and equal citizens as manifested in referenda or in more indirect but still recognizable ways and (b) some recognizable form of accountability remains in place.*[5]
c. ***J. Rawls:*** *Our exercise of coercive political power is proper and hence justifiable only when it is exercised in accordance with a constitution the essentials of which all citizens [as free and equal] may reasonably be expected to endorse in the light of principles and ideals acceptable to them as reasonable and rational.*[6]

[4] Ibid. 178; see Alessandro Ferrara, 'Political Liberalism Revisited: A Paradigm for liberal Democracy in the 21st Century' (2016) 42 Philosophy & Social Criticism 681, 684 (accepting a proposal from Michelman for a slight rewording of this text from its original form in *The Democratic Horizon*).

[5] Ferrara, *Democratic Horizon* (n. 3) 178.

[6] My rendition above combines two close similar formulations in Rawls, *PL* 137, 217.

In Ferrara's texts 'a' and 'b' we can easily read intentions to advance legal constitutionalism—dualist democracy—as a remedy both for occlusion of authorship ('free and equal subscription to texts that impose legal limits' to count sufficiently as authorship of compliant laws) and for shortfall of agreement ('constitutional essentials that meet the consent of free and equal citizens' to supply a sufficiency of agreement). In Ferrara's text 'b' we also easily see a parallel with Rawls's text 'c'. What we shall further find, though, in part through a closer comparison of Ferrara's thought with Rawls's, is that constitutional remedies for inhospitable conditions can carry differing side-effects on legal practice, depending on which type of inhospitable condition, 'occlusion' or 'shortfall', we take them as being meant to cure. That observation will lead us to a problem that neither Ferrara nor Rawls, I believe, can ever hope finally and fully to solve.

3. A Programme of Comparison

The evidently intended echo of Rawls's 'c' by Ferrara's 'b' makes all the more intriguing two fairly glaring discrepancies between these two texts. Where Rawls sets a condition for the justification of any and all exercises of political coercion, Ferrara writes more narrowly of the legitimation of structures of 'governance'—meaning by that term the extensively delegated, comitological mode of production of a great deal of the regulatory law that Europeans these days have little choice but to obey. And where Rawls prescribes a purely substantive-hypothetical standard for a set of legitimacy-worthy constitutional essentials (they must meet a test of expected endorsement by citizens judging reasonably on the basis of principles approvable by reason), Ferrara looks for historical manifestations of actual citizen consent.

As a possible clue to a cause of these discrepancies, consider that a different one of our two types of inhospitable conditions might be motivating the respective proposals of Rawls ('c') and Ferrara ('b') for a retreat to constitutional essentials as the space of political coming together: 'occlusion' for Ferrara and 'shortfall' for Rawls. Ferrara's proposal comes in a chapter specifically directed to the challenge to democratic correctness posed by increasingly obtrusive facts of regulation of daily life by agencies 'beyond the nation'.[7] Rawls's comes in response to the question of the justifiability of democratic political coercion in religiously, philosophically, and morally pluralized societies.[8] Thus cued, we

[7] Ferrara, *Democratic Horizon* (n. 3) 164.
[8] Rawls, *PL* xx, 136, 216–17.

may ask about differing and possibly even conflicting implications, for democratic theory and practice, stemming from the difference of triggering inhospitable conditions for the similar-looking formulations of Rawls and Ferrara.

Rawls and Shortfall of Agreement

On what possible basis, Rawls wants to know, can a democratic political order call upon all citizens for a general posture of willing compliance with laws decreed by majorities, however badly off the track of justice, fairness, or tolerance some undoubtedly well-disposed dissenters might find some of those laws to be? Rawls saw that as the generative 'problem of political liberalism'.[9] In answer came the principle of legitimacy sufficiently established by a guaranteed compliance of political power with a few abstractly stated basic-law 'essentials'.[10]

In pluralistic conditions, the premise for this proposal obviously cannot be a supposition of a free convergence by literally everyone in sight on a substantial conception of the moral-minimum conditions for collaboration in a country's practices of coercion by law. Rawls suggests only the possibility of such a convergence by everyone reasonable and rational—by, in other words (the implication is inevitable), everyone for whose freedom and equality we are most urgently required to care by a morality of mutual recognition by all of all as free and equal. We thus here enter the gap that separates the Rawlsian fact of 'reasonable' pluralism from the more obstreperous fact of 'hyper' pluralism that Ferrara quite properly insists on including under what I have called the 'shortfall' class of inhospitable conditions. (Dealing with these more extreme conditions, Ferrara rightly remarks, was 'beyond Rawls's intention' for his proposed constitution-centred liberal principle of legitimacy.[11] Any attention by Rawls to this further challenge would have to be sought elsewhere in his writings—most obviously in *The Law of Peoples*.)

We may notice, now, how this limitation on the Rawlsian legitimacy principle's intention jibes nicely with the principle's adoption of a strictly hypothetical-counterfactual test of the constitution's acceptability to citizens *conceived as reasonable*, to be contrasted with Ferrara's stipulation (text 'b') for actual ('manifested') consent by citizens *as they are*. We will see below how this difference bears further consequence for the meanings to be ascribed to the

[9] Ibid. xx.
[10] See Introduction, pp. 3–5, Chapter 1, pp. 18–19.
[11] Ferrara, *Democratic Horizon* (n. 3) 91.

constitutional essentials and for our reliance on courts of law authoritatively to construe and apply them to hard and testing cases. But that point is better left until after we have looked a bit further into the path taken by Ferrara to his own constitution-centred proposal for the achievement of democratic legitimacy.

Ferrara and Occlusion of Authorship

Ferrara's texts 'a' and 'b' do not expressly address the question of tying political justification or the possibility thereof to a supposition of the reasonability of citizens (however strictly or loosely understood). The proposal of text 'a', for a substitution of authorship of constitutional essentials for authorship of laws directly to be obeyed, comes initially not as a response to shortfall of agreement but rather as a response to occlusion of authorship by citizens of the laws that directly govern daily life. The question Ferrara expressly says he wants his proposition to answer is: 'How can we make sense of collective self-rule by citizens when governance replaces representative government?' It comes not in his book's chapter 4, on hyperpluralism and possible remedies therefor, but rather in chapter 7, directed to the challenge to democratic correctness posed by increasingly obtrusive facts of regulation of daily life by agencies 'beyond the nation', where the accustomed constitutional-democratic lines of control and accountability are blurred perhaps to the vanishing point.[12]

At a point in history where this fact finally has to be faced without evasion, our test for democracy *vel non*—so urges Ferrara—can right-thinkingly take a different turn from that of insistence on credibly clear channels of citizen control over all the laws that directly rule their daily lives. Democracy then may then still meaningfully be said to persist—the 'ethos' and 'passions' of democracy can still be satisfied—so long as we can see the citizens as freely and equally the authors of a relatively few and moderately abstract set of constitutional essentials to which the daily regulators' actions will reliably be held to conform. No doubt 'strong' democratic proceduralists may find this an impermissible relaxation from what democracy as a political cause ought always to be held to demand.[13] Ferrara, though, has waiting for them a cogent rejoinder. He would reply that satisfaction of his constitution-centred principle makes a difference worth fighting for, even by them, from the standpoint of motivating

[12] Ibid. 164.

[13] See e.g. Benjamin R. Barber, *Strong Democracy: Participatory Politics for a New Age* (U. Calif. Press 1984).

values that democracy means to advance: 'the common good', 'equality', 'individualism', and beyond and above those also a covering value of 'openness' including aspects of 'hospitality' and 'generosity'.

4. Dualist Democracy and Judicial Review: Ferrara Versus Rawls?

Ferrara and Rawls both claim to follow Bruce Ackerman's conception of democracy as 'dualist', upholding in its legal order a separated higher track of law that is to be controlling upon subordinate day-to-day laws made by the constituted legislative bodies. For Ackerman, as for Ferrara, the first aim of the dualist legal-systemic design is to temper concerns about occlusion of authorship. A sufficiently constraining higher law, itself historically issuing directly from the people (even if the subsequent ground-level laws immediately governing their actions do not), can suffice, both say, to fulfil democracy's stipulation for authorship of a country's laws by its people. Now, that view may seem quite compatible with—even complementary to—the Rawlsian view (text 'c') of the constitution's service as a sufficient containment to shortfalls of agreement through its assurance of unfailing due regard to the basic liberties. And indeed a commingling of the two constitutional missions may be read in Rawls's own remark about judicial review. 'A supreme court', Rawls writes, 'fits into ... dualist constitutional democracy as [an] institutional device[] to protect the higher law.'[14] Does he mean protect it as vehicle of popular self-government, or protect it as justification-bearing guarantee? It could be either or both (and very likely Rawls did mean both).

So where, then, do we see finally any possible conflict between Rawls and Ferrara, on this point of the uses of the constitution? Rawls no less than Ferrara is a declared endorser and follower of Ackerman's higher/ordinary law construction, thus placing judicial review in the service of liberal-democratic legitimation. So what if they both get to the same place from different initial motivations? The response I ask you now to consider—but not yet to make your final conclusion—is that despite resemblances they might not both be getting to the same place. Where the two views may come apart is not at the choice pro or con the institution of judicial constitutional review in a democracy—they both support it—but in their implications for the conduct by the courts of their office of constitutional enforcement.

[14] Rawls, *PL* 233.

The topic is rich and complex and I can deal with it here only in cursory, conclusory terms. So to get right to the marrow: where, as with Ferrara, an alleged deficiency of citizen authorship of laws is the trouble to be cured by retreat to the more abstract level of constitutional essentials (but it cannot be too vaporously abstract), the corresponding job of the overseeing court will be to 'protect' the higher law as historically enacted by the people. No matter how loose or even figurative a conception of popular enactment Ferrara might accept, he cannot finally escape a tie to some form of 'originalism' in judicial constitutional interpretation. He cannot then abjure an expectation from reviewing courts of overt commitment to some mode or method, be it ever so highly abstracted or extenuated, of extracting from enactment history the actual legislative will of the people themselves.[15]

With Rawls, though, the case looks different. The issue *he* means to address, by his proposal to deflect the question of consent to government from everyday laws to constitutional essentials, is not historical-authorial, it is moral-theoretic. It is the issue of the moral licence of majorities to impose the coercion of ground-level laws on assertedly free and equal dissenters. That licence is said by Rawls to depend on the questioned law's conformance to constitutional essentials acceptable to everyone conceived as reasonable and rational. The corresponding call for overseeing courts can only be to bend the scripted constitutional essentials (along with any overlay of judicial doctrines of their application) as far as possible towards values that the judges 'believe in good faith ... that all citizens as reasonable and rational' could endorse;[16] and of course that can only mean by the test of some political conception of justice that the deciding judge—studious, attentive, wise, patriotic, and tolerant as the judge might or might not be—will always bring to the work of decision. The call, in short, is for judicial resort to the so-called 'philosophical' approach to constitutional interpretation, which currently stands as originalism's polemical opposite.[17] So there we have it: originalism for Ferrarians in search of vindication of democratic authorship, the philosophical approach for Rawlsians in search of moral vindication for the rule of legislated law.

That cannot, however, be the end of the story. If we ask what would be the one leading point of difference that Ferrara has with Rawls, the answer surely must lie in Ferrara's refusal to flinch from facts of hyperpluralism. Any fair

[15] For a luminous exposition of the varieties of extenuated or pretentious originalism currently on offer in American debates, see James E. Fleming, *Fidelity to Our Imperfect Constitution: For Moral Readings and Against Originalisms* (OUP 2015) (hereafter Fleming, *Against Originalisms*).

[16] Rawls, *PL* 236.

[17] See Fleming, *Against Originalisms* (n. 15) 22.

cover-to-cover reading of Ferrara's book will show him searching, from start to finish, for a political-liberal-compatible accommodation to these 'deeper cultural cleavages'—posing thus primarily a problem of justification of ordinary laws and only secondarily (if at all) of authorship of a higher law. The fair conclusion (see text 'a') is that Ferrara (like Rawls) puts the Ackerman dualist conception into service as a response both to occlusion of authorship and to shortfall of agreement.

But then which implication for judicial review will he tell us to choose: 'originalist' or 'philosophical?' If it truly is *both* types of inhospitable conditions that we liberal democrats must always be aiming to meet through the device of the dualist-legal constitution, then that question seems destined to remain forever open, dangling before us and leading us ever onward towards an ever-receding liberal-democratic constitutional horizon.

6
On Reconciling the Two Understandings of Judicial Review

Alessandro Ferrara

Frank Michelman correctly points out how my *The Democratic Horizon* depicts at the same time a 'constitutional horizon' of sorts. In fact, the main adaptive move set in place by democracy in order to survive prohibitively adverse conditions in the late twentieth and early twenty-first centuries revolves around the constitution-centred 'democratic dualism' theorized by Ackerman and Rawls and Michelman himself. In Chapter 5, Michelman starts by grouping the inhospitable conditions that challenge democracy in recent decades (some of which he himself identified in a famous essay)[1] into two groups: (a) conditions linked with an 'occlusion of authorship', i.e. a deterioration of control by citizens over the regulatory environments confronting them, and (b) conditions conceived as a 'shortfall of agreement', i.e. as an increasing, and ever more insistent and politically evident, diversity in the political, moral, social, and religious conceptions endorsed by citizens.

While Michelman acknowledges my intent to address both the challenges from shortfall and from occlusion, and also the apparent close kinship of my view to Rawls's formulation of the liberal principle of legitimacy, he also asks whether in the end these views 'carry differing side-effects on practice' because premised on the superior urgency of different ones of the two kinds of inhospitable conditions. More specifically, because my own, as well as Ackerman's, primary object of concern would be occlusion of authorship—an impression perhaps linked, in my case, with Michelman's focusing on a formulation coming from a chapter of *The Democratic Horizon* devoted to supra-national governance—then I would be bound to give priority to the supreme or constitutional court's function 'to "protect" the higher law *as historically enacted by the people*'.[2] And then, even allowing for my readiness to understand popular

[1] Frank I. Michelman, 'How Can the People Ever Make the Laws? A Critique of Deliberative Democracy', in James Bohman and William Rehg (eds), *Deliberative Democracy* (MIT Press 1997) 145.
[2] Chapter 5, p. 88.

Legitimation by Constitution. Alessandro Ferrara and Frank I. Michelman, Oxford University Press. © Alessandro Ferrara and Frank I. Michelman 2021. DOI: 10.1093/oso/9780192855121.003.0007

enactment in highly metaphorical terms, such priority somehow would ultimately commit me to a penchant for some, however thin, 'form of "originalism" in judicial constitutional interpretation'.[3] If, says Michelman, we take occlusion of authorship as the sole condition to be remedied by a reframing of the traditional consent of the governed as a dualistic legitimation-by-constitution, then there must follow a commitment of the highest judicial interpreter of the constitution to the development of 'some mode or method, be it ever so highly abstracted or extenuated, of extracting from enactment history the actual legislative will of the people themselves'.[4]

Things then would look different for Rawls, taking *his* primary remedial aim (for a shift from the classical Lockean consent of the governed to the dualist liberal principle of legitimacy) to be directed at the shortfall of agreement rather than at the occlusion of authorship. For in that case (following Michelman) 'the corresponding call for overseeing courts can only be to bend both the scripted constitutional essentials and the doctrines of their application as far as possible toward values that the judges "believe in good faith ... that all citizens as reasonable and rational" could endorse'.[5] This justification-supportive function assigned to the highest judicial interpreter of the constitution can be discharged only by testing challenged laws against some general conception of political rightness—and consequently it generates a penchant for 'the so-called "philosophical" approach to constitutional interpretation, which currently stands as originalism's polemical opposite'.[6] To sum up, the paradigm of legitimation-by-constitution, depending on whether it is understood as a remedy for the occlusion of authorship or for the shortfall of agreement, generates divergent understandings of the function of judicial review and, consequently, diverse interpretive approaches.

Or so it seems. In the closing paragraph of Chapter 5, Michelman acknowledges once again that Ackerman's dualist conception of democracy is adopted by me 'as a response *both* to occlusion of authorship *and* to shortfall of agreement'.[7] Consequently, both versions of the highest courts' mandate are somehow reflected within my account of democratic legitimacy. The tension, however, would surface again, because, Michelman says, the philosophical approach required for remedying the shortfall of agreement is bound to clash

[3] Ibid.
[4] Ibid..
[5] Ibid. (quoting from Rawls) p. 88.
[6] Ibid.
[7] Ibid. pp. 88–89.

with the originalist approach required for retrieval of the will of the people as author of the constitution.

And why do these two understandings of the function of the highest judicial interpreter of the constitution ultimately generate diverging inclinations towards a however mitigated originalism and a more 'philosophical' interpretation? Because, in spite of all leanings towards an 'abstract' originalism, still the primary task of a supreme judicial interpreter entrusted with unblocking occlusion necessarily must include reference, Michelman says, to some trace of the sovereign will, reconstructed either from the duly interpreted original constitution or from some subsequent constitutional moment—a 'must' from which a supreme judicial interpreter entrusted with the alternative task of remedying the shortfall of agreement in a reasonably non-rejectable way is remarkably free. In the first mode, the highest interpreter of the constitution is asked to tell the public what the sovereign people *did* will, in the second to articulate what it *should* will.[8]

I believe that the opposition between these two ways of understanding the function of judicial review within a dualist paradigm of constitutional democracy is less unbridgeable than it looks at first sight, if only we pause to think that whatever the people willed—whether by way of enacting a constitution or its subsequent modification—was always necessarily willed against a set of background assumptions, of a cognitive nature, themselves not immune from critical scrutiny. As an example, let me offer the transition from *Plessy v. Ferguson* to *Brown v. Board of Education* as indicative of two quite different applications of the 'equal protection' clause of the Fourteenth Amendment, both offered by the highest interpreter of the Constitution of the United States, respectively in 1896 and 1954.[9]

Even if we imagine, along with Michelman, that the priority of unblocking the occlusion of authorship commits one to think that the Supreme Court in *Brown* should have anchored its opinion in the reconstruction of an unequivocal, historical act of will of the democratic sovereign, still the following account could be articulated. The democratic sovereign endorsed 'equal protection' at the time of the Fourteenth Amendment, but whereas in 1868, and as late as in 1896, the 'badge of inferiority' associated with racial separation was considered inexistent (or existent 'solely because the colored race chooses to put that construction upon it', as the court stated in *Plessy*),[10] half a century

[8] See Frank I. Michelman, 'Political Liberalism's Constitutional Horizon: Some Further Thoughts' (2017) 4 Rivista internazionale di filosofia del diritto 607.

[9] See *Plessy v. Ferguson*, 163 U.S. 537 (1896) and *Brown v. Board of Education*, 347 U.S. 483 (1954).

[10] *Plessy v. Ferguson*, 163 U.S. 551 (1896).

later the interpreter of the constitutional script found, in the light of evidence partly of a social-scientific nature, that 'separate educational facilities are *inherently* unequal' and violate the 'equal protection of the laws', because segregation is '*usually* [my italics] interpreted as denoting the inferiority of the negro group'.[11]

Regarding segregation, then, the Warren Court neither articulated what the people *should* will (thus making itself vulnerable to the charge of itself occluding the citizens' authorship of the laws) nor violated historical evidence by attributing to the people a non-segregationist, substantive understanding of 'equal protection' foreign to nineteenth-century America. Indeed, the background assumptions under which that democratic will to provide 'equal protection of the laws' was formed—i.e. the assumption that segregation along racial lines could be compatible with equal citizenship—had not yet been conclusively challenged. Arguably, the Supreme Court took *a third course*, not contemplated in Michelman's disjunctive rendering of the two possible judicial mandates. In *Brown v. Board of Education*, the supreme constitutional interpreter did rightly impute an actual and original act of will to the democratic sovereign—namely, the will to establish 'equal protection of the laws', since 1868—but at the same time, in the same act of adjudication, updated, in the light of a changed historical context, the cognitive assumptions against which such original will was formed. Consequently, the burden of proof incurred by the judicial interpreter is not *normative* (about what the people ought to will in light of some reasonably non-rejectable philosophical argument) but *empirical* (about what are the relevant facts in the light of today's best knowledge).

In sum, *tertium datur*, and the two alternatives that Michelman presents as destined to endlessly clash admit of bridging, along the following lines: in the process of recalibrating its interpretation of the Constitution in the light of a new historical context, the highest judicial interpreter *neither* imputes to the people an original intent to desegregate schools and a substantive conception of equality (a will and a conception that certainly were inexistent at the time of the Founding and of the enacting of the Fourteenth Amendment), *nor* develops a non-rejectable philosophical argument about how the equal protection clause should henceforth be interpreted. By modifying the background cognitive assumptions relevant for interpreting the Constitution, the highest judicial interpreter goes some way, if not all the way, towards bridging the gap between the two kinds of mandate pointed out by Michelman.

[11] *Brown v. Board of Education*, 347 U.S. 494 (1954).

The same line of reasoning can be applied to *Obergefell v. Hodges*.[12] If we follow Michelman's argument, we should choose between defending the court's opinion in *Obergefell* as a valid application of an abstract-originalist approach and applauding it as a valid application of the 'philosophical' approach. However, if we accept my thesis of a cognitive background of shared assumptions, on which both judicial interpretation of the Constitution and the will of 'we, the People' inevitably depend, then we could make sense of *Obergefell* in the same terms as *Brown* or *Loving*. In *Loving v. Virginia*, rejection of Virginia's anti-miscegenation laws was justified on the basis of (a) affirming 'equal protection' as expressive of the will of the people, (b) questioning racial difference qua 'ground'—up to then reputed 'natural'—for restricting freedom to marry, and (c) finding racial classifications *objectively* (as opposed to *subjectively*) discriminatory.[13]

Just as in the case of *Brown* on segregation, likewise in the case of *Obergefell* the judicial interpreter—according to my reconstruction—is required to show convincingly not so much that the people concretely willed same-sex marriage, but that the people's historical will to grant equal protection was formed in a context where certain assumptions regarding sexual preference still prevailed, and therefore led to legal conclusions that now, in the light of contrary evidence, ought to be reversed.

To put the point in more general philosophical terms: 'we', as one generational segment of 'the people', acting through the constituted power of the highest judicial interpreter of the constitution, may be bound by the *normative will* of our predecessors, for example their will to ground our communal political life in freedom and equality, as secured under a certain list of enumerated rights, but cannot be argued to be bound by their *cognitive horizon*. We can, through that understanding, offer relief to Michelman's worry that a court interpreting the constitution with a view to conforming it to principles the court might now judge as reasonably non-rejectable, thereby commits its own occlusion of democratic authorship, its own pre-emption of the self-legislative capacity of the citizens. As Michelman has put the case elsewhere, for a supreme or constitutional court to interpret the 'scripted constitutional essentials' with the aim of producing a non-rejectable bridging of reasonable disagreements over constitutional matters 'contradicts the principle of reading and applying the scripted essentials to match the will or understanding of any historical author'.[14]

[12] *Obergefell v. Hodges*, 576 U.S. (2015)
[13] *Loving v. Virginia*, 388 U.S. 1 (1967).
[14] Frank Michelman, 'A Constitutional Horizon?' (2016) 42 Philosophy & Social Criticism 640, 648.

My suggestion of the third course exemplified by *Brown* and *Obergefell* can go some distance to relieve this concern. It furthermore matches well the Rawlsian paradigm for a well-ordered constitutional democracy, where no branch of government is above challenge. In light of Rawls's rejection of judicial as well as parliamentary supremacy, any seemingly 'philosophical' interpretation, for example, of 'equal protection' provided by the higher judicial interpreter must be taken as at least *putatively* reflective of the will of the people—even if only in a fallibilistic sense, unless and until the people (through the other branches and according to the procedures provided by the constitution) sets the amending procedure under way and corrects an erroneous, partial, or otherwise unwelcome interpretation on the part of the court. 'Judicial occlusion', as it were, is always temporary: ways to offset it are provided by the law.

In the case of the United States, and as documented by Ackerman in *The Civil Rights Revolution*,[15] it could be counter-objected—against this Rawlsian understanding of the power of the highest judicial interpreter of the Constitution as ultimately checked by the secondary constituent power of the citizens to amend the Constitution—that the formal mechanism for amendment has become, over the twentieth and twenty-first centuries, prohibitively difficult for the people to operate. Such alteration of the constitutional picture produces a new predicament, in which the mere lack of an amendment procedure in response to a pronouncement of the Supreme Court is less indicative of acceptance than it used to be until the New Deal.

By itself, such counter-objection does not invalidate my response to concerns about occlusion by judiciary, but it does raise a serious problem. Given an ever more fictive accessibility of the formal amendment procedure, what possible substitutes could in the future avoid occlusion of authorship due to what is in theory (but maybe not in practice) a merely provisional judicial supremacy? A balance has been altered, by complex historical processes, and the power of the judicial interpreter of the constitution has consequently been enhanced and awaits rebalancing. This discussion is totally open and could be next on the ongoing agenda for rethinking the paradigm of political liberalism.

[15] See Bruce Ackerman, *The Civil Rights Revolution* (Harvard U. Press 2014) 40–41.

7

Judicial Constitutional Application: A Rejoinder

Frank I. Michelman

In *Political Liberalism*, John Rawls adopts from Bruce Ackerman the idea of a political democracy as a two-layered legal structure, where a higher-ranking body of norms, the constitution—itself attributed to authorship by the people, and in their name enforced as law by judicial bodies acting as their agents—is held distinct and apart from subordinate, day-to-day law produced by the constituted legislative bodies in a representative-democratic institutional formation.[1] In *The Democratic Horizon*, Alessandro Ferrara joins with that conception of democracy as 'dualist'. In an essay of 2016[2]—the original of this book's Chapter 5—I worried that Ferrara's deployment of the dualist-democracy idea had caught him betwixt and between two irreconcilably contradictory approaches to the work of constitutional application conducted by reviewing courts, which I named as 'originalist' and 'philosophical'. By associating Rawls—as I did in that paper—primarily with the philosophical (but not also the originalist) side of the divide, I effectively excused him from the dilemma in which I said Ferrara was caught. That is one feature of that paper (and Chapter 5) that I here wish to modify. Another is my proposition there of a strict and simple non-compatibility between the two interpretive approaches. The case, as I aim to show below, is more complex than that, and in a way more congenial to Ferrara's reflection (Chapter 6) in response to my concern.

1. The Debate up to Here

In *The Democratic Horizon*, Ferrara had been concerned to show how the dualist conception of democracy could serve in response to challenges

[1] This chapter is drawn from Frank I. Michelman, 'Political Liberalism's Constitutional Horizon: Some Further Thoughts' (2017) 4 Rivista internazionale di filosofia del diritto 599.

[2] See Frank I. Michelman, 'A Constitutional Horizon?' (2016) 42 Philosophy & Social Criticism 640 (hereafter Michelman, 'Constitutional Horizon').

Legitimation by Constitution. Alessandro Ferrara and Frank I. Michelman, Oxford University Press. © Alessandro Ferrara and Frank I. Michelman 2021. DOI: 10.1093/oso/9780192855121.003.0008

posed by certain oncoming social realities to idealizations of government in the constitutional-democratic West. I noted in response[3] how these challenges, as recounted by Ferrara, can be sorted into two main types, which I distinguished as 'occlusion of authorship ('occlusion' for short) and 'shortfall of agreement' ('shortfall' for short). 'Occlusion' covers concerns about a daily subjection of citizens, by forces of globalization and privatization and the so-called comitological mode of governance in Europe, to sundry regulatory regimes of which they cannot plausibly see themselves as authors. 'Shortfall' covers the challenge posed to the professedly democratic societies of the West by the increasingly visible and insistent presence here of populations who do not at all or do not fully include themselves or their ways within the Western historical-cultural tradition of liberal constitutional democracy.

In keeping with his perception of this latter condition as an extended or intensified case of the 'fact of reasonable pluralism' underlying political liberalism's attraction to the dualist conception of democracy, Ferrara names it as one of 'hyperpluralism'. Ferrara then pushes beyond where Rawls had left the matter. He finds, in this condition of hyperpluralism, the ground of a moral need, in liberal-leaning societies, for a loosening of the Rawlsian requirement of a constitution acceptable to all in the light of normative ideals and principles held by them, to take in some citizens who go along partly or perhaps even wholly on prudential grounds. But still Ferrara does follow Rawls in placing the lion's share of the weight of democratic legitimation, in pluralist/hyperpluralist conditions, on the idea of a widespread and uncoerced (if not in the deepest sense freely willing) convergence by all on a set of broadly liberal higher-law essentials. That continued reliance on the constitution as a justificatory platform for government by consent must have a bearing—so my argument has run—on a responsible court's approach to the work of constitutional application in contested cases. And that returns us, then, to my detection of an inherent tension in Ferrara's reliance on the dualist conception of democracy for relief against both the challenge from shortfall and the challenge from occlusion.

If (I said) what you are trying to repair with the dualist-democracy idea is a fact of pluralism/hyperpluralism and resultant shortfall of agreement, then you will be committed to a *philosophical* mode of constitutional interpretation. If what you seek to repair is a rupture of self-government by the people, then you will be committed to an *originalistic* mode of constitutional interpretation.

[3] See Chapter 5, pp. 82–84.

But the originalistic and philosophical modes are contraries, I objected; they cannot both at one time fully occupy the space of a unified, coherent judicial practice.

Where occlusion of authorship is the trouble to be cured by a shift of the focus of justification from everyday law to constitutional higher law, it seems the corresponding assignment to the overseeing court must be exactly, as John Rawls remarked, to 'protect' the higher law enacted by the people.[4] We must expect from the reviewing court the use of some mode or method of extracting from the words and other facts of enactment history the real legislative will of the constitutional authors. That is not so, however—or so I contended—when the problem to be cleared by the shift of focus is that of the moral licence of majorities to impose the coercions of ordinary law on assertedly free and equal dissenters. The problem then supposedly is handled by assurance that courts of law will rule out any contested ordinary legislation that fails to conform to some set of constitutional essentials that *the court can see as* acceptable to everyone conceived as reasonable and rational. And then the corresponding call for overseeing courts can only be to steer interpretation of the scripted constitutional essentials and the doctrines of their application as far as possible towards values that the judges 'believe in good faith ... all citizens as reasonable and rational' could endorse;[5] and of course that can only mean by the test of some justice conception that the deciding judge will always bring to the work of decision.

Between the calls for philosophical and originalist approaches to judicial constitutional interpretation, I claimed, there stands an unbridgeable gap of concept and principle. It is one thing to search out the historical-factual truth about a legislative will, limber as you may find that will to be to shifts in contexts of application. It is quite a different thing to ask which one out of the semantically defensible applications of the recorded words will best comport with some trans-historical normative standard (e.g. the standard of acceptability to any and all free and equal citizens hypothetically conceived as reasonable and rational). And never, I said, can the twain quite meet. 'The principle of bending and applying the scripted constitutional essentials as required in

[4] Rawls, *PL* 233 ('A supreme court ... fits into ... dualist constitutional democracy as [an] institutional device[] to protect the higher law').
[5] Ibid. 236.

reason' to sustain a liberal justification for the force of law, I said, 'still contradicts the principle of reading and applying the scripted essentials to match the will or understanding of any historical author.'[6] And so, I concluded, Ferrara wades into troubled waters by putting the dualist conception of democracy into service as a response *both* to occlusion *and* to shortfall. How, then, I asked, will he choose between the originalist and philosophical approaches to judicial review?

In response to my concern, Ferrara (Chapter 6) has offered a third course to place alongside my posited binary choice between deciding what the sovereign people 'did' will (the originalist approach, responsive to occlusion) and deciding what the people 'should' will (the philosophic approach, responsive to shortfall). The third course is for the reviewing court indeed to ascertain the original will of the people, but in a version updated to take on board intervening changes in background assumptions presumably informing that will. Thus, for example, the seeming conflict of applications of the US Constitution's equality clause in the *Plessy* case of 1896 ('separate but equal') and the *Brown* case of 1954 ('separate ... inherently unequal') is not to be understood as reflecting a choice between a 'normative' ('should') and an 'empirical' ('did') inquiry, but rather as reflecting a difference between earlier and later applications of one, unchanging dictate from the people's utterance of 1868. The difference in applications would be owing to an intervening shift in relevant background assumptions—in this instance, assumptions regarding the likelihood of uptake of a 'badge of inferiority' from state-imposed segregation of facilities by race. Thus, in *Brown*, the Supreme Court

> neither imputes to the people an original intent to desegregate schools and a substantive conception of equality ... nor develops a ... philosophical argument about how the equal protection clause should henceforth be interpreted. [Rather, by] modifying the background assumptions relevant for interpreting the Constitution, the highest judicial interpreter goes some way, if not all the way, towards bridging the gap between the two kinds of mandate pointed out by Michelman.[7]

[6] Michelman, 'Constitutional Horizon' (n. 2) 648.
[7] Chapter 6, p. 93.

2. Towards Common Ground: Intertemporal Fixation of Meaning

One could raise here a question about whether Ferrara's third course quite cleanly evades the 'originalist' horn of my posited binary choice.[8] That is not, however, the bone I wish to pick on this occasion. Rather, I want now to come to Ferrara's aid in a project of bridging the gap, but from a direction opposite to his. Where he points to an opening of interpretation-for-the-sake-of-authorship towards philosophically minded constructions, I want now to establish a necessary closure of interpretation-for-the-sake-of-justification around an ineluctable core of historical fixation of meaning.

Deployment of the dualist-democracy idea, as a way of bridging across shortfall of agreement, corresponds to what we may call a 'proceduralizing' conception of the work done by substantive constitutional law—in contradistinction, that is, to a more familiarly obvious 'regulatory' conception. In the sight of the regulatory conception, the work of substantive constitutional law straightforwardly is that of constraint of political outcomes in preselected directions. Bills of constitutional rights are meant to reduce the chances that state activities will infringe unduly on certain claims or interests of persons or other public values, or will fail unduly in the active furtherance of such values. The regulatory conception thus works from an expectation of advance-designed effects on political outcomes. A constitutional-legal guarantee of 'the freedom of speech' is meant to enhance the likelihood that a condition already known to be named (be it more or less generally or abstractly) by the words between the inverted commas will actually prevail. Such a linkage of predictive hope to semantic confidence has occupied a central place in the wide tradition of constitutional-democratic thought.

The regulatory conception thus starts out from a posit of certain set-in-advance preferred and dispreferred directions for political outcomes—'the freedom of speech' preferred; its absence or negation dispreferred. The proceduralizing conception, by contrast, starts out from a posit of inevitable, recurrent, situated disagreements and uncertainties among citizens about exactly which directions, in which circumstances, are rightly preferred. It sets for substantive constitutional law the aim of maintaining, against these facts of disagreement, a rule of law that can be (i) rightly binding on free and equal dissenters from fair and deliberative legislative majorities, while also being

[8] Compare Ferrara's third course with (e.g.) the theory of 'living originalism' currently espoused by Jack Balkin. See Jack M. Balkin, *Living Originalism* (Harvard U. Press 2011).

(ii) fully respectful of the dissenters' freedom and equality—which is to say, of their presumptive capacities, no less than with the majorities, for responsible engagement with morally fraught matters of public law and policy.

In the result, we still have before us these two non-identical aims for substantive constitutional law, the regulatory and the proceduralizing—the one directed to an effectuation of directive principles for exertions of political power laid down in the past, the other directed to transcendence of major disagreements *now* over the direction of such power—with an obvious possibility of conflict between the two: 'should' opposing 'did' or vice versa. On that point, I do not yield or retract. But now I want to add the following dialectical twist. The two aims are not only thus divergent as I have said, but they are also joined together by the obvious and simple truth that the proceduralizing aim cannot get off the ground without presupposition of a regulatory success.

In a slogan: *proceduralizing ambition presupposes regulatory effect*. 'So long as' the legal system in force requires and assures that legislative majorities will keep with *these* stated bounds—so says the proceduralizing conception, pointing by 'these' to the constitution, the basic law—the system should in all reason be found acceptable among free and equal citizens, and so we may all justifiably insist on each other's compliance with the laws that duly issue from the system. But that 'so long as' sends us, then, right back to the regulatory conception of substantive constitutional law. It returns us to the link between semantic confidence and predictive hope that comprises the very core and essence of the regulatory conception. Just there do we catch our glimpse of the spark of originalism that I now want to say must always already be firing in any Rawls-style set-up of the higher-law constitution as linchpin in a practice of political-liberal justification of the force of law to free and equal dissenters from majoritarian legislation. 'So long as' sets the originalistic inner bound on any practice of philosophic-inclined constitutional interpretation that would come within the idealizing pull of the Rawlsian principle of legitimacy.

For a bit of confirmation, I can give you words from a prime and also definitely Rawls-minded expositor of the philosophic approach.[9] James Fleming describes the approach as a mode of interpretation in which judges progressively 'strive for the true meaning or best account'—of what? Not of what a Rawlsian legitimation-worthy constitution hypothetically 'should' say, but rather of what 'our' constitution 'does' say—if

[9] See James E. Fleming, *Fidelity to Our Imperfect Constitution: For Moral Readings and Against Originalisms* (OUP 2015) 20–21 (noting the connection to Rawls's work of his favoured 'constitutional-constructivist' approach to constitutional interpretation).

sometimes only somewhat broadly and abstractly—to wit, '*our* ... ends-dedicated scheme of ... rights phrased more often than not as referring to general goods and principles'.[10] The philosophic approach, Fleming says, 'does not involve judges or other interpreters doing moral and political philosophy without regard to the commitments of our constitutional order'.[11] Or compare this restatement of Fleming's view offered by Professor Balkin: constitutional words and sentences 'bear an implicit moral or political logic', and so constitutional interpreters should read them 'as examples or instantiations of a prior or more general moral or political theory that underlies the Constitution'.[12] Take it all together, it does not quite add up—nor could it and still comport with the Rawlsian constitution-centred principle of legitimacy—to the flat-out stance 'against originalisms' proclaimed by Fleming's book title. *Some* originalisms—the 'abstract' or 'living' originalisms—are still in place.

In the clash between an abstract originalist approach and what I will now call an 'unbound' philosophic approach to constitutional interpretation, the issue would be over exactly what business awaits the court in a contested constitutional case at law. Is it to be an application of 'this' constitution—'our' constitution—received as a body of more or less abstractly stated but nonetheless temporally fixed and pre-scripted norms? Or is it rather to be an application of a trans-temporal idea of what a properly scripted, political-liberal, justification-bearing constitution 'would' provide for the case at hand? Our two identified uses of the democratic-dualist conception—to clear occlusion and to bridge across shortfall—do indeed initially point towards divergent answers to that question. In the end, however, it cannot be *a choice between* these opposing implications with which political liberalism has to deal. We must rather face up to the question of how to put them together in a unified coherent practice of constitutional-legal application.

That conclusion follows from the point, which I hope here to have established, that political-liberal resort to the dualist conception to overcome shortfall of agreement does *itself* (even putting aside any aim of a cure for occlusion) necessarily implicate a reference to meanings already settled in law. Proceduralizing ambition, to repeat, presupposes regulatory effect. Thus do I join with Ferrara in the necessary political-liberal project

[10] Ibid. 80–81 (emphasis supplied).
[11] Ibid. 80.
[12] Jack M. Balkin, 'History, Rights, and the Moral Reading' (2016) 96 Boston University Law Review 1425, 1434–1435.

of tracking between fixation and openness in the essential terms of a justification-worthy constitution. We are in that regard, as in others, companions—although here starting out from opposite sides of the bridge we each are seeking to build. Or should I rather say, the bridge whose possibility we each are seeking to envisage?

8

Backgrounding the Debate: Judicial Occlusion and Remedial Strategies

Alessandro Ferrara

A new twist has been impressed on our debate, at the end of Chapter 7, by Frank Michelman. Under consideration, to that point, had been an apparent conceptual gap between (a) a *shortfall*-remedying version of judicial review, aimed at tracking an acceptable 'philosophical' intimation of what the constitution *should* say on a subject of reasonable disagreement, and (b) an *occlusion*-remedying version aimed at retrieving traces of the *actual* will of the author of the constitution. Writing from a purely conceptual or analytic point of view, Michelman had found that gap unabated, not quite closed by my third-course strategy of distinguishing the binding normative will of 'the people' and its not-binding cognitive presuppositions. The 'originalist horn' of the dilemma would somehow be 'evaded' and not fully be done justice to.[1]

But then comes, from Michelman, what I would describe as a practical turn in his thought. In lieu of pursuing further our conceptual debate on the possibility of bridging that gap in theory, Michelman turns to explaining why (possibility now for the moment aside) the unavoidable challenge for political liberals is to bring together, in a 'unified coherent practice of constitutional-legal application', these two contrary seeming takes on the mandate of a constitutional court. He thus joins with me in the project of building or perhaps, more modestly, 'of seeking to envisage' a bridge between the two approaches.[2]

He does so by calling for laying the foundation stone on the opposite bank of the river from where I have started. While I tried to show that 'interpretation-for-the-sake-of-unblocking-authorship', if enriched with an assessment of the cognitive presuppositions of the people's will, becomes more similar to a philosophical argument, Michelman, in response, offers to show that the model of 'interpretation-for-the-sake-of-justification' in fact requires, in order to

[1] See Chapter 7, p. 100.
[2] Ibid..

Legitimation by Constitution. Alessandro Ferrara and Frank I. Michelman, Oxford University Press. © Alessandro Ferrara and Frank I. Michelman 2021. DOI: 10.1093/oso/9780192855121.003.0009

perform its justificatory function in legal terms, a moment of closure connected with 'an ineluctable core of historical fixation of meaning'.[3]

How does Michelman's alternative approach to building the bridge then work? He distinguishes two functions of a constitution: a 'regulatory' and a 'proceduralizing' function. The *regulatory* function aims at ensuring for the future that the state's legislative, judicial, and administrative actions comport with certain guidelines laid down in advance by the constitution's authors; a constitutional guarantee of 'the freedom of speech' aims to ensure that no regulation in times to come infringes on the principle—it might be a broad or abstract principle—to which the authors referred under that name. Michelman's *proceduralizing* function, instead, aims at ensuring the conformity of government to guidelines reflecting some political conception of justice judged currently supportable by an overlapping consensus of reasonable and rational citizens.

My 'third course' between the originalist ('regulatory') and philosophical ('proceduralizing') versions of the court's mandate converges with Michelman's view insofar as he considers his two versions of the interpretive mandate of a supreme or constitutional court (each linked with an assumed priority of either the regulatory or the proceduralizing function of the constitution) to be 'joined together by the obvious and simple truth that the proceduralizing aim cannot get off the ground without presupposition of a regulatory success'.[4] As he concisely puts it: 'proceduralizing ambition presupposes regulatory effect'.[5]

I thoroughly endorse Michelman's indication of a pressing need for bridging the divide between the two versions of the interpretive mandate of a constitutional court. As a footnote, let me add the consideration that the divide in the end boils down to a split between a *descriptive* reconstruction (of historical traces of the will of the people) and an *evaluative* assessment (of the desirability of constitutional interpretive outcomes in light of their potential for cutting across divisive and controversial substantive orientations) on which recent philosophy has cast doubt.[6] I also share Michelman's point that 'political-liberal resort to the dualist conception to overcome shortfall of agreement does *itself* (even putting aside any aim of a cure for occlusion) necessarily implicate a reference to meanings already settled in law'.[7] We are indeed constructing the same bridge from different ends.

[3] Ibid.
[4] Ibid. p. 101.
[5] Ibid. p. 101.
[6] See Hilary Putnam, *The Collapse of the Fact/Value Dichotomy* (Harvard U. Press 2002).
[7] Chapter 7, p. 2–3.

Furthermore, underlying our diverse but convergent efforts at reconciling two views of the constitution's function and of the mandate of its highest judicial interpreter, a shared sense can be detected of the urgency to respond to unsettling historical developments. Among them, in our late-modern, complex, and diverse democratic societies, is an elevated level of concern about an occlusion of democratic authorship *at the hands of the judiciary*, and especially of constitutional courts, calling for some kind of rebalancing of the prerogatives of the entitled authors and the commissioned interpreters/guardians of the constitution. With the intent to enrich the previous discussion, the rest of this chapter will focus on this inextinguishable predicament of constitutional democracies and on three possible remedies for current unrest.

1. Judicial Occlusion of Democratic Authorship?

An extended literature proclaims the occlusion of democratic authorship by the constitutional judiciary.[8] Much of it comes from champions of so-called 'political constitutionalism', who take issue with judicial review and counterpropose different ways of relocating that function within the purview of legislative assemblies.[9] Here, I want to consider the issue through the coordinates of political liberalism and its conception of democracy as intrinsically and ineluctably constitutional.

By that conception, no branch of government in a well-ordered society can enjoy unchallengeable final authority. In line with Rawls's rejection of judicial as well as parliamentary supremacy,[10] the interpretation, for example, of 'equal protection of the laws' by the highest judicial interpreter remains *putatively* reflective of the will of the people, in a fallibilistic sense, until the people (through the other branches and according to the procedures provided by the constitution) set the amending procedure under way and correct a possibly erroneous,

[8] For examples of authors who voice that concern without necessarily endorsing 'political constitutionalism', see Jamin B. Raskin, *Overruling Democracy: The Supreme Court versus The American People* (Routledge 2003); Judith Resnik and Lane Dilg, 'Responding to a Democratic Deficit: Limiting the Powers and the Term of the Chief Justice of the United States' (2005–2006) 154 University of Pennsylvania Law Review 1575; Sanford Levinson, 'How the United States Constitution Contributes to the Democratic Deficit in America' (2006–2007) 55 Drake Law Review 859. See also Wojciech Sadurski (ed.), *Constitutional Justice, East and West: Democratic Legitimacy and Constitutional Courts in Post-Communist Europe in a Comparative Perspective* (Kluzer 2002).

[9] See Richard Bellamy, *Political Constitutionalism: A Republican Defence of the Constitutionality of Democracy* (CUP 2007); Richard Bellamy and Dario Castiglione (eds), *Constitutionalism in Transformation: European and Theoretical Perspectives* (Blackwell 1996); Jeremy Waldron, *Law and Disagreement* (OUP 1999) and *The Dignity of Legislation* (CUP 1999).

[10] See Rawls, *PL* 233 and 237.

partial, or otherwise unwelcome interpretation on the part of the court. As Rawls succinctly summed up his rejection of judicial supremacy: 'The constitution is not what the Court says it is. Rather, it is what the people acting constitutionally through the other branches eventually allow the Court to say it is.'[11] Moments of judicial occlusion of democratic authorship are provisional only: ways to move past them are provided by the law.

It is important to examine one counter-argument against this Rawlsian take on the power of the highest judicial interpreter as checked by the citizens' prerogative to amend the constitution according to the procedures provided for by the law of their country. The counter-argument turns on the observation that historically and in several contexts many of the mechanisms for amending the constitution have become cumbersome and impractical to the point of being largely inoperative. As documented by Ackerman and others for the case of the United States, over the twentieth and twenty-first centuries it has become prohibitively difficult to set the institutional machinery of Article V in motion.[12] This alteration of the constitutional picture, due among other causes to the rise of the presidency to a prominent constitutional role, the acceleration of time, the complexity of twentieth-century administrative and legislative processes, all combining with the high supermajority thresholds and multiple veto points prescribed by Article V, means that the mere absence of an amendment action in response to a contested pronouncement of the Supreme Court cannot be taken as indicative of popular acceptance, as it might have been in former times. Since the days of the New Deal and up to the civil rights era, constitutional transformation has been largely carried out via 'landmark statutes', as well as via exemplary opinions of the court (e.g. *Brown* and *Loving*), with the sole exception of the Twenty-Fourth Amendment.[13] The diagnosis of a juristocratic occlusion of the democratic will of the people receives much of its current force from the widespread perception of the unlikelihood, any time soon, of a formal remedy to this *contretemps* (say, in the United States, by formal amendment of Article V).

Perhaps a high-water mark of complaint has come on the occasion of the *Obergefell* case of 2015 on same-sex marriage. Not only have the justices who filed a dissenting opinion made that claim, but also such political philosophers

[11] Ibid. 237.

[12] See Bruce Ackerman, *The Civil Rights Revolution* (Harvard U. Press 2014) 40–41(hereafter Ackerman, *Civil Rights Revolution*) and Richard Albert, *Constitutional Amendments: Making, Breaking, and Changing Constitutions* (OUP 2019) 119–120.

[13] See Ackerman, *Civil Rights Revolution* (n. 12) 70–72 and 80–82; see also William N. Eskridge, jr and John Ferejohn, 'Super-statutes' (2001) 50 Duke Law Journal 1215.

as Jeremy Waldron have joined in. Chief Justice Roberts, joined by Justices Scalia and Thomas, dissenting, lodged an objection that 'five lawyers have closed the [democratic] debate and enacted their own vision of marriage as a matter of constitutional law. Stealing this issue from the people will for many cast a cloud over same-sex marriage, making a dramatic social change that much more difficult to accept.'[14] Calling the Court's opinion 'an act of will, not legal judgment', and noting that it abruptly 'invalidates the marriage laws of more than half the States', the dissenting justices maintained that the majority of the Court not only had seized for itself a question the Constitution leaves to the people, but had done so at a time when the people were engaged in their own vibrant debates on that question, and then only to answer it not by neutral principles of constitutional law, but by their own 'understanding of what freedom is and must become'.[15]

Waldron, echoing many of the points raised by the dissenting justices, sharpens the complaint by drawing a comparison between the question of the constitutionality of the segregation and anti-miscegenation laws, held invalid in *Brown* and in *Loving*, and that of limiting access to marriage to heterosexual couples. While the ruling on segregation did not change the commonsense meaning of education, and that on interracial marriage did not change the commonsense meaning of marriage (so argues Waldron), the ruling on same-sex marriage does strike at the common understanding of marriage as it has stood from time immemorial.[16]

To this observation, Waldron adds that transformations of the institution of marriage can and do 'take place informally, as changing patterns of behavior over time'. This was the case, for example, with the declining emphasis on procreation as the purpose of marriage or with romantic love replacing arranged marriages as the inspiring model for marriage. Other transformations, instead, have taken place through deliberate social decisions—the main example being the introduction of divorce. The point is that such deliberate choices, including the one introducing same-sex marriage, have generally been of a legislative nature—Colombia and Brazil being the only countries, beyond the US, in which same-sex marriage has been introduced by a judicial decision. Now, the Supreme Court is certainly justified in overturning statutes that do infringe constitutional essentials, as was the case with *Loving*'s striking down

[14] *Obergefell v. Hodges* 576 U.S.___(2015), Roberts, CJ, dissenting, 2.

[15] Ibid. 3.

[16] Ibid. 7–8, 16; see also, for the same point, Jeremy Waldron, 'What a Dissenting Opinion Should Have Said in *Obergefell v. Hodges*', http://papers.ssrn.com/sol3/papers.cfm?abstract_id=2844811 17–18 accessed 27 November 2020).

anti-miscegenation laws in Virginia that prohibited interracial marriage. Why would the Court not be justified in overturning statutes that restrict access to marriage on the basis of sexual preference?

Somewhat surprisingly, Waldron's answer is that in the latter case caution ought to have been exercised by the court, in order not to proceed 'too far in advance of changing public opinion'.[17] Concerning same-sex marriage, Waldron maintains, opinions 'are very deeply felt—indeed, in the case of many people, associated with deeply felt religious views. What is needed for the modification of these opinions is time—above all, enough time for varied levels of personal experience and ideological conviction to shift and thaw hardened attitudes.'[18] Caution is demanded not just in consideration of the possibility of coming up with 'the wrong answer', but also 'because even if the Court gets the outcome right there is a cost to democratic self-determination in the process involved'.[19]

The conceptual content of the 'cost to democratic self-determination', however, is not specified convincingly by Waldron. Consider, first, this inference from the dualist conception of democracy: *if* the interpretive argument to the effect that it is unconstitutional for statutes to limit the freedom of same-sex persons to marry holds, in overturning those statutes the court acts as one separated branch of power in lieu of 'the people', no less than state legislatures do. The court, even if not directly elected, is no less an expression of the people than representative legislative institutions: that is the gist of a political-liberal view of the separation of constituted powers. When Waldron, after illustrating the momentous change ushered in by *Obergefell* adds 'this is a change for the people to make, not their judges',[20] he is simply assuming that the people is represented primarily by legislation and not also by the judicial interpreter of the constitution.

Second, the Court correctly emphasizes that time is irrelevant in matters of 'rights', crucial though time might independently be for the public acceptance of certain consequences:

> [W]hile the Constitution contemplates that democracy [in the form of ordinary congressional law-making] is the appropriate process for change, individuals who are harmed need not await legislative action before asserting a fundamental right.[21]

[17] Ibid. 9.
[18] Ibid. 9.
[19] Ibid. 9.
[20] Ibid. 18.
[21] *Obergefell v. Hodges* 576 U.S.___ (2015), 5.

Waldron's point that same-sex marriage constitutes a more radical transformation of marriage than interracial marriage at the time of *Loving* seems to hold no other force beyond Waldron's own personal conviction. Interracial marriage mobilized the very same sort of resistance, based on the idea that it was 'against nature'. As late as 1965, in the official records of the *Loving* case, the following statement can be found, underwritten by Virginia trial court Judge Leon Bazile:

> Almighty God created the races white, black, yellow, Malay, and red, and placed them on separate continents, and but for the interference with his arrangement there would be no cause for such marriages. The fact that he separated the races shows that he did not intend the races to mix.[22]

Yet Waldron and all who lament occlusion of democratic authorship at the hands of the judiciary do have a point—not so much when they refer to the magnitude of change (as though a threshold of innovation existed, above which only legislatures are authorized to decide) as when they implicitly raise the conceptual challenge of telling apart the *interpretation* of the constitution from its *transformation*. Most defenders of the democratic propriety of *Obergefell* readily acknowledge that the Fourteenth Amendment-based arguments that led to overturning statutes prohibiting same-sex marriage could not justify overturning statutes prohibiting polygamy. How do we conceptualize that different legal response to the possibly equally strong subjective feelings of exclusion from marriage experienced by a gay couple and by a polygamous community? The difference cannot rest on the readiness of the larger public to accept the practice in question, lest we forfeit the constitutional character of the Constitution.

The key to answering that question lies in querying the term 'to conceptualize'. Perhaps the difference between interpreting and transforming cannot be captured by a concept at all, any more than the difference between a work of art that barely deserves such a name and one that displays excellence and breaks new ground can be captured conceptually. That difference, however, certainly

[22] Quoted in Neely Tucker, 'Loving Day Recalls a Time When the Union of a Man and a Woman Was Banned', *Washington Post* (13 June 2006) <http://www.washingtonpost.com/wp-dyn/content/article/2006/06/12/AR2006061201716.html> accessed 10.5.2017. Half a century earlier, Congressman Roddenbery in a congressional session declared that 'Intermarriage between whites and blacks is repulsive and averse to every sentiment of pure American spirit. It is abhorrent and repugnant to the very principles of Saxon government. It is subversive of social peace', Congressional Record, 62d. Congr., 3d. Sess., December 11, 1912, pp. 502–503. Declarations such as these, in the public forum by public officials, raise questions about Waldron's claim that *Loving* was less groundbreaking than *Obergefell*.

exists and exerts a normative force—it grounds what our judgements *ought to* recognize rather than reflecting the empirical convergence of our judgements. Just as the work of art possessed of the quality of *exemplarity*—let me avoid the Kantian term 'beauty', too internal to one specific aesthetic paradigm—produces a sense of the 'enhancement of life' (*Beförderung des Lebens*) in those who come in contact with it,[23] so the interpretation that 'enlivens' the constitutional text and brings it into creative contact with our context produces a sense of promoting and enriching our political life in a stable and just society of free and equal citizens, a sense of 'making the most' (to borrow Dworkin's fortunate phrase) of our living constitutional tradition.[24] Judgements that fail at interpretive excellence and superimpose unduly transformative aims onto the constitutional texture of the polity hit a wrong note, a disturbing rather than a life-enriching note. The soundness of reflective judgement cannot be *demonstrated*; that is why in many fields it is not binding. In film criticism, you follow your favourite critic, and her judgements are not binding on anyone. Not so, of course, with constitutional adjudication, which binds everyone, not excepting the holders of legislative power. And that, then, is why, instead of wishfully chasing the chimera of a strictly conceptual threshold between interpretation and transformation, a constitutional order should aim primarily at aptly designed avenues of correction through democratic politics, when the institution entrusted with judgement on the constitution errs.

Consequently, if and only if Waldron and others are correct in accusing the Ccourt of having unduly 'transformed' the Constitution, their attendant allegation that the Court has thereby occluded the exercise of democratic sovereignty by the people has substance. Likewise, Waldron's claim concerning an untimely decision—'too far in advance of changing public opinion'—can be now reconsidered as pointing to one missing element in the Court's judgment, namely a sense of the correct timing for a rendition of judgment. To Alexander Bickel we owe the famous line that the Court should be '100 percent principled 20 percent of the time',[25] meaning that it 'may strike down legislation as inconsistent with principle. It may validate ... legislation as consistent with principle. *Or it may do neither.* It may do neither, and therein lies the secret of its ability to maintain itself in the tension between principle and expediency.'[26]

[23] Immanuel Kant, *Critique of the Power of Judgment* (first published 1790), ed. Paul Guyer (CUP 2000) § 23, 128.

[24] Ronald Dworkin, *Law's Empire* (Harvard U. Press 1986) 228–232.

[25] Gerald Gunther, 'The Subtle Vices of the Passive Virtues' (1964) 64 Columbia Law Review 1, 3.

[26] Alexander Bickel, *The Least Dangerous Branch: The Supreme Court at the Bar of Politics* (first published 1962), 2nd edn (Yale U. Press 1986) 69. See also Mark Tushnet, 'The Jurisprudence of Constitutional Regimes: Alexander Bickel and Cass Sunstein', in K. D. Ward and C. Castillo (eds),

Thus, despite the interpretive coherence required when a contested issue is selected for decision, the risk of error (and in that sense of occlusion) originates not only from the plurality of contesting interpretations concerning what constitutional coherence requires, but also from the judgement that leads to selecting an issue for pronouncement. For example, Attorney General John Mitchell supported the Voting Rights Act's renewal, in 1970, with the observation that 'voting rights is not a regional issue',[27] meaning that voting could not be left up to the decision of local majorities. National uniformity was mandated by the constitutional relevance of the matter, no less than national uniformity on the allowance or disallowance of slavery was understood as non-negotiable by Abraham Lincoln a century earlier. Was the Supreme Court right in attributing to same-sex marriage the status of an issue (along with voting, segregation, interracial marriage) on which regional variation is not—or is no longer—admissible, when (by comparison) capital punishment is to this day an issue on which no one spends too much time wondering why the law shouldn't vary according to local majorities? Only if the answer is negative, can a moment of occlusion of democratic authorship be said to have occurred.

From the perspective of a normativity based on judgement and the force of exemplarity,[28] concept-based attempts to fix the appropriate moment for adjudicating contested issues (segregation, interracial marriage, same-sex marriage, capital punishment) must appear misguided, just as with attempts to differentiate between acts of constitutional interpretation and transformation. These contestations are matters for reflective judgement, and reflective judgement operates via *guidelines* (*Leitfäden*) that orient its outcome, not with concepts that bring the contested matter to final closure via subsumption under preordained categories.[29]

It is owing to this lack of concept-mandated closure that the challenge of occlusion-free judicial constitutional review remains all too real and present. The most promising strategy for meeting it consists of maintaining the openness of the process whereby instances of constitutional adjudication found wanting—inadequate either in substantive terms (e.g. the enunciation of new rights that the living segment of the people fails to see as cogently grounded in its will) or in the arbitrary timing of a cut-off to political debate and regional

The Judiciary and American Democracy: Alexander Bickel, the Countermajoritarian Difficulty, and Contemporary Constitutional Theory (SUNY Press 2006) 26.

27 Quoted in Ackerman, *Civil Rights Revolution* (n. 12) 166.

28 See Alessandro Ferrara, *The Force of the Example: Explorations in the Paradigm of Judgment* (Columbia U. Press 2008) 1–61.

29 Ibid. 59.

variation—can be remedied and rectified by an exercise of the amending power vested in the living segment of people. If the original balance—the highest interpreter says what the Constitution says, the people can correct that interpretation by amending the Constitution—has been upset by historical circumstances, a new balance must be found. To remain with the case of the United States, if the formal procedure mandated by Article V has become increasingly impractical, what possible substitutes could avoid adjudicative occlusions of authorship?

2. Three Remedial Strategies

We have reached here one of the crossroads for liberal-democracy in our time: rethinking the separation of powers in the twenty-first century. There are several facets to this problem. One is the identification of new powers, alongside the classical Montesqueian ones, that now, in societies typically more complex than those of the mid-eighteenth century, ought to be separated and balanced with one another.[30] Another need is for adjusted fine-tuning of the relation between the executive and the legislative power, given new challenges to social ordering.[31] And a third need, as disclosed by our discussion here, is for a rethinking and rebalancing of the relation of the judiciary to the other two classical branches, with an eye to mitigating the occlusion of authorship that derives from the increased difficulty, affecting the United States but also other democracies, of effectively revising the constitution via formal amendment rules.

Focusing on this third facet of the separation of powers, three main strategies come to mind for sustaining the values of judicial constitutional review without resulting occlusion of democratic constitutional authorship.

The first strategy consists in weakening the grip of judicial review on the outcome of legislation. The current standard model of judicial review operates in an 'all-or-none' fashion: a statute can be upheld by a constitutional court or can be declared unconstitutional. Although, in some jurisdictions, degrees of constitutionality are created by the fact that single parts of a statute can be

[30] On this point see Bruce Ackerman, 'The New Separation of Powers', (2000) 3 Harvard Law Review 634 (hereafter Ackerman 'New Separation'); Michel Troper, 'The Development of the Notion of Separation of Powers' (1992) 26, 1 Israel Law Review 1–15; Yaniv Roznai, 'The Newest-Oldest Separation of Powers' (2018) 14, 2 European Constitutional Law Review 430

[31] Two opposite views are: Ackerman, 'New Separation' (n. 30) and Eric Posner and Adrian Vermeule, *The Executive Unbound: The Post-Madisonian Republic* (OUP 2011).

upheld or invalidated, a single legal provision—whether the whole of a statute or a part thereof—can never be constitutional and unconstitutional at the same time. An ingenious remedy for judicial occlusion of democratic authorship lies in weakening the force of the pronouncements of supreme or constitutional courts. Instead of having the conclusive and immediate effect of invalidating the legislative act under scrutiny, such pronouncements could rather extend a strong institutional invitation, or even an obligation, for the legislative authorities to reconsider the matter, while perhaps also setting a benchmark for the adequacy of such reconsideration. It could also be imagined that the highest constitutional interpreter be entrusted with addressing a broader set of interlocutors than parliaments. For example, when socioeconomic rights are at stake, the court could be entrusted to act in the first instance as instigator and non-dictatorial overseer of engagements among stakeholders very broadly defined, among whom state actors hold no privileged position, in an ongoing process of interpretive clarification of what a constitutionally declared right of (say) 'access to health care services' consists of in substance and, simultaneously and reciprocally, of what sorts of steps by what classes of actors are concretely (in the current conditions of society, economy, and so on) in order towards the achievement of due and adequate service to everyone's core interest.[32]

This strategy for alleviating judicial occlusion of the democratic will pivots around a so-called 'weak-form judicial review', thematized in work by Mark Tushnet and discussed by Michelman in relation to the difficulty of constitutionalizing socioeconomic rights, which often seem to depend, for their enforcement, on the planning and managing capacity of economic institutions and on these institutions' influence on market processes. It remains to be seen if such a model of a weak, non-imperative form of judicial review could be exported, as Michelman seems inclined to suggest, from the realm of social rights to the more traditional area of rights securing negative freedom.[33]

[32] Frank Michelman, 'Legitimacy, the Social Turn, and Constitutional Review: What Political Liberalism Suggests' (2015) 3 Critical Quarterly of Legislation and Law 391. See also Rosalind Dixon, 'Creating Dialogue about Socioeconomic Rights' (2007) 5 International Journal of Constitutional Law 391.

[33] Weak-review generalized to all realms of constitutional adjudication is no complete novelty. Already in the 1930s, with the intention of supporting New Deal legislation in ways different from the Rooseveltian plan for 'packing the Supreme Court' with progressive justices, Senator Wheeler put forward a scheme which would allow Congress to override an adverse opinion by the Supreme Court if the override was supported 'by a two-thirds majority in both houses, as long as an election intervened between the Court decision and the override'. Mark Tushnet, *Taking the Constitution Away from the Courts* (Princeton U. Press 1999) 175 (hereafter Tushnet, *Taking the Constitution*).

More recently, Michelman has offered an important contribution to a reflection on adjustments to judicial review not limited to the area of social rights. He has distinguished three modalities of judicial restraint. First, judicial restraint as *quiescence* (as opposed to a court's *activism*) refers to a court's disposition 'to narrow the range of social disputes on which [it] will see fit to pronounce in the constitution's name'.[34] Second, judicial restraint as *tolerance* (as opposed to a court's *assertiveness*) refers to a court's willingness to provisionally abstain from imposing (often by a majority vote) its own vision of the 'most reasonable' among a plurality of balance-judgments concerning basic liberties and rights, provided that the competing balance-judgments—favoured by legislative and executive institutions or by associations of citizens—pass the threshold of being at least reasonable.[35] Third, a court can be said to exercise a *weak-form judicial review* if its pronouncements are not ultimately binding for the other branches, notably for legislative institutions, but simply injunctions to reconsider the contested matter—a form of judicial review that, however, falls short of satisfying the requirement, embedded in Rawls's 'liberal principle of legitimacy', that constitutional essentials, fixed beyond uncertainty, function as benchmarks of legitimacy.

We can furthermore, in coherence with the political-liberal paradigm, aim to avoid occlusion by acting on the temporal dimensions of judicial review. In Michelman's words, 'case-bound determinations of constitutional meanings and applications from an undoubtedly strong-form court need not take full and legal control from the instant of their first utterance'.[36] A convenient time span between the first utterance of a pronouncement and its final binding effect, in combination with a due regard for quiescence and tolerance on the part of the court, may provide a chance for a constitutional dialogue with the other branches and may offer, at the same time, a more flexible instrument for the purpose of allaying judicial occlusion than amending the constitution.

A second strategy for relief of judicial occlusion consists of a more radical modification of judicial review: namely, abolition. In Tushnet's eloquent phrase, we simply would 'take the Constitution away from the courts'.[37] We would relocate to parliaments, or to special segments of legislative institutions, the function of overseeing the Constitution's living nature, i.e. its persisting

[34] Frank Michelman, 'Political-Liberal Legitimacy and the Question of Judicial Restraint' (2019) 1 Jus Cogens 61.
[35] Ibid. 72.
[36] Ibid. 71.
[37] Tushnet, *Taking the Constitution* (n. 33).

alignment with the people's deep seated normative intuitions supposed to exercise a regulatory function over lower level legislation.

While some proponents of this remedy—Richard Bellamy and Jeremy Waldron[38]—come from constitutional contexts where the legislative institutions have historically been less subjected to imperative judicial review, the most thought-provoking articulation of this strategy comes from Tushnet. As he puts it: 'Doing away with judicial review would have one clear effect: It would return all constitutional decision-making to the people acting politically.'[39] The institutional realization of this reclamation of the Constitution for normal lawmaking remains to be detailed, but its core intuition consists of putting an end to what Tushnet calls 'judicial supremacy'—namely, the notion that the provisions of the Constitution cannot have any other meaning than the meaning authoritatively attributed to them by the Supreme Court. A sensible scheme for reform, in his opinion, would allow representatives elected in contests between alternative platforms to contribute to shaping those meanings in the name of the people.

A *third* strategy for remedying democratic occlusion follows a trajectory opposite to the previous two. It recommends leaving judicial review in place while strengthening the ability of other constituted powers, including the executive, to act on behalf of the living segment of the people, unconvinced by or actively opposing the court's interpretation of the constitution. A few years ago, in a different political context, Ackerman outlined this strategy under the name of 'Popular Sovereignty Initiative'.

From his review of the major transformative constitutional moments in the history of the United States—the *Founding*, the *Reconstruction*, the *New Deal* and the *Civil Rights Revolution*—Ackerman draws a fourfold teaching. First, Article V need not be interpreted as the one and only path to constitutional reform. Although it provides the *via regia*, it could be supplemented by other ways, for instance by 'landmark statutes' of congressional origin. Second, each of the above junctures of American constitutional history can be understood as a way-station towards the affirmation of the *nationwide* dimension of the people's will, over against the idea of the people's will as a function of some fraction of state-based local political wills. Third, the Presidency, formally not included in the process of constitutional amendment as envisioned in Article V, in the twentieth century has in fact come to play an increasingly influential

[38] Waldron specifically levels his argument only against strong-form of judicial review, see his 'The Core of the Case Against Judicial Review' (2006) 115 Yale Law Journal 1354.

[39] Tushnet, *Taking the Constitution* (n. 33) 154.

role, on account of its being the one elective office whose constituency spans the entire country: 'Modern Americans put their national identity at the center and expect the Presidency to take a leading role in the process of articulating the nation's future'.[40] Fourth, and consequently, limitation of the president's formal role in processes of constitutional change to the nomination of justices now stands as anachronistic, out of line with the historical context of the United States.

The strategy envisaged by Ackerman accordingly aims at absorbing into formal institutions the reality of the important role in fact and inevitably played by presidential leadership in the field of constitutional reconsideration, while curbing potentially populist excesses by tying the exercise of presidential influence to a close interaction with Congress. More specifically, Ackerman envisages the enacting of a special statute called the *Popular Sovereignty Initiative* designed to supplement and not to suppress Article V:

> Proposed by a (second-term) President, this Initiative should be submitted to Congress for two-thirds approval, and should then be submitted to the voters at the next two Presidential elections. If it passes these tests, it should be accorded constitutional status by the Supreme Court.[41]

Three aspects of this proposal are worth highlighting. The authority to initiate constitutional reform, in response to a perceived occlusion of democratic will, would be granted to the president only during his or her second term: this measure constitutes a check on the quality and strength of the mandate given by the electorate to the president. Furthermore, such new prerogative to formally propose constitutional amendments is further checked by the required congressional super-majority and the required dual approval at two subsequent presidential elections, in which the proposing second-term president will not be a candidate. Thus 'the test of time' extends a veil of ignorance over the original proponents of the amendment. Ackerman's requirement that the proposal, in order to be ratified, has to be approved by three-fifths of the electorate in two national referenda, run in conjunction with two consecutive presidential elections, is designed to inject a strong element of uncertainty in the partisan calculations that might possibly provide motivation for presidential and congressional action. It is simply too hard to predict the political climate of ten years in the future. Finally, the referendum format of ratification is designed

[40] Bruce Ackerman, *We the People*, Vol. 2, *Transformations* (Harvard U. Press 1998) 413.
[41] Ibid. 415.

to offset the residual weight attributed by Article V to state-bound processes of will formation. As Ackerman puts it, 'each voter will be treated as an equal citizen of the nation', in that 'his judgment on the referendum-question will not count more if he happens to live in Wyoming than in California'.[42] This strategy would leave day-to-day judicial review at whatever level of strength it might otherwise occupy, while offsetting potential occlusive effects by allowing for the living segment of the popular sovereign to express a corrective will through the other branches.[43]

It is too early to assess the relative merits of these three strategies, especially in the absence of a clear and detailed account of their institutional specifications. For all of them, the shadows of the Trump presidency constitute a challenge, though in a different sense for those who advocate a paring back of judicial review than for those, like Ackerman, who advocate strengthening the presidency.

In sum, and abstaining from detailed evaluations: the case for entirely relocating constitutional review from the judiciary to the legislatures or the electorate (and so, inevitably, to the contestations of political parties) runs into the trouble of entrusting the rules of the democratic game, i.e. the Constitution, to the players themselves in the midst of playing the game. I find Michelman's suggestions very interesting where social rights are concerned, and potentially capable of a differentiated application—incorporating different gradients of restraint—in the case of fundamental rights. I do see much promise in Ackerman's counter-strategy of strengthening the constitutional agency of the other branches of constituted power as a way to rebalance a historically diminished capacity, on the part of the people-qua-sovereign, to correct the interpretation of the Constitution provided by its authorized supreme interpreter. As in many other cases, the important preliminary step is to understand the problem in the correct way. The merits of the alternative solutions will become clearer over time.

[42] Ibid. 410.

[43] In the section of 'New Separation' (n. 30) entitled 'Bringing the People Back in' (666–668), Ackerman has also discussed the possibility of 'a carefully constructed process of serial referenda' (668) as a way of bringing the people back in the legislative process in a non-populist way. Central to this strategy are the ideas of multiple balloting and of Fishkin's 'deliberative polling' as ways of accruing the deliberative quality of the referendum process.

PART III

GLOBAL ORDERS AND LIMITS OF LIBERALISM

The 'limits of liberalism' named in the title to this Part are of three kinds. First, they are limits to the appeal—limits, as we might say, to the reach of the reasonable reason—of comprehensive or perfectionist liberalism. Conceptions centred around individual rights, sceptically tinged toleration, the principle of utility, Kantian autonomy—even around discursive generalizability of norms across a population of free and equal individuals—can serve as starting points only within certain cultural coordinates far from universal. They cannot work to buttress a regime of liberty when transplanted to other contexts, and indeed they become oppressive when unilaterally generalized—oppressive in the sense that, in spite of well-meaning projects of democratization, these liberal conceptions rest their correspondent institutions on principles that in some parts of the world are not endorsed.

Second, the phrase refers also to limits of anti-perfectionist, political liberalism as thus far herein articulated. To its opening question of how possibly to provide for 'a just and stable society of free and equal citizens who remain profoundly divided by reasonable religious, philosophical, and moral doctrines', political liberalism responds with a cluster of ideas—political conceptions of justice, of the person, and of the citizen; reasonability and public reason; legitimation-by-constitution (the liberal principle of legitimacy); the public forum; reciprocity and the duty of civility—that have questionable resonance in settings apart from societies shaped by Western traditions. A central question for this Part of the book is whether or how these limitations can be overcome by conceptually overhauling—while still in some form retaining—these core presuppositions of political liberalism. The exchange of views here concerns the best way to rethink these central notions of the paradigm when legitimacy in hyperpluralist conditions is in question. Again, two distinct tonalities can be heard—Ferrara's more optimistic about the possibility of reconciling even such differences in the political-liberal spirit, Michelman's somewhat more sceptical view of our chances of bridging all the relevant gaps.

Third, the 'limits of liberalism' can take on also another shade of meaning. We have seen in Part I how John Rawls followed Bruce Ackerman's conception of democracy as 'dualist' in proposing his liberal principle of legitimacy. Then, in Part II, we took up Ackerman's proposal for an additional path to constitutional amendment (the 'Popular Sovereignty Initiative') as a plausible response to concerns about adjudicative occlusions of democratic constitutional authorship in the United States. Here in Part III, where the topic is the applicability of political liberalism to global contexts, Ackerman's work can be read to offer, in partial response to concerns about a limited reach for *liberalism* in the world as it stands today, a more encouraging thought about a broader reach for *constitutionalism*. In his *Revolutionary Constitutions*, Ackerman takes note of how the Iranian constitution, while it 'gives the Guardian Jurist far greater power to repel the advances of his democratic adversaries' than a liberal West could tolerate, still does oblige the Supreme Leader to earn that authority through the recognition of his fellow clerics and political officials. From this observation, Ackerman draws the teaching that Iran, because it requires even 'the most powerful officials to engage with institutional rivals for the final say over the future course of political development',[1] must be counted a constitutional regime, in spite of the theocratic bent of its constitutional culture. Constitutionalism thus stands for a principle prior to that of the rights and liberties of the liberal Enlightenment. While all forms of liberalism—including Rawls's political liberalism—are premised on the equality of citizens and of their rights, constitutions respond to a more basic principle that power does not emanate from one centre alone, but is to be exercised by institutionally serious rivals who engage in an ongoing contestation over the country's future. While liberalism sets benchmarks for a polity of free and equal citizens who pursue their visions of happiness, constitutionalism, in whichever variant, is 'larger than liberalism' and reaches worldwide where liberalism cannot reach. Constitutionalism, on this view, could arguably provide a grammar of trans-liberal political decency.

As John Rawls, cued by Bruce Ackerman, initially worked out his political-liberal turn on dualist democracy (that is, in the 'liberal principle of legitimacy' of *PL*), it was with the case in mind of a twentieth-century,

[1] Bruce Ackerman, *Revolutionary Constitutions: Charismatic Leadership and the Rule of Law* (Harvard U. Press 2019) 360. For different lines of interpretation, see Nader Sohrabi, *Revolution and Constitutionalism in the Ottoman Empire and Iran* (CUP 2011); Asghar Schirazi, *The Constitution of Iran: Politics and the State in the Islamic Republic* (Tauris 1997); and H. E. Chehabi, 'Religion and Politics in Iran: How Theocratic is the Islamic Republic?' (1991) 120, 3 Daedalus 69–91.

constitutional-democratic nation-state. A 2018 workshop at Boston College, on 'The Legitimacy of Transnational Orders: Discussing the Idea of a World State', marks the point at which, for the authors of this book, a debate about the resilience of legitimation-by-constitution to the threat from hyperpluralism slips across whatever gap of relevant difference may separate the two cases of the hyperpluralizing nation-state and a global-scale institutional order.[2] Ferrara and Michelman each prepared for that workshop a draft on possibilities and problems of transposition from the one case to the other of the idea a legitimation-bearing, higher-law constitution.

Both drafts took off from assumptions that trouble-making facts of hyperpluralism at the global scale must certainly match and even exceed those currently overtaking various separate countries of the constitutional-democratic West, about which both had written previously. In his book of 2014, *The Democratic Horizon*, Ferrara had proposed, as political liberalism's best response to these oncoming 'inhospitable conditions',[3] the idea of a legitimation-bearing 'constitution for a multivariate polity'.[4] As part of a 2016 published symposium on Ferrara's book, Michelman had briefly voiced some doubts about the multivariate idea.[5] In his draft for the 2018 world-state workshop, Ferrara reflected on a possible extension of the multivariate model idea to a global-scale institutional order. Michelman, responding, reverted to his own prior hesitant reception of that model.

The chapters in Part III of this book stem directly from those drafts we prepared for the Boston College meeting, which in turn had drawn from our prior published writings. We rewrote the chapters for this book in the light of ongoing conversations between us. And while the chapters are separately authored, their contents reflect a measure of prearranged coordination, so as to let the overall debate develop on the page in a way that is orderly and clear. Thus, Michelman's Chapter 9 sets out terms of political-liberal analysis and argument on which the authors agree, both as an account of what the political-liberal philosophy is up to and as representation of a coherent political ideal to

[2] We must at this point stay thus non-committal about any such gap, in part because, as will appear below in Chapter 10, Ferrara's multivariate-polity idea for the nation-state case had itself been inspired by John Rawls's proposal for a set of constitutional principles—a 'law of peoples'—for a potentially globe-spanning 'society of peoples'.

[3] Ferrara, *The Democratic Horizon: Hyperpluralism and the Renewal of Political Liberalism* (CUP 2014) 6–12 (hereafter Ferrara, *Democratic Horizon*) (citing Michelman 'How Can the People Ever Make the Laws? A Critique of Deliberative Democracy', in James Bohman and William Rehg (eds), *Deliberative Democracy* (MIT Press 1997) 154).

[4] Ferrara, *Democratic Horizon* (n. 3) 105–108.

[5] See Frank I. Michelman, 'A Constitutional Horizon?' (2016) 42 Philosophy & Social Criticism 640, 647–648.

which both authors are sympathetically drawn. Ferrara's Chapter 10 addresses some questions raised by Michelman's account of a possible transposition of the political-liberal model of legitimation-by-constitution to the transnational level. At the domestic level, the constitutional essentials supposedly reflect some underlying shared political conception of justice, such as Rawlsian justice as fairness. Ferrara offers reasons to doubt an assignment of equivalent status—that of a shared conception of justice for a well-ordered global society—to Rawls's proposed eight chartering principles for a society of peoples. On a Rawlsian conception, argues Ferrara, principles of justice for a worldwide political association—in order to be more normatively binding than just the outcome of the incidentally converging wills of the signatory states—would have to reflect some political conception of justice for the global level; and justice as fairness cannot play that function, on account of its individual-egalitarian premises not shared across the globe.

In Chapter 10, Ferrara does propose a guide—the good or flourishing of humanity as a whole—to a compelling political conception of justice to underlie a constitution for a society of peoples. Michelman then follows, in Chapter 11, with a proposition for a 'political conception of a people', arguing that this, too, is required for an extension to the society of peoples of Rawlsian legitimation-by-constitution. From that argument, Michelman further derives, as a consequence, a problematic-looking model for the society of peoples as what he calls a 'chequerboard empire'. In Chapter 12, Ferrara explains why that is not a necessary conclusion or, in his view, the best transitional result to be looking for when compared with that of a multivariate-polity model for the society of peoples. Ferrara ends by noting both areas of agreement and points still under debate between the two of us.

9

Hyperpluralized Constituencies: The Challenge for Political Liberalism

Frank I. Michelman

1. A 'Realistic Utopia'

For John Rawls, a conception of justice comprises a set of precepts for a fair scheme of distribution, among members of a human society, of the sorts of claims, relationships, and statuses in that society that the members reasonably, rationally, and primarily value and seek. But a table of the terms and measures for a fair distribution does not yet, Rawls thought, fulfil the mission of political philosophy while conceived 'in abstraction from institutional forms'.[1] Philosophy, in his view, is obligated no less for some further institutional reflection in keeping with those terms and conducive towards those measures. The quest, Rawls said, is for a 'realistic utopia'.[2] That meant that the terms and measures of a just distribution would have be such as to fit some workable institutional conception, one within practical reach, one that 'we can understand and act on, approve and endorse'.[3]

Now, this 'we' signals not just an author's address to whoever might be reading at the time, not just a casual callout by one party to a conversation to a happenstance group of others standing by. More pointedly, and quite explicitly, this 'we'—for whose capacity to approve and endorse, understand and act upon the justice-serving institutional prescriptions Rawls makes his stipulation—are Rawls's stand-in for J.-J. Rousseau's classic 'men as they are under laws as they might be'.[4] This 'we' calls out to people, actual or envisaged, who already now, or at some time in the future, will have 'grown up under' an institutional framework sufficiently approximating to the one the philosopher treats as justice-serving.[5] Rawls aimed to show how certain institutions historically known to

[1] John Rawls, *A Theory of Justice* (Harvard U. Press 1971) 171 (hereafter Rawls, *Theory of Justice*).
[2] Rawls, *The Law of Peoples* (Harvard U. Press 2001) 6, 11 (hereafter Rawls, *Law of Peoples*).
[3] Ibid. 6–7.
[4] Ibid. 7, 13.
[5] Ibid. 7.

Legitimation by Constitution. Alessandro Ferrara and Frank I. Michelman, Oxford University Press. © Alessandro Ferrara and Frank I. Michelman 2021. DOI: 10.1093/oso/9780192855121.003.0010

us—specifically, those of a liberal constitutional democracy—can be rationally and freely embraced by those who come of age under their tutelage, while at the same time carrying into execution the conditions of the utopia: liberty and justice for all. Rawls aimed—here using his own special formulation—to show how such institutions could be stable across generations' worth of time, and furthermore stable 'for the right reasons'.[6]

Given the stipulations, maybe the game seems easy. Hegemony does its work. Those who grow up under a given institutional framework will have internalized its ways and means, both as to justice and as to fundamental interest. The pre-liberation peasantry in Russia, no? Well, no. Rawls didn't make it *that* easy.

2. Reasonable Pluralism

When, in *Political Liberalism* and succeeding works, Rawls takes up the question of the possible legitimacy of political regimes (in the sense of their moral justifiability to all those subjected to the force of their laws), he does so with a special regard to societies of persons perceiving themselves and each other as each one a 'free and equal' moral agent, all caught together in conditions of a 'reasonable pluralism' of comprehensive views. 'Free and equal' we will return to later. 'Pluralism' means, to Rawls, the cohabitation within a society of multiple and conflicting moral, religious, and metaphysical ('comprehensive') views. Such a social fact guarantees that coercive policies pursued by democratic parliamentary majorities will sometimes arouse deep objection from dissenters respecting matters they deem fundamental to morality, justice, faith, or the simple truth of how things are in the world. A social fact of pluralism poses in that way a complication to democratic political legitimacy among free and equal citizens. With the introduction of a further social fact of 'reasonable' pluralism,[7] the complication goes deeper. Guaranteed, then, is not only some frequency of heartfelt dissent from the policies of political majorities themselves not unreasonable, but of dissent that reasonable majorities cannot in good conscience brush aside as *itself un*reasonable and on that ground unworthy to be considered. That otherwise tempting path of evasion of the moral question of majority domination over free and equal resolute dissenters, is thus closed off.

[6] Ibid. 12–13. Meaning that 'the reasons from which citizens act include those given by the account of justice they affirm'. Rawls, *PL* xxxix, 143.

[7] See ibid. xviii–xix, 37 (distinguishing a 'fact of pluralism' from a 'fact of reasonable pluralism').

But where an assumption or expectation of reasonability on multiple sides of a question of social policy does thus block one avenue of escape from the problem of disagreement, it may also open up another. If it is *only* 'reasonable' pluralism with which political morality need be concerned—if it is only those conflicting views within bounds of reasonability that demand democratic respect—then that sets a limit to the range of objections to their policies with which putatively reasonable majorities need be morally concerned. And that opens, then, as explained in Chapter 5, the space of possibility for legitimation-by-constitution ('the liberal principle of legitimacy').[8] That solution still depends, though, on an expectation that a state-scale body of citizens, all of them judging reasonably within their mutually recognized social context of reasonable-pluralist conflict, will be able to concur on the full moral worthiness of a constitutional regime exposing them and others to concretely repugnant legislative outputs, without compromise to the freedom and equality of any. Or—now to bring into play another Rawlsian term—without oppression of any.

3. Oppression

In the political-liberal moral vocabulary, *oppression* is the human evil that *political* liberals are distinctly—by self-comparison, say, with 'comprehensive' liberals—committed to avoid.[9] A 'continuing shared understanding on one comprehensive religious, philosophical, or moral doctrine [and that would include, say, "the reasonable liberalisms of Kant or Mill"] can be maintained only by the oppressive use of state power'. Thus writes Rawls, naming this 'the fact of oppression'.[10] Political-liberal toleration is thus, exactly, the refusal and avoidance of oppression. In toleration's absence, oppression results. There is no compromise; our choice lies between the two.

And yet the assumption of the constitutionally convergent reasonability of citizens, on which rests the possibility of legitimation-by-constitution, seems itself fraught with oppressive potential. While liberal reasonability must then be wide enough to clear a path through a great deal of sectarian-liberal prejudice, it cannot be infinitely wide or else the whole construction of the 'liberal principle of legitimacy' (LPL) falls apart. Liberal toleration is still liberal, and

8 See Chapter 5, pp. 85–86.
9 See Rawls, *PL* xix–xx.
10 Ibid. 37.

that must impose a constraint-with-a-bite on liberal reasonability. A '*liberal* principle of legitimacy' is necessarily, after all, one ensconced within a detectably liberal political outlook.

A spectre of oppression thus haunts any and all political formations, global or domestic, whose edicts must be expected sometimes to touch on claims that *we* scions of the constitutional-democratic West—but, alas, decidedly not everyone else affected—are bound to regard as morally fundamental matters of basic liberty among persons free and equal: the condition we have named in Part II of this book as 'hyperpluralist'. How is that spectre to be met? Perhaps, if at all, as Rawls beautifully writes, by the political-liberal philosophy's relentless application 'to itself' of its own 'principle of toleration'.[11] And that, then, makes a suitable entry to the question of a rerun—or perhaps better, in Alessandro Ferrara's upbeat term, a 'renewal'[12]—of political-liberal thought in order to explain the possible (eventual, if not immediate) liberal legitimacy of a globe-spanning political formation whose various constituencies are right now even more sure to be hyperpluralistically divided than are the populations today living in the countries of the historically constitutional-democratic West.

4. Six Pre-constitutional Commitments of Political Liberalism

Any such renewal, it appears, would have to pivot on a refurbished account of the essential content of a higher-law constitution for the political formation in question. That is because any tinkering with received political-liberal wisdom to meet the threat from hyperpluralism will still have to retain the general ideas of legitimation-by-constitution and dualist democracy contained in the Rawlsian liberal principle legitimacy. A reworking of political-liberal ideas to meet the threat will still have to base the possibility of the justification of the force of ground-level law on that of a constitutional framework that is, as framework, acceptable to all affected constituencies. (If it did not, it would have lapsed from *political*-liberal to *comprehensive*-liberal political wisdom.) As a way of nailing down this point, it will behove us now to review summarily a series of commitments within liberal political philosophy—understood as

[11] Ibid. 9–10.

[12] Alessandro Ferrara, *The Democratic Horizon: Hyperpluralism and the Renewal of Political Liberalism* (CUP 2014) 6, 14 (hereafter Ferrara, *Democratic Horizon*).

Rawls, Ferrara, and I all would understand it—leading into the political-liberal idea of legitimation-by-constitution.

As a first and basal commitment: there is a non-reducible, irrecusable *something* that the liberal-utopian 'we' understands by the idea of treating persons politically as free and equal. That something falls in the general neighbourhood of an equality of respect for each individual person as (*per* Rawls) a 'self-authenticating source of valid claims',[13] at least partly in view of an attribution to each of certain powers of moral-cum-rational agency and a higher-order interest in the development and exercise of these powers over a complete life.

As a second commitment: for any political formation empowered to issue coercive regulatory legislation, *we* (meaning herein always still that same bunch from the constitutional-democratic tradition) are bound to raise the question of its legitimacy—that is, of the ground of justification for that government's coercion of moral and other dissenters, among a population of subjects free and equal, in conditions of a reasonable pluralism of moral, religious, and metaphysical orientations and outlooks.

As a third commitment: we are bound, in such conditions (if we would avoid oppression of fellow free and equal political cooperators), to seek a ground of justification that is, in Ferrara's phrase, 'political' not 'perfectionist'.[14] And let us, then, also here anticipate Ferrara's definition of 'perfectionist' to take in any and every 'teleological' conception, meaning (along with Rawls)[15] any conception that 'understand[s] justice and legitimacy ... as the maximal possible realization of' some value the conception posits as supreme, whatever might be that value.[16]

As a fourth commitment: the only form now clearly known to *us* of a non-perfectionist basis for the justification of a state's coercive political power is procedural and contractualistic. It has at its crux the idea of the justification of the force of ordinary laws by a convergence on the essential content of a 'higher' law—a 'constitution' (written or unwritten) to direct and constrain the actions of the state, to which *constitution* (at least) everyone affected can rationally, reasonably, and freely give assent as a basis for the institution among them of coercive political rule.

As a fifth commitment: for *us*, only a *democratic* constitution can hope to meet the standard of universal reasonable acceptability among citizens free and equal. By a democratic constitution we mean, above all other meanings, a

[13] Rawls, *PL* 32.
[14] See below, Chapter 10, pp. 140–141.
[15] See Rawls, *Theory of Justice* (n. 1) 22.
[16] Chapter 10, note 294.

constitution through which the members of the populace who will be subject to the ordinary laws of the political formation in question—the laws to which they will hold themselves and others justified in pressing for compliance—can count themselves collectively responsible for those laws. As Rawls writes, in a passage I deem of importance: 'Political power is always coercive power applied by the state,' but in a democratic regime that power 'is at the same time the power of free and equal citizens as a collective body. Thus political power is citizens' power, which they impose upon themselves and one another as free and equal.'[17] And the idea of legitimation-by-constitution, then, responds to the question of how such impositions can be justified among free and equal citizens in visionary-pluralist conditions.

As a sixth commitment: where direct deliberative democracy is impracticable, democracy can only be 'dualist' or 'constitutional'. Your and my links of responsibility for the ordinary laws are then given by our concurrences (actual or reasonably ascribable) on a constitutional pact that constrains and directs the aims and outcomes of subordinate legislation, not in detail but still substantially enough so as (along with whatever further participation by us in daily politics our constitution may provide) to render us thereby sufficiently responsible for that legislation.[18]

That completes my summary review of postulates and lemmas of the political-liberal philosophy, leading into its idea of legitimation-by-constitution. As an upshot from these postulates and lemmas: for any coercively empowered political authority, a detectable presence of a higher-law constitution, written or unwritten, freely approved or approvable by every constituent member or subject of that authority, would seem to be doubly required: once and primarily by commitment *fourth* on the fallback to procedural justification (so as to keep clear of perfectionist oppression), and then once more, secondarily, by commitments *fifth* and *sixth* on democracy in modern conditions. Absent the mediating effect of a higher-law constitutional-procedural pact on which a free consensus might still be available, political liberals would be left hanging onto the hope—or rather, the fantasy—of a day-to-day democratic politics whose every concrete legislative choice of policy or method will evade objection from some or other socially enfranchised comprehensive view on grounds sincerely experienced from within that view as morally, metaphysically, or religiously fundamental.

[17] John Rawls, *Justice as Fairness: A Restatement*, ed. Erin Kelly (Harvard U. Press 2001) 40–41.
[18] See Chapter 5, pp. 86–87.

5. Expectations and Assumptions in the Liberal Principle of Legitimacy

The possibility we have now to consider is that the fallback to procedural justification, itself unavoidable for political liberals (commitment *fourth*), might not necessarily commit us to the LPL cast in the exact terms laid down by John Rawls in *PL*. We now recall that statement:

> Our exercise of coercive political power is proper and hence justifiable only when it is exercised in accordance with a constitution the essentials of which all citizens [as free and equal] may reasonably be expected to endorse in the light of principles and ideals acceptable to them as reasonable and rational.

The question before us is how (if at all) those stated terms of the LPL might possibly be reworked in ways that (i) would render the principle amenable to the hyperpluralist condition in which not all the constituencies with whom we would share a single regime of political rule are able freely to endorse *our* bedrock ideas of 'equality among all citizens, gender equality, the idea of the citizen as a self-authenticating course of claims, freedom of conscience',[19] while the same reworking (ii) still would leave the principle able to do its work of warranting the legitimacy *for us* of regimes that meet its terms. (*We* are still here, after all, no less rightfully demanding of consideration for *our* principles and ideals than any other party to the problem.)

Now, one can detect three different indices or thresholds of expectation in the LPL as propounded by Rawls, allowing us to recast our question slightly to ask which (if any) of these might possibly be subject to adjustment, so that the principle as thus adjusted could meet both our conditions (i) and (ii). We can name these as the indices of *motivation for acceptance* of a constitution, of *the spread of acceptance* across the population, and of *the powers of the regime* for which constitutional guarantees are to bear the weight of justification. *Motivation for acceptance* ['endorse in the light of principles and ideals']: must the motivation be always and only the citizen's discernment of the constitution's instantiation of 'principles and ideals' embraced by her? And then how morally lofty or universal-regarding, how far cleansed of grubby or self-serving instrumental concerns, must be the citizen's reasons in order to count here as the requisite principles and ideals? *Spread of acceptance* ['all citizens']: even if acceptance strictly in the light of principles and ideals is to be expected on the

[19] Ferrara, *Democratic Horizon* (n. 12) 91.

part of some or even most citizens, must that expectation really extend to *all* citizens? What if some non-trivial fraction decide relatively freely (as these things go in real life) to join in the established civic order, not on ideal-moral grounds but out of some combination of a spirit of accommodation, an instinct to temporize, and maybe also some grosser calculus of expediency? Must that fact undermine the moral licence of the rest to call upon all for compliance with the regime's duly enacted laws? *Powers of the regime* ['coercive political power']: are there degrees of coerciveness, or other relevant differentia, among the kinds of powers a political regime might be authorized to exercise? Is there some threshold of regime empowerment below which *we* could reasonably and rationally relent on *our* bedrock demand for constitutionalization of the Rawlsian-liberal basic liberties?

By way of illustration of possibilities for adjustment of these expectational thresholds in Rawls's constitution-centred principle of legitimacy, we now take up for initial, brief examination (chapters to follow this one will take the examinations further) two proposals for relaxation now currently in circulation. One of these comes from Alessandro Ferrara, the other from John Rawls. What both proposals share is a retained commitment to an acceptance *sufficiently* motivated, across constituencies *sufficiently* widespread, of a constitution *sufficiently* thick with assurances (considering the powers of the regime) to sustain the justificatory burden. The political-liberal attachment to legitimation-by-constitution, and hence to a dual system of law, thus remains, in both proposals, ostensibly in place.

6. A Constitution for a Multivariate Polity?

In his book *The Democratic Horizon* (2014), Alessandro Ferrara addressed the quandary posed by claims to full legitimacy (in the Rawlsian sense of that term) for constitutional-democratic regimes whose constituencies now include—and apparently will do so on into an indefinite future—substantial population fractions whose willing support for a liberal constitution must finally rest on purely instrumental, prudential, or accommodationist motivations.[20] Whereas Rawls reserves full and final justification for state regimes to those just then approvable 'for the right reasons'[21] by all citizens subject to the force of their

[20] See ibid. 17.

[21] Rawls wrote of 'stability for the right reasons', but it was also his view that the stability of a regime would be a necessary condition for its reasonable and rational approvability. See Rawls, *PL* 141–143.

laws (thus, as participants in a simultaneous, overlapping moral-procedural consensus), Ferrara asks us to contemplate also a full justificatory koshering for state regimes whose permanent condition would be such that, for some citizens, they could qualify only as modi vivendi given the options realistically on offer.[22]

The higher-law constitutional pact for such a state would be one designed for what Ferrara called a 'multivariate polity'. Such a pact is one for social unification, but without even the thinned-out unanimity on a relatively few 'ideals and principles' envisaged by Rawls's principle of legitimacy. This complex unity (such as it would be) would take in not only wholehearted endorsers of the society's scripted (liberal) constitutional essentials—and so of the system of political rule those essentials constitute—but also an extended circle of resigned but still reflectively willing prudential cooperators with that system. A harder case would be that of people who find themselves blocked from even such qualified endorsement by their principled attachments to non-liberal, even anti-liberal ways. Still, the multivariate national polity could make allowance even for them by allowing for a 'degree[] ... of legal pluralism' within the state—subject, however, to some proviso that the norms to be extracted by these semi-autonomous groups from their dedicated forms of life and culture would not conflict outright with liberal constitutional essentials deemed 'central'.[23]

Among our three indices of expectation in the Rawlsian LPL, this proposal works by relaxing those of motivation to accept and spread of acceptance. An aptly drawn multivariate constitution, Ferrara has suggested, might attract a *sufficiently* free acceptance from a *sufficiently* large population fraction, plus a *sufficiently* reconciled accommodationist or strategic acceptance from enough of the rest, to satisfy a principle of legitimacy that must be taken as liberally reasonable, *given* the fact of inhospitable conditions unlikely ever to abate.

As Ferrara is well aware, the thought is one that invites resistance from opposing directions. From one side comes protest that the multivariate constitution gives away the liberal cause entirely. Seyla Benhabib, for example, complains against the multivariate proposal that the whole idea risks 'throwing

[22] Such is my understanding of Ferrara's rejection of any 'assumption that the liberal-democratic polity must move homogeneously and all of a piece through a preordained sequence of stages: from the fact of ... conflict to modus vivendi to constitutional consensus and finally to overlapping consensus', thus to accommodate the moral acceptability of polities 'where most citizens share an overlapping consensus on the basic structure and constitutional essentials, but then jointly relate in a modus vivendi way with minorities whose comprehensive conceptions overlap to a lesser extent with the reasonable ones and endorse only a subset of the constitutional essentials'. Ferrara, *Democratic Horizon* (n. 12) 16–17.

[23] Ibid. 107–108.

out the baby with the bath water'. Not all constitutional essentials, she writes, 'can be open to revision and questioning at all times without distorting the essentials of liberal democracies beyond recognition'.[24]

From an opposite direction, though, Ferrara's multivariate constitution may be said still to gravitate around the constitutional-democratic heritage. It still, in its way, does marginalize politically those within *our* countries for whom that heritage is foreign. Ferrara does not really suggest otherwise, but only that the multivariate constitution, still thus liberally tethered, is 'the best response to the tenuousness of consensus and the ubiquity of dissent that political liberalism can offer'.[25] But if—as appears to be true—the arrangement then cannot be deemed fully oppression-free, the question must remain as to whether political liberalism's best possible response is adequate to the salvation of that philosophy in hyperpluralist conditions.

7. Constitution for a Law of Peoples?

We turn now from Ferrara back to Rawls.

'A *liberal* principle of legitimacy', we have said, 'is necessarily … one ensconced within a detectably *liberal* political outlook.'[26] That still leaves open, though, a question about the political-relational contexts in which a liberal political philosophy must tie the possibility of the justified exercise of political authority to an assumption of liberal reasonability on the part of all participants. John Rawls drew a sharp line, in that regard, between the context of justification of the force of law within a going constitutional democracy (call this 'context CD'), and that of the qualification of a state or its corresponding 'people' for inclusion in an international system whose members commit to mutual protection, while also exercising mutual restraint, in support of each others' several secure existences as self-directing political associations ('context IS'). In *Political Liberalism* (1993), writing in context CD, Rawls reserved the liberal seal of full and final approval for those, and only those, state regimes to which all a society's members—*as* self-consciously free and equal persons, reciprocally recognized as such—could freely give their endorsement as

[24] Seyla Benhabib, 'The Multivariate Polity or Democratic Fragmentation: On Alessandro Ferrara's *The Democratic Horizon: Hyperpluralism and the Renewal of Political Liberalism*' (2016) 42 Philosophy & Social Criticism 649, 653.
[25] Ferrara, *Democratic Horizon* (n. 12) 108.
[26] This chapter, Sec. 3.

morally acceptable. In *The Law of Peoples* (1999) ('*TLOP*'), Rawls, writing now in regard to context IS, set a more generous outer bound of toleration, so as to take into an international system some decidedly non-liberal (but still what a liberal political philosophy could qualify as 'decent') national societies, whose political regimes would not meet the *PL* requirement for full and final moral justification.

Thinking still from a liberal point of view (applying, as it were, the political-liberal principle of toleration 'to itself'), Rawls proposed, as suitable for schemes of political cooperation encompassing both liberal and non-liberal societies, a set of eight principles by which to constitute, as he said, 'the basic charter' for a 'Law of Peoples'.[27] In the Rawlsian oeuvre, these eight principles from *TLOP* hold a position corresponding to that filled in *Theory of Justice* by the two principles of justice as fairness. Just as those two compose a set of deep-lying principles of right for any primary governmental formation in a state-scale territory, so do these eight compose the same for a globe-spanning political 'society of peoples'. (We skip over for the moment, but take up soon below, what Rawls had in view by speaking of this political society as one of 'peoples' rather than (say) 'nations' or 'states'). Assuming that the political-liberal reliance on legitimation-by-constitution is still 'on' for the international political formation in question, it must, then, be these eight 'principles of the law of peoples' that are to define the essentials for any legitimation-bearing constitution for that formation.

Rawls's eight principles of the law of peoples are as follows:

1. Peoples are free and independent, and their freedom and independence are to be respected by other peoples.
2. Peoples are to observe treaties and undertakings.
3. Peoples are equal and are parties to the agreements that bind them.
4. Peoples are to observe a duty of non-intervention.
5. Peoples have the right of self-defence but no right to instigate war for reasons other than self-defence.
6. Peoples are to honour human rights.
7. Peoples are to observe certain specified restrictions in the conduct of war.
8. Peoples have a duty to assist other peoples living under unfavourable conditions that prevent their having a just or decent political and social regime.

[27] Rawls, *Law of Peoples* (n. 2) 37.

It thus appears (from principle 6) that any legitimation-bearing constitution for a society of peoples would essentially contain a guarantee of due regard for human rights—seemingly corresponding, then, to the place of guarantees respecting the basic liberties in the constitutional essentials for a nation-state.[28] But then it further turns out that Rawls's sketches of what he has in mind as society-guaranteed human rights are all qualified so as quite decidedly *not* to cover, in all their aspects and applications, the bedrock liberal commitments to freedoms of conscience and expression and to civic equality. Human rights in the law of peoples, Rawls stipulates expressly, are not the same rights that citizens must have in any 'reasonable constitutional democratic regime', but rather comprise a 'proper subset' of those, a special class of 'urgent rights'.[29] Thus, in the law of peoples, a human right to equality equates to 'formal equality as expressed by the rules of natural justice (that is, that similar cases be treated similarly)'; a human right to life means 'to the means of subsistence and security'; a human right to liberty means to 'freedom from slavery, serfdom, and forced occupation, and to a sufficient measure of liberty of conscience to ensure freedom of religion and thought',[30] but 'equal' liberty of conscience need not be granted; for example, some religions, 'though tolerated, may be denied the right to hold certain positions'.[31]

The appearance here of an elision of the core idea of the liberal constitutional essentials is not an accident of loose exposition; it is deliberate, crucial to Rawls's purpose in this work. It is a direct reflection of Rawls's aim to extend the tent of the protections and obligations of the covenants of the society of peoples to take in certain constituencies beyond the outer bound of what can count as liberal societies. Human rights in the law of peoples are accordingly to be defined and trimmed so as not to be 'politically parochial', 'peculiarly liberal', or 'special to the Western tradition'.[32] The law of peoples cannot say, directly or by inference, that 'human beings are moral persons and have equal worth in the eyes of God'; or that 'they have certain moral and intellectual powers that entitle them to ... rights'. To posit thus would be to bring in 'religious or philosophical doctrines that many decent hierarchical peoples might reject as liberal or democratic, or as ... prejudicial to [non-Western] cultures'.[33]

[28] See Rawls, *PL* 227–230.
[29] Rawls, *Law of Peoples* (n. 2) 79, 81.
[30] Ibid. 65.
[31] Ibid. 65 n. 2, 70.
[32] Ibid. 65.
[33] Ibid. 68.

We need not just now delve deep into Rawls's conception of decency for a political society. What matters crucially for our purpose is that 'decent' falls short of *liberal* in ways that *we* are bound to regard as touching on constitutionally essential matters of fundamental justice. Because then the question is: where does that leave liberal *us* for whom constitutional non-attention to such matters must give rise to non-negotiable objection? (See the liberal principle of legitimacy and note the words 'only when'.) And the answer I would give is: just about where we were before.

That is because Rawls's society of peoples is operative only on the field of political concerns that we customarily speak of as 'international relations' or, as Rawls says, the field of concerns about the conduct of their respective 'foreign policies' by states corresponding to potentially constituent peoples; thus, the law of peoples is 'law governing the basic structure of the [political] relations between peoples'.[34] This law deals with such matters as the adjective law of treaties, territorial boundaries, just war and rights of self-defence, duties of assistance of some peoples by others, the international law governing migration flows and controls, and—of obvious salience for our purposes—the grounds and limits of justified collective intervention by the society or by some member peoples into a member people's internal affairs. None of this poses a threat to fulfilment of the commitments of fully liberal peoples to respect and regard for individual persons as each one a free and equal, self-authenticating source of claims and to the rights entailed by that commitment. (How could it possibly? Could a given constituent people's most zealous performance of that commitment ever conceivably give rise to a violation of principle 6 of the law of peoples?)

Why, then, it may be asked, does the law of peoples even include principle 6 at all? It does so precisely by way of defining the sole ground for a warranted collective intervention into a constituent people's internal affairs, by the society of peoples or a willing coalition of its members. Given that sole and specific function for principle 6, a restriction of it so as *not* to cover the full scope of liberal-individualist basic liberty, in all its aspects and applications, may well figure for political liberals as a virtue, not a vice in the overall conception. Indeed it *must* so figure, insofar as we agree with Rawls that '[some peoples] sincerely affirming a non-liberal idea of justice may still reasonably think their [societies] should be treated equally in a reasonably just law of peoples'.[35] If so, then so also conversely: we *as political-liberal* must accept that it would be unreasonable on

[34] See ibid. 10, 33, 57.
[35] Thus closely paraphrasing ibid. 70.

our part to expect from these decent-not-liberal peoples a free acceptance of a higher-law constitution, for a political society in which they share full membership with us, into which is inscribed an idea of individual human persons as each a free and equal self-authenticating source of valid claims.

Rawls's proposal for a law of peoples—and specifically the context-dependent curtailment it would administer to liberal ideas of human rights—may now be seen to instantiate the possibility of adjustment of the third index of expectation we have spotted in the Rawlsian LPL, that of the powers of the regime.[36] So long as the impact of the exercise of the sum of those powers upon any notionally free and equal person inhabiting any committedly liberal society or regime falls below the threshold of 'coercive', the Rawlsian LPL has no application to that case. Rather to the contrary, Rawls holds that it is, in such cases, unreasonable for us as *political* liberals to demand acceptance of *our* core idea of liberal individualism by non-liberal but decent peoples comprising our associates in the society of peoples. What makes that unreasonable for *us* is not an abstract absolute principle of toleration, but rather *our* principle of toleration, reasonably applied in view of the relatively light touch of the powers of the regime in question upon the basic liberties of any citizen anywhere.

That is how I understand Rawls's argument in *TLOP*. No doubt the argument is highly contentious among liberals of various stripes; but let us accept it. It still leaves unresolved the problem of the possibility of legitimation-by-constitution of any supra-national governmental authority exercising powers that would fall coercively upon liberal-minded inhabitants of liberal-minded societies. In cases of that kind—which might compose the bulk of the cases chiefly of interest to our generation of researchers into global political institutions—it still seems that liberal constituent peoples cannot reasonably accept anything short of the full liberal bedrock guarantee as an essential part of the constitution for the global authority, while decidedly illiberal peoples must take a directly contradictory stand.

8. 'Peoples', not 'Citizens'

But now why 'peoples', in that last preceding sentence? Why has the spotlight of concern shifted away from individual 'citizens', as in *PL*, to collective 'peoples'? Full treatment of this question lies beyond the scope of my discussion here. I can, though, offer the suggestion to read the choice of Rawls to speak in these

[36] See this chapter, Sec. 5.

contexts of 'peoples' as a way of affirming a point Rawls would derive from *our* own ideal of public reasonability—to wit, that *our* deductions of the necessity of a democratic rulership regime (commitments *fifth* and *sixth*) might have to be forgone in the face of a sufficiently strong case for the reasonable necessity of political cooperation across a range of political-cultural communions not limited to congregants of liberal political cultures but extending some distance beyond them. The spotlight on *peoples* faces us squarely with the thought that not all of the human company with whom we have sufficient moral reason to relate politically share an attachment to democracy as we understand it. But then it carries too, as I read it, a further, deeper, and for *us* more problematic implication. Rawls thus reminds us that what *also* does not hold sway, in all those parts of humanity with which we nonetheless might have prevailing reason to seek political-institutional alliance, is a conception of humanity in the end composed of biologically individuated persons each one of whom stands as its own self-authorizing source of valid claims. From which it seemingly must follow that not all the rights and interests that are unshakably fundamental for us, in *our* attachment to that conception, are going to pass muster as essentially includible in the terms of a legitimation-bearing constitution for any such trans-liberal political-institutional formation.

10

Can Legitimation by Constitution Apply Beyond the State?

Alessandro Ferrara

In Chapter 9, Frank Michelman has ingeniously addressed the difficulties incurred by the political-liberal paradigm when its central insights—reasonability, legitimation-by-constitution, public reason, anti-perfectionist normativity—are projected onto the possibility of a 'just and stable' polity beyond the bounds of a nation-state.

1. On Preserving the Basic Political-Liberal Commitments at the Global Level

Before responding to the points outlined by Michelman, let me briefly recall the six political-liberal commitments, understood by both of us as the normative guidelines that supposedly undergird and orient 'legitimation by constitution' in general, whether considered within or beyond the bounds of a nation-state. First, political liberals are committed to the irrecusability of equal respect for each person qua 'self-authenticating source of valid claims'. Second, whenever and wherever political power is exercised by an institution, backed up by the coercive force of law, an account of the justifiability of such exercise is owed to all those subjected to it. Third, such accounts are to be 'political', cast in terms of values and ends appreciable by all (or at least the vast majority) of those subjected to the actions in question. Fourth, political justification accordingly will take the form of showing the questioned action's compatibility with a constitutional script (written or unwritten), the essentials of which could draw the free assent of all (or a vast majority) of those affected. Fifth, the only arrangements that for the citizens of liberal-democratic countries can meet the above requirements are those comprised within the span of a 'democratic' constitution, 'by which the members of the populace who will be subject to the

Legitimation by Constitution. Alessandro Ferrara and Frank I. Michelman, Oxford University Press. © Alessandro Ferrara and Frank I. Michelman 2021. DOI: 10.1093/oso/9780192855121.003.0011

ordinary laws of the state ... can count themselves collectively responsible for those laws'.[1] Finally, a sixth commitment, once again prima facie binding only for liberal-democratic constituencies, stipulates that 'where direct deliberative democracy'—supposing that to be *our* first choice where practicable—is not practicable, the next best alternative is a democratic dualist or constitutional arrangement of the kind mentioned in our fourth commitment.

Michelman's elegant and concise rendition of these premises for legitimation-by-constitution prompts two comments. On the one hand, concerning the *sixth* commitment, one might want to consider the democratic-dualist arrangement as something more than a second best for the cases when direct deliberative democracy proves impracticable. Legitimation-by-constitution can arguably be understood as a response to a nexus of inhospitable conditions, highlighted very poignantly by Michelman in his 1997 essay and to which I added some items.[2] In my opinion, these conditions are so deeply ingrained in our contemporary context that direct deliberative democracy practically never works in its non-dualistic version. For these reasons, dualist democracy perhaps should be seen as the one view of democracy most responsive to the present predicament, but the preferability of either direct deliberative democracy or dualist versions of it lies beyond the scope of our present debate.

On the other hand, when considering ways to transpose the Rawlsian model of legitimation-by-constitution beyond the domestic polity—including Rawls's own proposal in *The Law of Peoples*—it might seem at first glance that only the first four of Michelman's commitments are binding for all the parties to a non-perfectionist scheme for global governance; and that, in order for commitments five and six to be deemed applicable, we would have to presuppose the existence of a fully-fledged global democracy nowhere in sight at the moment. In the rest of this chapter, I hope to show why this is not the case and no curtailment of our commitments is necessary in order to extend Rawls's paradigm.

A possible way of rescuing the full slate of the six commitments on a transnational scale has been described by Michelman as the attempt, on the part of Rawls, 'to extend the tent',[3] i.e. to enlarge the number of the political regimes admitted as parties to a global polity chartered by a (written or unwritten) constitution. In this chapter, I would like to build on Michelman's concise

[1] Chapter 9, pp. 127–128.

[2] See Frank Michelman, 'How Can the People Ever Make the Laws? A Critique of Deliberative Democracy', in James Bohman and William Rehg (eds), *Deliberative Democracy* (MIT Press 1997) 154, and Alessandro Ferrara, *The Democratic Horizon: Hyperpluralism and the Renewal of Political Liberalism* (CUP 2014) 8–12.

[3] Chapter 9, p. 134.

rendition of Rawls's scheme for a supra-national polity composed of 'peoples', and explore further the difficulties that besiege any attempt to transpose those six commitments, and specifically the idea of legitimation-by-constitution, at that level.

2. The Debate Concerning Supranational Governance: Perfectionism Redux?

One important preliminary consideration is that Rawls's scheme for transposing political liberalism and public reason beyond the original domestic level constitutes a quasi-unique exception in the intense debate that materialized in the wake of 1989 and the subsequent rise of a multi-polar world fraught with resurging nationalisms and explosive religious divides. That new climate stimulated an upsurge of reflection, in all the disciplines concerned with politics and law, on a question left up for utopian speculation during the past two millennia: *what is a just world*? That promising vista, however, has been clouded by the shadow of a return of traditional perfectionist arguments and deductive models, which derive the legitimacy of institutions from comprehensive, putatively well-grounded conceptions of human dignity, reason, objective values, transcendentally derived principles.[4] Let us here briefly note a recent tide of arguments that draw their normative force from some antecedently posited, or transcendentally derived, normative notion. Take, for example, the idea that human rights, as upshots from reasoning premised on basic needs and interests shared by all human beings, are antecedently prescriptive for any and all legitimate lawmaking, at the national or supranational level. That idea is not found only in the controversial, natural-law type perfectionism of Dworkin and Griffin.[5] It takes in also the sort of 'institutional understanding' propounded by Pogge, who conceives human rights as moral demands so exceptionally weighty that they 'normally [should] trump or outweigh other moral

[4] The term 'perfectionism' is used here as a synonym for the *comprehensive* quality of a conception of justice and of its attendant notion of legitimacy. In that sense, its meaning is broader than the one associated by Rawls with perfectionism as a specific moral view in John Rawls, *A Theory of Justice* (Harvard U. Press 1971) 325–332. Rather, perfectionism encompasses *all* the teleological conceptions that, regardless of the value(s) they posit as supreme, understand justice and legitimacy (qua standard for assessing the merits of institutions) as the maximal possible realization of that supreme value (see ibid. 24–25). A 'perfectionist' view of justice and legitimacy is then understood generically as the opposite of a 'political-liberal' conception of justice and legitimacy, though it may take many specific forms. See also Jonathan Quong, *Liberalism Without Perfection* (OUP 2013) 26–30.

[5] See Ronald Dworkin, *Justice for Hedgehogs* (Harvard U. Press 2011) 332–344 and James Griffin, *On Human Rights* (OUP 2008) and the interesting collection by Roger Crisp (ed.), *Griffin on Human Rights* (OUP 2014).

and non-moral concerns and considerations' in debating, designing, and conducting our social institutions and personal lives.[6]

Political liberalism stands distinctly opposed to all such leanings towards rights-foundationalism—in this respect (if not in all others) having the company also of Jürgen Habermas. In critical remarks addressed to Rainer Forst, but applicable to Pogge's view of human rights as well, Habermas eloquently objects to importing '*morally justified* rights' into the framing of a constitution—because then (writes Habermas), 'the liberal priority of human rights would be translated into the paternalism of an assembly of morally pre-programmed founders who cannot proceed democratically because the system of rights and the democratic procedure ... would be a function of their antecedent moral wisdom that they bring to bear prior to any political considerations'.[7]

Other authors' perfectionist propensities revolve around democracy: Held and Archibugi implicitly take democracy, recast as 'cosmopolitan democracy', as the one and only valid scheme of legitimate rule, thereby failing to accommodate even that basic duality of liberal and decent peoples envisaged by Rawls as the cornerstone of an acceptable post-Westphalian international order. They do refrain from deducing schemes of global governance from comprehensive and contentious philosophical notions; yet, from the pages of Held's *Democracy and the Global Order* or Archibugi's *The Global Commonwealth of Citizens*, one receives the impression that progress towards a morally satisfactory, politically integrated state of the world presupposes an increase in the number of countries that adopt fully democratic governance and not simply abide by some fair terms of supranational cooperation.[8] By contrast, and unlike religious believers

[6] Thomas Pogge, *World Poverty and Human Rights Cosmopolitan Responsibilities and Reforms* (first published 2002) (Polity Press 2008) 54. In Simon Caney, *Justice Beyond Borders: A Global Political Theory* (OUP 2005), a similar way can be found of proceeding from 'universal moral values' to principles of justice that specify what human rights follow from these antecedent moral entitlements (25–96). Caney then moves on to spell out distributive entitlements required by justice on a global scale (102–140), and then finally to derive an argument in favour of a specific 'kind of world order' from these considerations (148–182). For an original attempt to avoid perfectionism and actually bypass both perfectionist and agreement-based conceptions of human rights, see Beitz's 'practical conception of human rights', aimed at reconstructing the implicit meaning of human rights within the practice of international political interaction as carried out by the relevant actors, in Charles R. Beitz, *The Idea of Human Rights* (OUP 2009) 102–121. Beitz's conception, however, falls short of articulating an understanding of the *normativity* of human rights (a point substantially conceded ibid. 115). For one of the most interesting 'political' approaches to human rights, and critique of the perfectionist approaches (based on the so-called 'Mirror View'), see Allen Buchanan, *The Heart of Human Rights* (OUP 2013) 50–84.

[7] Jürgen Habermas, 'Reply to my Critics', in James G. Finlayson and Fabian Freyenhagen (eds), *Habermas and Rawls: Disputing the Political* (Routledge 2011) 296.

[8] See e.g. David Held, *Democracy and the Global Order: From the Modern State to Cosmopolitan Governance* (Stanford U. Press 1995) 232–233 (hereafter Held, *Democracy and Global Order*) and Daniele Archibugi, *The Global Commonwealth of Citizens: Toward Cosmopolitan Democracy* (Princeton U. Press 2008) 86–87.

who lean towards equating a morally perfected world with every human being's converting to their own religion, political liberalism (applying, as Rawls says, liberal tolerance to itself) rejects the view that progress towards legitimate global governance is coextensive with other societies' coming to adopt our liberal-democratic patterns. Such a view would clash with the pluralistic stance that forms the core of liberalism and with the anti-perfectionism of 'political liberalism'. Bohman's creative rethinking of transnational democracy as a democracy of *dêmoi*, which never aims at merging them into a global *demos*, rests on the 'republican ideal of freedom as nondomination as constitutive of the powers of citizenship'[9] and on the perfectionist assumption that 'human rights require democracy in order to be exercised'.[10]

More examples could be cited. My point is that, when discussing the possible legitimacy of transnational orders, we should come armed with a political-liberal wariness of backsliding into perfectionist conceptions responding to values and premises antecedently posited and contentious, oppositely to the commitments that Michelman has reconstructed in Chapter 9.

3. Extending Political Liberalism Beyond the Nation-State: Three Difficulties

Attempts to understand the legitimacy of transnational forms of authority along the lines of political-liberal and anti-perfectionist 'legitimation-by-constitution' face questions concerning the extension of three key terms to contexts beyond the bounds of the liberal-democratic nation-state.

First comes the expression 'citizens', as it occurs in the idea that political power is exercised properly when wielded in accordance with a constitution the essentials of which all *citizens* may reasonably be expected to endorse in the light of principles and ideals acceptable to them as reasonable and rational. There are no 'citizens of the world' (nor would there be in a Rawlsian society of peoples) except in a metaphorical and moral, not a political or legal, sense. *Second*, though, comes the expression '*all* citizens'—denoting thus a severalty of individuals (Michelman's 'first and basal' liberal-democratic commitment')—whose reasonably expectable concurrence is to be required on the framework terms of exercise of political power. That demand won't resonate with most

[9] James Bohman, *Democracy Across Borders: From Dêmos to Dêmoi* (MIT Press 2007) 173.

[10] Ibid. 115. Creatively combining Meadian and Kantian themes, Bohman envisages a 'human political community' as 'the community to whom those who are denied their basic rights can appeal', ibid. 120.

national polities in the world, including those 'decent' yet non-liberal ones with whom we may wish to be parties to a scheme of supranational governance. On the latest account offered by Freedom House, the liberal-democratic countries are only 83 out of 195, while the 'decent' ones (assuming that Freedom House's 'partially free' countries coincide with Rawls' decent peoples) are an additional 63.[11] Thus, in a hypothetical extension of Rawls's principle of legitimacy beyond the bounds of the liberal-democratic nation-state, to impose our 'first and basal commitment' onto others who do not share it cannot but count as oppression, rather than as a legitimate instance of a democracy among peoples. *Third*, then, comes uncertainty about what exactly, in the case of a law of peoples, will take the place of the shared or overlapping principles and ideals by which reasonable citizens in constitutional-democratic societies supposedly can converge on an acceptable set of constitutional essentials.

Elsewhere, I have offered more extensive comments on how to address these three questions.[12] The first ('citizens') yields easily, in consonance with a tradition dating back at least to Kant's idea of a *foedus pacificum* and reaching through to Rawls's society of peoples, to a scaling up of the constituent parties, from the level of actors in civil society to that of the peoples containing them. In such a way, we can also stand by our *sixth* commitment, to dualist constitutional democracy. What changes, in the transition from the domestic to the global level, is the designation of the parties to the dualist constitutional arrangement, not their political relation of freedom and equality. With Rawls's eight principles for the society of peoples, as with the Charter of the United Nations, these constituent units are not individuals scattered across the included peoples, but rather are *peoples* 'acting through their governments'.[13] These various peoples, some democratic and some merely 'decent' (however demandingly or inclusively we define 'decency'), relate to one another in the same way as do the free and equal citizens paradigmatic for liberal-democratic constitutionalism. Thus, the relations of equal respect, toleration, freedom of expression, religious neutrality or *laicité* undergirding the central (now potentially global) institutions and the transnational laws, are fully retained. Only the nature of the parties—individuals in the case of domestic constitutional

[11] See Freedom House, *Report* 2020 accessed at <https://freedomhouse.org/report/freedom-world/2020/leaderless-struggle-democracy> on 15 May 2020.

[12] Alessandro Ferrara, '"Most Reasonable for Humanity": Legitimation Beyond the State' (2019) 1, 2 Jus Cogens 111.

[13] See John Rawls, *The Law of Peoples* (Harvard U. Press 1999) 23 (hereafter Rawls, *Law of Peoples*). Rawls's choice of 'peoples' as constituent units of his supra-national form of association is motivated by their superior receptiveness, compared with states, to 'moral motives', reasonableness and reciprocity (see ibid. 17, 28–29). The qualification 'acting through their governments' signals that a 'people' is intended in its capacity as *demos* rather than *ethnos*.

democracies, *demoi* or states in the global case—have changed. We are really envisaging a 'polity of polities'.

The second difficulty ('all citizens') compounds the first. Once the tent is enlarged to non-liberal decent peoples, it appears no less crucial, in the new global polity of polities, than it was for the domestic liberal polity, to understand how oppression is to be avoided. It becomes then apparent that the constitutional script, written or unwritten, that unifies a supra-national polity of polities will have to be susceptible (as per our third commitment) of being endorsed by *all*, not just a subset, of the concurring peoples. This convergence is to be obtained by way of thinning out the normative components of the constitutional script meant to become the touchstone of the legitimacy of the constituted supranational institutions and authorities. The human rights to be mandatorily honoured will only be those presently listed in articles 3 to 18 of the UDHR—no mention being made of equality among citizens, of freedom of expression and of association, of a right to democracy and participation, or of education.

As a way to honour a standard, for those peoples who share it, of the consent of all citizens qua individuals, while avoiding imposition of it upon those who do not, *The Law of Peoples* envisages that the society's constitutional core—the chartering principles for the society—would be endorsed in two distinct, and sequentially ordered, instantiations of the original position. On a first run, only peoples sharing a liberal-democratic culture would approve the principles, via the consent of their free and equal citizens. Then, in a second run, the rest of the decent peoples (so identified on the basis of their respect for a reduced list of human rights and a commitment of their political processes to a 'decent consultation hierarchy') would also approve of it, albeit not necessarily by procedures we would call democratic.[14] It is then not entirely correct to state that our commitment to a democratic and dualist format of the rule of law has been revised. To repeat, while the scale of the constituencies has changed, the terms of the relations among them have not. It is now polities in their entirety that relate to one another on a free and equal basis.

Concerning the third question, of what, in the constitution of the polity of polities, will take the place of the principles and ideals by which reasonable citizens in constitutional-democratic societies converge on an acceptable set of constitutional essentials, the path to an answer may lie through the sense to be assigned to the term 'constitution'. We have seen that human rights will be part of it. Also the other principles of the society of peoples (i.e. equal sovereignty, *pacta sunt servanda*, duty of non-intervention, right to self-defence, *jus in bello*,

[14] See ibid. 32–38. For the extension of the original position to 'decent peoples', see ibid. 68–70.

duty of assistance), may be shown to be acceptable for all the concurring peoples whether liberal-democratic or decent.

Other aspects of this world-constitution, however, could be more controversial at the moment. Rawls opts for a minimal list of 'human rights proper', because the remaining ones seem more culture-specific and dependent on institutional arrangements far from universal, but the list could be reconsidered over time; the duty of assistance (say) could be extended to cover a global redistributive scheme, as Pogge and Beitz have suggested. At all events, it makes sense to require that such a list be validated through consent (not just philosophical or juridical argument).[15] Third, new dimensions could be added to this tentative constitution. For example, Pettit has persuasively suggested that a republican emphasis on non-domination could be woven into Rawls's non-cosmopolitan scheme, in the form of an intimation—which could, in my opinion, pass the test of global public reason, perhaps even that of the dual original position—that states concurring in a *foedus-pacificum*-like association also share a threefold commitment to (i) resist domination of their citizens, (ii) abstain from dominating other states, and (iii) do what they can to prevent others from dominating third states.[16] Nothing prevents a more robust agreement on the constitutional core of a society of peoples to include also these considerations—if such views were to pass the test of global public reason.

4. The Status of the Eight Principles

What matters most, however, is the method. If we stick to the six commitments of political liberalism, we are barred from grounding the legitimacy of transnational orders in controversial philosophical notions not shared by all the signatories, i.e. states in representation of *demoi*. The *foedus pacificum* need not be underwritten by *all* the existing states, including the tyrannical ones and those which reject human rights *tout court* or other principles of peaceful coexistence. As in the Rawlsian scheme, one could envisage a transnational order that includes a majority of willing states (liberal and decent), and then understand

[15] The identification of the human rights which are 'human rights proper', and thus have priority over state sovereignty, is one of the weakest points in *The Law of Peoples*. Such selection bursts the 'political' credentials of the paradigm—in that human rights are said to be binding also for peoples who are not parties to the society of peoples and thus never subscribed to them. On the idea of a *Second Declaration of Fundamental Human Rights* as more responsive to the new historical function expected to be exerted by a declaration of human rights in the post-1989 world and as more in line with the paradigm of political liberalism, see Alessandro Ferrara, 'The Idea of a Charter of Fundamental Human Rights', in Claudio Corradetti (ed.), *Philosophical Dimensions of Human Rights* (Springer 2012) 173.

[16] See Philip Pettit, 'A Republican Law of Peoples' (2010) 9, 1 European Journal of Political Theory 70.

the whole world as a multivariate political entity that includes also other kinds of polities, with which the parties to the *foedus pacificum* relate along purely prudential lines. This view seems initially more inclusive than proposals to build a transnational structure of governance from the smaller number of the already democratic states:[17] the *foedus pacificum* then would include, from the start, the majority of the political units of the world—about 75 per cent of the existing states, according to Freedom House's report—which is in itself a remarkable result.

The methodological crux, not entirely explicit in *Law of Peoples*, is then the following. Domestically, the constitutional essentials are supposedly endorsed by the citizens for reasons of principle sourced in one of a liberal family of political conceptions of justice, across which can be found an overlapping consensus on a sufficient set of constitutional essentials. However, justice as fairness (taken as representative of the liberal family[18]) is unable to perform that function on a global scale—presupposing, as it does, a society of free and equal individual claimants to bottom-line concern and respect (controversial among decent peoples), and incorporating also a principle of distributive equality that would be widely controversial if applied among peoples on a global scale. Will, then, the eight principles of the society of peoples function as an equivalent of the two principles of justice in 'justice as fairness'?

Michelman decidedly embraces this view in Chapter 9: as he puts it, these principles 'hold a position corresponding to that filled in *A Theory of Justice* by the two principles of justice as fairness',[19] that of 'a set of deep-lying principles of right for any primary governmental formation', whether in a 'state-scale territory' or in a 'globe-spanning political "society of peoples" '.[20] Although the analogy thesis is certainly suggestive, and is considerably supported by Rawls's prefatory remark about 'proceeding in a way analogous to the procedure in *A Theory of Justice*'[21] (which seems to suggest that the two sets of principles play an analogous function), in the end I rather incline to considering the eight principles *not* as principles in a conception of transnational justice, but only as a core of constitutional essentials (as it were) for the society of peoples. Three reasons support this attribution of a weaker normative status to them.

[17] See Held, *Democracy and Global Order* (n. 8).

[18] In his 'Introduction to the Paperback Edition', Rawls explicitly acknowledges that whilst he continues to consider justice as fairness as the most reasonable view of justice 'for us', it is not to be denied that 'other conceptions also satisfy the definition of a liberal conception' and thus that within a contemporary pluralistic society there coexist not only several rival comprehensive conceptions of the good, but also 'different and incompatible liberal political conceptions', *PL*, xlvii.

[19] Chapter 9, p. 133.

[20] Ibid.

[21] Rawls, *Law of Peoples* (n. 13) 36.

First, differently than in *A Theory of Justice*, where the two principles of justice emerge victorious from an original-position confrontation with strong utilitarian and intuitionist competitors, no serious contenders challenge the eight principles in either of the two instantiations of the original position in *The Law of Peoples*. In the first instantiation, the eight principles simply are said to reflect certain 'familiar and traditional principles of justice among free and democratic peoples'.[22] In the second, Rawls expressly stipulates that 'the parties are not given a menu of alternative principles and ideals from which to select', but rather these 'familiar and largely traditional principles' are simply drawn 'from the history and usages of international law and practice'.[23] The two instantiations of the original position thus resemble more closely a sort of supranational constitutional convention, where representatives (who already roughly know what their constituencies desire) come to an agreement, than they resemble the original position as found in *A Theory of Justice*.

Second, the eight principles are open-ended, avowedly 'incomplete' and non-exhaustive,[24] in a way that the two principles of justice as fairness are not. For example, Rawls mentions the need to supplement the eight principles with further ones designed to address the 'forming and regulating' of federations of peoples or the 'standards of fairness for trade and other cooperative institutions',[25] including standards 'to keep the market free and competitive'.[26] It would indeed be counter-intuitive to have an incomplete political conception of justice as a basis for subsequently outlining the constitutional essentials of a polity. This is the single strongest reason why the eight principles, in spite of Rawls's remark, are best understood not as applications at a 'constitutional stage' of a prior-established conception of (transnational) justice, but simply as a set of terms validated by the consent of the contracting parties.

Third, the fact that the 'additional' principles, left by Rawls for subsequent elaboration, are in no way projected by him to occupy a normative rank subordinate to the original eight—as (say) applications thereof—seems to strengthen the idea that the original eight principles are themselves to be understood more as the core of a world-constitutional script for organizing the fair and equitable cooperation of the peoples included in the society of peoples, than as the core of an underlying shared conception of justice.

[22] Ibid. 37.
[23] Ibid. 41.
[24] Ibid. 37.
[25] Ibid. 38.
[26] Ibid. 43.

In sum: if the eight principles are to be *normatively* understood as constitutional essentials for a polity of polities, then some further normative grounding will be needed for them. They cannot be taken simply as the precipitate of the factual political will of the signatory states. So the question arises: how could they then be endorsed out of reasons of principle that make them different from a modus vivendi?[27] What would be the equivalent, at the global level, of the anticipation of a freestanding political conception of justice, capable of bestowing on the society's charter a higher normative status than the one stemming from political agreement as routinely observable in the coexistence and cooperation of different domestic constituencies?

5. Humanity's Flourishing, the Dual Concept of Humanity, and Global Public Reason

Let us go back to Rawls's texts with this methodological reflection in mind. In *The Law of Peoples*, the dual instantiation of the original position is the key justificatory device. The normative cogency of the outcome of this twofold procedure—the eight principles—should not be understood as resting on merely rational grounds, as though the fairness of just relations among the political units of the world were to derive solely from considerations of mutual advantage. The dimension of the reasonable ought to be figured in as well. Indeed, starting from 'Kantian Constructivism', and especially in *Political Liberalism*, the normative credentials of justice as fairness are said by Rawls to rest on the reasonable, actually on its being the conception of justice 'most reasonable for us'. That can stand as Rawls's single most groundbreaking formulation of a non-perfectionist view of the *domestic* political order: the exercise of coercive political power is legitimate insofar as it is in harmony with a constitution the essentials of which can be endorsed by citizens severally, as sufficiently in tune with a political conception of justice deemed by them 'most reasonable for us'.

When we address legitimacy at the transnational level, we need then to answer a question that remains unaddressed in *The Law of Peoples*. If the eight principles are to be understood as essentials for a world-constitution, and if the individualistic underpinnings of justice as fairness (and its liberal cousins)

[27] For an interesting public-reason approach to the legitimacy of authority and coercion 'in a world of states', see Gerald Gaus, *The Order of Public Reason: A Theory of Freedom and Morality in a Diverse and Bounded World* (CUP 2011) 470–479.

disqualify it from being the political conception of justice underlying such a world-constitution, which political conception of justice should these constitutional essentials be reflective of?

One obvious requirement for that conception is that it plausibly should qualify as 'most reasonable' not for a single national *demos* but for humanity as a whole. In *The Force of the Example*, I have identified the conception of justice most reasonable for humanity not with a scheme for intra-societal justice writ large—how could such a scheme ever work for such a heterogenous set of societies as found at the global level?—but with a 'concrete universal', namely the normative idea of the good or flourishing of *humanity*, understood as the set of all the human beings that have existed, are presently living, and will live in the human condition.

As required, the idea of humanity invoked here is a 'political' idea, distinct from comprehensive views of humanity that in the past have demanded allegiance on religious or secular grounds: humanity as created by God in his likeness, humanity as the collection of the possessors of reason, humanity as those who can use symbols, humanity as the set of beings whose instinctual deficit is made up by culture. We seek a view of humanity compatible with the diversity of cultures present on the planet—of humanity as the conceptual point where the concrete and the generalized other coincide. We suppose that the representatives of the various human societies, who consent to a certain scheme of cosmopolitan governance centred around the preservation of peace, the protection of human rights, the redressing of unjust distributive arrangements, the preservation of the viability of the planet for human life, are doing so for the benefit not just of the society they represent (if so, they would be devising a mere global modus vivendi based on mutual advantage) but with a view to creating the best achievable world for all human beings. We suppose that even the representatives of peoples that do not endorse the ideal of political equality still have a shared sense of some predicaments of the world being potentially better for humanity as a whole than the alternatives. In sum, the empirical consensus of the associating peoples is to be understood as harmonious with the flourishing of humanity, taken as the most inclusive imaginable human grouping.

The flourishing-of-humanity standpoint meets the requirement to be impartial with respect to the particularisms of single contending demotic identities, while also avoiding retreat to a level of vapid and useless abstraction. The good or flourishing of humanity is a *concrete universal* whose substantive content can vary over time. It is arguably not the same today as it was at a time when nuclear weapons were unknown, or when the total aggregate output of the production processes still posed a limited threat to the integrity of the natural environment, or when science knew no way to interfere with genetic processes, or when the devastating impact of global pandemics had not yet impacted our political awareness.

In partial correction of what I argued in *The Force of the Example*, I do not here equate humanity with the sum total of existing societies as they are, with all their injustices and vices. That remainder of facticity can be overcome by appeal to humanity in its entirety, which the expression 'most reasonable for humanity' tries to capture. According to this more expansive concept, we conceive humanity as the set of all human beings who have lived, are living, and will be living on the earth. Among them, presently living ones are the only human beings endowed with agency, yet this does not make them the sole arbiters of what constitutes the flourishing of humanity. In the light of this more expansive concept, the flourishing of humanity, consists, among other things, in bringing to fulfilment projects, aspirations, and values typical of past generations, and preserving the future generations' chances to live a life of quality not inferior to that of their predecessors. The human lives no longer and not yet with us have to be figured in that normative equation, just as, on a domestic scale, legitimacy requires that the will of the voters today take into account the constitutional will of the transgenerational people.[28]

Would, then, the adoption of a scheme for a world-constitutional regime based on the eight principles (plus possible additions to them) allow, contrary to first impressions, for retention of all of our political-liberal commitments? It seems that *we* political-liberals could accept such a scheme as reasonable and rational for us, while still harbouring a realistic-utopian hope of someday closing the gap between our own liberally more demanding constitutional essentials and these eight principles for the initiation of a global regime right now.

The good or flourishing of humanity could thus play a twofold role homologous to that of justice as fairness (and its family cousins) in the political-liberal just and stable society of free and equal citizens. That is (a) it can undergird the stated principles by which the legitimacy of institutions and authorities is assessed, while (b) keeping those principles from backsliding into the articles of a merely prudential modus vivendi.

But still the question may persist: should *we*, political-liberals of democratic countries, find it rational and reasonable to endorse a scheme of transnational governance premised on a set of principles falling significantly short—as far as principle 6 goes, concerning a subset of fundamental human rights—of the list

[28] On the domestic scale, the proper balancing of the will of an entire, transgenerational people and of its living segment (the voters) is at stake in debates over judicial review. See Chapter 8, pp. 106–133.

of rights-respecting essentials that we are prepared to endorse domestically? A positive answer will say that such a development is at any rate more congruent with our range of locally prevailing conceptions of the good (thus more rational for us), and with our sense of a fair scheme of cooperation among the liberal and decent polities of the world (thus more reasonable for us) than any alternatives, including: (a) a Westphalian lawless space of anarchic coexistence among Leviathans; or (b) a bi-imperial world order (the Cold War), with its intra-empire limited sovereignty; or (c) a possible pluri-imperial new global order, with a few superpowers and their client states competing for hegemony. It is also more rational for us to pursue the creation of such a multivariate global polity than to pursue *un*realistic-utopian projections of a democratic cosmopolis premised on the notion of each human individual counting as a free and equal member of a global scheme of government. Appealing though such projections may be for each of us as a committed constitutional democrat, they fail to keep the spirit of Rawlsian realistic utopianism.

6. Conclusion

In that spirit, then, let me complete the ideal-theoretic picture of a global rule of law—where liberal-democratic and decent peoples cooperate on the basis of principles that (a) can generate articles for the charter of a global polity, (b) allow a quasi-global public reason to be operative, and (c) respond to a political view of the flourishing of humanity—with a note on the non-ideal process that might lead to that outcome.

Institution-building rests on communicative infrastructure and the primitive accumulation of social capital among free and equal future participants. Such a process can realistically proceed on a regional level, in the footsteps of what the EU, for all its limitations, has achieved in a few decades. Regional unions of existing states may develop ties among them, assuage previous fractures and lines of tensions, as the EU has done with its own 'warring states', to use a Chinese expression. Regional unions can implement relations of equal respect among the member societies and stabilize practices of public reasoning. Finally, they can act as intermediate associations to moderate the unilateralism of competing great powers like Russia, China, and the United States, and of self-standing world powers like Japan, Australia, post-Brexit UK, and Canada.

To be sure, a world government is neither in sight nor even ideal-theoretically conceivable in our philosophical horizon. What our grandchildren might witness, however, could be a world where, along with the great, self-standing existing powers, which are unlikely to merge into any global organization significantly different from the current UN, regional associations such as the EU, ASEAN,[29] SAARC,[30] the African Union,[31] and USAN[32] succeed in bringing together most of the other existing states. A positive aspect of these regional aggregations is that democratic states exist in all of them, possibly inspiring movements towards democracy in the decent ones, by way of providing close-by, culturally contiguous, living exemplars of the operation of democratic principles. Coalitions of these regional associations may prove effective in taming the unilateralism of the great powers and in eroding the significance of their veto-power in the UNSC, and each of them may with good reasons claim a permanent seat in lieu of the presently rotating ones. Taken together, these regional associations may push the political unification of humanity one important step further, by reducing the 195 political units to a little more than a dozen actors and above all by testing the practice of transnational democracy in a variety of cultural contexts.

[29] The *Association of Southeast Asian Nations*, founded in 1967, includes Indonesia, Malaysia, Philippines, Singapore, Thailand, Brunei Darussalam, Vietnam, Laos, Myanmar, Cambodia.

[30] The *South Asian Association for Regional Cooperation*, founded in 1985, includes Afghanistan, Bangladesh, Bhutan, India, Maldives, Nepal, Pakistan, and Sri Lanka.

[31] The *African Union* was founded in Addis Abeba in 2001. It includes Algeria, Angola, Benin, Botswana, Burkina–Faso, Burundi, Cameroon, Cape Verde, Central African Republic, Chad, Comoros, Congo, RD Congo, Côte d'Ivoire, Djibouti, Egypt, Equatorial Guinea, Eritrea, Ethiopia, Gabon, Gambia, Ghana, Guinea Bissau, Guinea, Kenya, Lesotho, Liberia, Libya, Madagascar, Malawi, Mali, Mauritania, Mauritius, Mozambique, Namibia, Niger, Nigeria, Rwanda, Saharawi Arab Democratic Republic, São Tomé and Principe, Senegal, Seychelles, Sierra Leone, Somalia, South Africa, Sudan, Swaziland, Tanzania, Togo, Tunisia, Uganda, Zambia, Zimbabwe.

[32] The *Union of South American Nations*, founded in 2008, includes Argentina, Bolivia, Brazil, Chile, Colombia, Ecuador, Guyana, Paraguay, Peru, Surinam, Uruguay, Venezuela, and Mexico and Panama as observers.

11

A Political Conception of a People (and its Consequence)

Frank I. Michelman

In Chapter 9, noting the Rawlsian shift from 'citizens' to 'peoples' as the constituent members in the global political formation envisaged by Rawls as the society of peoples ('SOP'), I drew from this move an intended Rawlsian teaching: because (as I wrote) 'not all the human company with whom we have sufficient moral reason to relate politically share an attachment to democracy as we understand it,' political liberals would have to forgo any insistence on democracy as a condition of legitimacy for SOP. Alessandro Ferrara has now, in Chapter 10, neatly turned that inference of mine on its head. It is precisely, as Ferrara now shows, because and insofar as we *do* thus conceptually 'scale up' the constituent units of the SOP from individuals to peoples, that we can *still* ascribe to that formation an operationally democratic make-up at both the constitutive and workaday levels—at the former, as a requirement for unanimous acceptability of the constitution among the constituent peoples and, at the latter, as a requirement for an equality among them of political franchise, majority voting, and so on.

Does that mean, then, that the matter of the variant internal distributions of authority *within* the peoples, qua constituencies for the SOP, simply disappears from the field of political-moral concern, as we go about constructing a set of essentials for a constitution for the SOP? In a political-liberal construction of the SOP, it cannot mean that. The reason, in brief is this: a political-liberal conception of a globe-spanning political order of peoples requires for its construction a political conception of a people; a political conception of a people can only be found in that people's convergence on the set of constitutional essentials accepted by them as the most reasonable for their own political association, which is to fill also the place of a constituent member in the SOP; and the powers of the SOP, then, cannot be such as to clash with the internal

Legitimation by Constitution. Alessandro Ferrara and Frank I. Michelman, Oxford University Press. © Alessandro Ferrara and Frank I. Michelman 2021. DOI: 10.1093/oso/9780192855121.003.0012

constitutional guarantees of any constituent people (or state). Fuller explanation follows.

Just as political liberalism requires for its normative and institutional constructions at the nation-state level a 'political conception of the person' as political cooperator (say, as endowed with the two moral powers and a highest-order interest in their development and exercise), so does that philosophy require for its parallel construction of the SOP a political conception of a people. The reasons are the same in both cases: to fill in the minimum motivational assumptions required to make determinate the unanimous choice of principles in the original position or positions, and to set conditions for the 'common reason' against which a set of constitutional essentials, sufficiently thick to sustain the weight of legitimation for its correspondent political regime, can be tested for acceptability to all reasonable constituents. A *political* conception of a constituent—person or people as the case may be—thus means, in Rawlsian political constructivism, a *motivating* conception but still one that can count in its context as non-perfectionist.

Ferrara has suggested that a common reasonability for the SOP can derive from certain aims that humanity uniformly may be counted on to share: 'the preservation of peace', 'the viability of the planet for human life', and so on.[1] This persuasive attribution of motivational reasonability from the standpoint of humanity is meant by Ferrara as a way to anchor the eight constitutional principles of the SOP to an underlying moral consensus of the constituent peoples, not just to a modus vivendi convergence of transient political wills. The attribution serves, in that way, as a political conception of humanity. It does not, however, supply the political conception *of a people* that is also required by the political-constructivist project of political liberalism. Picking up where Ferrara leaves off, that attribution of a common human reason does not in itself suffice to motivate a *democratic* institutional order (among the peoples, as Ferrara explains) as a constitutional essential for the SOP. It does not explain, say, why, for the SOP, a constitutional commitment to rule by experts elected by the world's twenty leading universities would not work better towards achievement of the humanly shared aims.

What, then, does motivate the democratic modus operandi (between and among the constituent peoples) that Ferrara successfully restores as an eligible constitutional essential for the SOP? It can only be the idea—ultimately always a core idea in political liberalism—of a political formation as a scheme of cooperation among diversely motivated constituent agents whose own

[1] See Chapter 10, pp. 148–151.

self-authenticating projects risk running into mutually destructive conflict. Just as, in the case of the liberal nation-state, the constituent persons are accordingly politically conceived as endowed with the moral powers and corresponding interests, so, in the case of the SOP, the constituent peoples are to be politically conceived as distinctively motivated, self-authenticating agents. It is from that attribution that then will flow the demand for what will correspond in the SOP to the principle of the fair value of political liberty in justice as fairness, but now among peoples rather than persons as constituents. But then comes the question: if political self-authentication for citizens in the nation-state case consists in exercise of the moral powers, and if this same valorization of individual moral agency cannot be non-oppressively attributed across the entire constituency of the SOP, what, then, *can* be the political-not-perfectionist idea of self-authentication for peoples as constituent units in the SOP? In the answer to that question will lie the political conception of a people, required for a Rawlsian political construction of the essentials of a constitution for a society of peoples.

We can see the likely answer when we focus on the ambition of political liberalism (as represented by Rawls's proposition for the two original positions in *The Law of Peoples*) to work as a unified and consistent philosophy across the two cases of the nation-state regime and the SOP. A people's self-authentication in the SOP can then be seen to lie in its attachment to its own political constitution, written or unwritten, and to the societal common reason made manifest in that constitution. The political conception of a people, then, is that of a human society—that is, a congregation of a severalty of human instances—united, for purposes of cooperation at a basic-structural level, by *a constitution* expressive of *that society's* politically pertinent common human reason. As the case may be for one or another society by its own self-understanding, the human instances composing the severalty may figure as individuals—but possibly also as families, bloodlines, social or economic or divinely imposed ranks or classes, trade and business guilds or associations, assemblies of faith and religion, and add whatever you like to the list of possibilities. Whichever it is, the common reason manifest in that society's constitution will then vary accordingly.

I do not find John Rawls writing anything quite like that in *The Law of Peoples*. Pointing strongly in a like direction, though, is the very idea of identifying the 'decent' non-liberal peoples—the peoples with whom we from the constitutional-democratic tradition have prevailing reason to seek an institutionalized scheme of political cooperation—with those sustaining in their politics what Rawls calls a decent consultation hierarchy. A decent consultation hierarchy is after all, a *constitutional* arrangement, written or unwritten.[2] A 'people' is being politically conceived here as an executant, not of its moral powers, exactly, but of its constitution. A people's convergence on its constitution stands in place of a citizen's deployment of the moral powers, as the expression of that people's motivational individuality qua people.

If that is right, then the constitution of the SOP would not be in accord with a reason common across the society's constituent peoples, if it were to empower the SOP to act coercively on any individual (or firm or association) in any way that the individual's own country's constitution secures its own constituents against. (Political liberalism thus applies to itself, in a double sense, its own principle of toleration.) That deduction goes hand in hand, as I have argued in Chapter 9, with the initial limitation of the SOP's field of concern to the conduct of their respective foreign policies by the constituent peoples.[3] It is thus an aspect of what Ferrara, following Rawls, calls the incompleteness of the Rawlsian eight constitutional principles for the SOP. But the deduction goes further, by imposing strict guardrails on future additions to competencies aiming towards completion. Take, for example, a possible future body of SOP legislation setting rules and standards for trade. As applied to members of any one of Rawls's liberal peoples, those rules and standards would have to fit with the constitutional law of that people respecting rights of property and economic freedom reasonably deemed apt (in the words of Rawls) 'to allow a sufficient material basis for a sense of personal independence and self-respect [required] for the development and exercise of the moral powers'.[4]

Now, to say so is not to rule out prospects for future supplementation and expansion of the scope of the SOP, along lines suggested by Ferrara, from its initial restrictive setting by the eight principles. It is rather to set imaginations going on the paths such expansion might take. SOP trade regulations (to continue with this example) could not, at the outset, have the attribute of direct effect claimed by European officials and courts for European law. Rather, they would have as their direct addressees the respective state regimes of the

[2] A similar point is made by Ackerman. Based on his analysis of the Iranian revolution, he argues that a non-monocentric structure of legitimate authority is what distinguishes constitutionalism from despotism: 'Dictators also encounter resistance to their commands, but they refuse to recognize that such shows of opposition are legitimate. Constitutional regimes, in contrast, require the most powerful officials to engage in ongoing competition with institutional rivals for the final say over the future course of political development.' Bruce Ackerman, *Revolutionary Constitutions: Charismatic Leadership and the Rule of Law* (Harvard U. Press 2019) 360.

[3] See Chapter 9, pp. 134–135.

[4] Rawls, *PL* 298.

constituent peoples. The regulations could still aim to reach through to the conduct of ground-level social actors, through the medium of conforming legislation enacted by the nation-states. The expanding SOP constitution could even obligate the nation-states for such conforming legislation, *but only as long as* attended by a proviso that no state would be required to act in a manner inconsistent with that state's constitutional essentials.

Any SOP regulatory laws, in order to be made effective by nation-state legislation against ground-level actors in that state, would then have to make it through the sieve of that state's constitution. Supposing a wide latitude for differences among state constitutions that today can claim to satisfy the standard of broad acceptability to that state's citizens or subjects as reasonable for them, there are a multiplicity of such sieves standing in the way. We must accordingly anticipate the likelihood of SOP regulatory policies passing through some of these constitutional sieves while being blocked by others. From the respective standpoints of the several citizen bodies in the nation-states, what we would have going would be all and only bodies of laws rendered legitimate for them by compliance with their respective nation-state constitutions. For any constituent people whose politics measure up (say) to the Rawlsian LPL, their state will have in force a legitimation-bearing constitution acceptable to that state's citizens as rational and reasonable (for them), and the progress of SOP powers will not disturb that condition.

The result would be what Ronald Dworkin might have called a chequerboard empire under the SOP.[5] From the standpoint of a political-liberal-minded world citizen (assuming there yet could be any of those), that might look depressingly like a modus vivendi. From Ferrara's guardedly hopeful remarks on prospects for expansion from the SOP initial stage, though, I take a thought that we should not necessarily dismiss out of hand such an intermediate chequerboard empire as worse than nothing or unworthy of pursuit. We would not thereby be giving up on hopes for a progression, under combined pressures of pragmatic accommodation and mutual learning (much explored by recent European theorists of constitutional pluralism[6]), from that initial modus vivendi at least to a constitutional consensus—and beyond that (who knows?) maybe then all the way on to a full moral consensus among an emergent democratic citizenry of the world.

[5] Compare Ronald Dworkin, *Law's Empire* (Harvard U. Press 1986) 178–184 (on possible objections to 'checkerboard laws').

[6] See e.g. Klemen Jaklic, *Constitutional Pluralism in the EU* (OUP 2014).

12

From Decency to Democracy: Leading by Example

Alessandro Ferrara

In Chapter 11, Michelman has ingeniously addressed a further puzzle incurred by the political-liberal paradigm when directed to the possibility of a just and stable polity beyond the nation-state: how to fill the space, required for such an extension of that paradigm, of a 'political conception of a people'. He ends with a prospect for a 'chequerboard' model for a present-day society of peoples—one whose regulatory laws could not be self-executing (as they could be in my proposed model for a multivariate transnational regime), but would 'have to make it through the sieve' of the member-states constitutions in order to have traction on the lives of the citizens of the local states.

Comparing these two prospects for a transnational, general political order—the multivariate and the chequerboard—we can see that common ground largely prevails and differences are a matter of emphasis. Behind my thought of the multivariate model lies the prospect, as I see it, for a liberalizing world order emerging non-oppressively out of an already existent array of regional associations. Over a span of few generations, I have suggested, these could attain a level of integration that even the EU has not yet reached. None of them—the EU, ASEAN (*Association of Southeast Asian Nations*), SAARC ('*South Asian Association for Regional Cooperation*), the African Union, and USAN (*Union of South American Nations*)—will be able to secure the participation of any of the great global powers (USA, China, Russia), or even of the medium, nation-state size powers (e.g. Japan, Australia, post-Brexit UK, Canada). But then these associations could significantly shape the global political environment within which the great and medium powers develop their strategies, constraining unilateralism at times of world-crises.

The point of this realistic-utopian prefiguration is that it maximizes the impact of the 'force of the example', so to speak. If we try to generalize from the model of the EU, other regional associations of states conceivably would

Legitimation by Constitution. Alessandro Ferrara and Frank I. Michelman, Oxford University Press. © Alessandro Ferrara and Frank I. Michelman 2021. DOI: 10.1093/oso/9780192855121.003.0013

need ample spans of time in which to tighten and deepen their own forms of political integration, over which they could be drawing inspiration from each other's experiences. To this process I referred by the phrase 'testing the practice of transnational democracy in a variety of cultural contexts'.[1] In each of these extra-European regional associations, one or more democratic regimes will exist alongside a majority of decent ones. One might, then, look for stimulation, from these neighbouring-state exemplars of transitional paths and experiences, of additional transformations from decency to democracy. Perhaps living examples from culturally germane contexts can better inspire such transformations than can abstract argumentation from abroad. Such a seeding of exemplars of embodied democratic life, across varied cultural contexts, is perhaps a key contribution that these regional associations could offer to a resurgence of democratic regimes in a world where democracy has recently been in apparent retreat.[2]

Michelman's chequerboard alternative starts out from the worry, often heard within the EU, that supranational administrative and regulatory activities may encroach not just on the local majorities' current democratic will, but also on the member states' constitutional essentials. Accordingly, he qualifies his own envisaged realistic-utopian pathway in terms of one characteristic: the lack of self-executing character of any regulatory laws of the transnational regime. The regime could be possessed of regulatory powers, but its regulatory laws would have direct effect only on the member states. As Michelman details further, 'the expanding SOP constitution could even *obligate* [my italics] the nation-states for ... conforming legislation', presumably applying sanctions for non-compliance. We would be in a scheme of government, not governance.[3] However, the member states' obligation to legislate domestically in execution of the global centre's regulatory intimations would depend on such regulations passing muster under the member state's constitution. The operation of such a global-constitutional script would generate what Michelman, twisting a Dworkinian expression to a positive connotation, calls a 'chequerboard

[1] Chapter 10, pp. 151–152.

[2] For a more detailed account of exemplary normativity, see Ferrara, *The Force of the Example: Explorations in the Paradigm of Judgment* (Columbia U. Press 2008) 17–41, and 'Exemplarity in the Public Realm' (2018) 30, 3 Law & Literature 387.

[3] Although both government and governance ultimately purport to coordinate the conduct of the actors comprised within their jurisdiction, government can impose sanctions for non-compliance in a way that is precluded to structures of governance. For a definition of governance along these lines, see Ferrara, *The Democratic Horizon: Hyperpluralism and the Renewal of Political Liberalism* (CUP 2014) 171–182. For different accounts of the distinction, see David Held and Mattias Koenig-Archibugi (eds), *Taming Globalization: Frontiers of Governance* (CUP 2005). For a radical critique of the notion of governance, see Claus Offe, 'An "Empty Signifier"?' (2009) 16, 4 *Constellations* 550–551.

empire' under the SOP: local member states would apply their own constitution as a sieve through which not all the edicts of the global centre would pass. The overall picture of the transnational rule of law would resemble a chequerboard, not a homogeneous surface.

This chequerboard arrangement is certainly not a modus vivendi. Legitimation-by-constitution remains in place locally, thanks to this qualification of the obligation of local enforcement. In the end, concludes Michelman, we could hope that 'pragmatic accommodation and mutual learning' will set in motion a dynamic leading eventually to 'a constitutional consensus' and perhaps even beyond, 'to a full moral consensus among an emergent democratic citizenry of the world'.[4]

To repeat, a lot of common ground exists between our two envisaged realistic-utopian pathways: a multivariate global rule of law and a transitional chequerboard empire. Both share the premise that, at the global level in present times, a democratic relation among free and equal participants necessarily counts as participants only states (or 'peoples' as *demoi*), not individuals; no just and stable society of liberally free and equal individuals is globally conceivable now. Various authors offer differing reasons for this conclusion;[5] both Michelman and I say simply, from a political-liberal standpoint, that liberal and decent constituencies do not at present hold compatible or overlapping conceptions of a just society. A people attaches the status of free-and-equal claimants to its individual members (as in the liberal democracies) or it does not (as in various decent societies). One cannot have it both ways.

Both of our envisaged realist-utopian pathways towards a world-constitutional regime pivot on an ideal of a publicly reasonable justification for regulatory actions of global scope. In the view of both, such actions will have to seek their justification in reasons accessible to all, i.e. to democratic and decent peoples alike. Finally, both envisaged pathways supposedly embed the seeds of their own overcoming—of their progressing, as Michelman puts it, towards 'a full moral consensus'. Both schemes count on political-cultural effects in the decent polities, both from the exemplary relation of their state with other free and equal states and from exposure to the differing internal modes of relations

[4] Chapter 11, p. 157.

[5] See e.g. Michael Walzer, 'Governing the Globe' (2000), in *Arguing about War* (Yale U. Press 2004) 171–191; Richard Bellamy's argument in favour of a 'republican intergovernmentalism' on the scale of the EU, which draws on a broader view of 'cosmopolitan statism' as a 'civic association of democratic nation states', in his *A Republican Europe of States: Cosmopolitanism, Intergovernmentalism and Democracy in the EU* (CUP 2019); see also Thomas Christiano's idea of a 'fair system of voluntary association among highly representative states', in his 'Democratic Legitimacy and International Institutions', in Samantha Besson and John Tasioulis (eds), *The Philosophy of International Law* (OUP 2010) 127.

among the individuals, groups, or classes (as the case may be) in the associated states.

What, then, are the differing emphases in Michelman's and my own distinct ways of rethinking the paradigm of political liberalism beyond the national scale? We should look at them as parallel efforts to adapt the Rawlsian paradigm to the hyperpluralist conditions sure to be attending on any global-scale, politically empowered SOP. *First*, then, the multivariate SOP regime, for all its accommodating pluralism, remains faithful to the Lockean claim that a body politic (on any scale) should be understandable as one body that moves in one direction.[6] By contrast, the political configuration in the chequerboard scheme has, at any given moment, a more openly random appearance, as blockages to central regulations from local constitutional sieves do or do not appear, from place to place and from time to time.

Second, the chequerboard scheme incorporates a structural tension between a state's political autonomy and its participation in the world-constitutional regime. The more normatively demanding the local constitution, the more expanded the (negative) freedom retained by the local state vis-à-vis the regulatory action of the global centre. Member states conceivably could then be induced to amend their constitutions in ever more demanding directions, just in order to protect their domestic rules of law from the encroachments of supranational regulation. No such effect attends upon the multivariate arrangement.

Third, the multivariate arrangement does, however, by its very acceptance of a prudential local submission to the legitimation-conferring central authority, open itself to an objection of failure to incentivize the emergence of a more principled sort of constitutional or moral consensus. A different, but parallel concern attends the chequerboard idea, about what would move the various states to bring their constitutions more in line with the world-constitutional script, when from such a movement more stringent obligations would follow to conform to regulatory inputs originating from a global centre.

To conclude, underneath these differing nuances, a basic, deep-seated conviction is shared among us two. Even, we say, in those regions of the world where liberal democracy, with its pivotal assumption of free and equal individual citizens, cannot reach, the battle for political decency is not lost. Where liberal democracy cannot reach, constitutionalism can, with its attendant ideas of the rule of law, of separated and balanced powers, of a duty

[6] John Locke, *Two Treatises of Government* (first published 1690, with an introduction and notes by Peter Laslett) (New American Library 1965), II, 8, § 96, 375.

to consult and with its inherent aversion to monocratic or imperial rule. Constitutionalism can keep the flame of decency burning, and with it the openness of the future to what *we* deem best—a stable and just society of free and equal citizens—without yielding now to the temptation to impose this view on recalcitrant others.

AFTERWORD TO PART III

A transnational political formation wielding coercive powers—among, upon, or within the included states, societies, or peoples—poses a clear challenge to political-liberal legitimation-by-constitution. Our respective essays in Part III have construed that challenge on the model of a problematic extension—*from* the domestic case *to* the transnational case—of certain core ideas including, most crucially, that of a political reasonability that can encompass all of a society's major constituencies. Taking those ideas as *relatively* comfortably assumed for the domestic case of a constitutional democracy (saving bracketed instances of advanced hyperpluralist development in some countries of the West), we have sought to figure out how much of legitimation-by-constitution can then be salvaged for the case of worldwide institutional reach, from which any such easy comfort is barred from the start.

The transnational case, however, also bears a reverse and potentially a wider significance for the political-liberal project of legitimation-by-constitution. Call it a blowback effect. The blowback is evident already when Ferrara draws, from Rawls's idealistically thinned-out institutional design for a transnational law of peoples, his own proposal for a multivariate polity; but this time not for a *global* political formation; rather, as political liberalism's best response to facts, when and as they appear, of *domestic* visionary division. Now, the blowback effect is not so easily cabined. First appearing in our sights as an opposite case to the domestic, the transnational then morphs to a mirror to us of our own divided conditions at home, and a caution not to wish or presuppose away the difficulties ever standing in the way of the idea, *tout court*, of a political reasonability to supersede or liquidate or hold at bay those divisions. We have thus come full circle from our initial appraisal of political liberalism as the paradigm of constitutionalism, and as the political philosophy committed, in our times, to holding together in one thought a recognition of the depth of the plurality of our political worlds and the quest for a political normativity respectful of that plurality.

That said, our exchanges here, arising as in fact they have as a series of *pièces d'occasion*, have reached no bottom lines. Readers might fairly wish from us something firmer by way of assessment both of the impact to date of the political-liberal initiative in the recent history of political ideas, and of the initiative's prospects and worthiness for further development in changing times. In that spirit, we offer each our own concluding reflection.

Concluding Reflections

A Glance Back and the Road Ahead

Alessandro Ferrara

At the end of this dialogue, it is the proper time to take stock, look at the larger picture, and sum up what our debate over *Political Liberalism* has sedimented in the way of convictions more (or less) settled, lacunas in urgent need to be filled, problems awaiting solution and inviting more specific inquiries in the near future.

It seems to me that the one most settled persuasion emerging from the previous chapters is that Rawls's legacy, twenty years after his passing away, is still vibrantly alive and inspiring. At the same time, only now the detailed contours of that legacy begin to be discerned with greater resolution.

A Theory of Justice, widely acclaimed for having reawakened normative political philosophy from the long lethargy it had entered since John Stuart Mill's *Considerations on Representative Government* (1861), developed to its extreme limit, thanks to the incorporation of what was then called 'the fact of pluralism', a still traditional scheme of foundational normative philosophy. In the language of films' reviews: philosopher sets a normative standard for judging the world, justifies it against competing standards, and expects the rest of us to agree. These dialogues have been premised on the idea, unreservedly shared by us and hopefully destined to acquire wider acceptance, that the core of John Rawls's path-breaking contribution to normative political philosophy consists of his moving *beyond* that model in a way unequalled by all fellow liberal normative philosophers, including Habermas and Dworkin. The later Rawls fully measured up to the challenge of rethinking normativity within a new philosophical horizon, opened up in the first half of the twentieth century by Wittgenstein, that considers futile the exercise of bridging the plurality of locally shared frames of meaning (language games) through appealing to some trans-local foundation. In hindsight, however, that philosophical sea-change has resulted by and large in a stalemated philosophical scene, populated either by deniers of the problem or by contextualists who give up on

Legitimation by Constitution. Alessandro Ferrara and Frank I. Michelman, Oxford University Press. © Alessandro Ferrara and Frank I. Michelman 2021. DOI: 10.1093/oso/9780192855121.003.0014

context-transcending normativity and limit their inquiries to reconstructions of locally prevailing codes.

Political Liberalism breaks that standstill. After downgrading the original position to a non-foundational 'device of representation',[1] Rawls innovatively grounds justice as fairness on the context-sensitive, singularized normativity of what is 'most reasonable for us'. The novelty of this approach to normativity—anticipated in the history of philosophy by Aristotle's notion of 'phronesis', by Kant's notion of 'purely reflective judgment' and, in political philosophy, by Rousseau's figure of the legislator—consists of its requiring that the free-standing validity of the two principles of justice as fairness be reconciled with the historical situatedness and political culture(s) of the addressees of justice, 'we the people' as involved in a process of self-constitution. Reflective equilibrium is the methodological resource that allows us to make sense of *when* such balance is achieved and has become 'irrecusable' for us without any pretence, however, of reflecting something outside of us.

Another settled conviction transpiring from this exchange is that *Political Liberalism* offers a novel articulation of what legitimacy means—the title-eponymous 'legitimation by constitution'—that ingeniously responds to the increasing unlikelihood, under conditions of hyperpluralism, institutional and social complexity, that a generalized 'consent of the governed' on single exercises of legislative, executive, or judicial power ever materializes. If the legitimacy of the acts of constituted powers rests, instead, on these acts' compatibility with a constitution, the essentials of which indeed may be expected to garner the consent of the citizens, then 'political liberalism' embeds an implicit and productive constitutional theory that calls for further elaboration.

Some of these developments already have received consideration above. In order for 'legitimation by constitution' to operate, the constitutional essentials must be legitimate in the first place, before they can cascade legitimacy all the way downstream. Thus, the nature of the 'irrecusability' that supposedly binds the 'constituent power of the people' had to be clarified. Then, judicial review as the institutional procedure that monitors and maintains the consistency of the lower-level machinery of government with the higher-level normativity of the constitution has been examined. And finally, our focus has shifted on the potential of the paradigm for being applied beyond the domestic level for which it had been conceived in the first place.

However, those are simply the initial steps on the way to bringing the legacy and potential of political liberalism to full fruition. Other aspects of Rawls's

[1] Rawls, *PL* 24.

implicit constitutional theory need to be spelled out and the major paradigms of twentieth-century constitutionalism will have to be engaged. These further aspects are facets related to the formation, and subsequent modification, of the constitutional essentials. Rawls is the one major liberal theorist who explicitly includes constituent power as a central concept in his construction. But he dedicates only a few paragraphs to this subject. He mentions Locke as a source for distinguishing the constituent power of the people 'to establish a new regime'[2] and to inscribe in a constitution the political ideal of governing itself in a certain way[3] from the constituted power of the officials and the electorate.

This move brings at centre stage not just the elucidation of the normativity under which constituent power supposedly operates—debated in our initial four chapters—but also the question, which instead exceeds the scope of this volume: how should the constituent power of 'the people', a collectivity which supposedly encompasses many generations all equally free under the same constitution, properly relate to the pro-tempore living segment of the people itself in its dual capacity of electorate (a constituted power) and co-author of the constitution (as co-possessor of a share of constituent power)?

In order to answer that question, in future work, light will have to be cast on at least three facets of a fully reconstructed and expanded Rawlsian constitutional theory. *First* and foremost, a lacuna that affects not only political liberalism, but most of modern and contemporary normative political theory, will have to be filled with the greatest urgency. In Chapter 2, the formation of a *demos* out of an *ethnos* via self-constitution was discussed in a preliminary and tentative way, but a 'political conception of a people' or of the bearer of constituent power will need to be outlined, as a supplement to Rawls's 'political conception of the person'.[4] Drawing on the distinction of *ethnos* and *demos*, the process of self-constitution needs to be clarified, through which a *demos* comes into being from one *ethnos* or a plurality of *ethnoi* that have come to first coalesce and then form a 'commitment to make joint commitments'.

At the same time, an account of the people's constituent power should embed full awareness of the fact that the formation of a *demos* out of an 'unconstituted' multitude is scarcely observable in a world already fully occupied by 195 sovereign states. It makes sense to presume that the conditions of the legitimate exercise of the constituent power of the people will have to be specified with reference to the observable manifestations of that power. One common

[2] Ibid. 231.

[3] Ibid.

[4] The expression 'a political conception of a people' is used here in a sense different from the one originally attributed to it by Frank Michelman in Chapter 11.

manifestation consists of the change of an existing form of government and its constitutional essentials—i.e. of fully-fledged *regime-change*. Another way in which constituent power manifests itself is through *secession*, or the splitting away of one or more segments of a *demos* (whether on a monoethnic or polyethnic basis), in order to give rise to a new *demos* in its own right. Furthermore, a manifestation of the constituent power of the people, on which *Political Liberalism* has remained silent, concerns the converse trajectory, by which a plurality of constituted, autonomous *demoi* merge into a larger *demos*, with the consequence of turning the previously autonomous *demoi* into ethnical segments of the new political unit. Finally, the constituent power of the people manifests itself as the power to significantly modify the essentials of the existing constitution without creating a new regime or *demos*: this is *amending* power.[5]

The distinction of the people and the electorate then presses onto our attention a *second* facet of a reconstructed Rawlsian constitutionalism. Insofar as these two political collectivities are kept distinct, their respective wills cannot be assumed to be blessed by a pre-established harmony. Thus their proper relation and reciprocal alignment ought to become the focus of reflection. Representation becomes a crucial concept. The voters have their representatives in elected legislators and executive officials. Who represents, instead, the whole transgenerational people qua author of the constitution? And is the meaning of 'representation' the same across the two cases? While Rawls's answer to the first question is that a supreme or constitutional court is vested with the (constituted) power to represent the will of the author of the constitution, and exercises that mandate through judicial review, it is less clear how such a mandate ought to be understood—the issue at the centre of Part II in this book—and how its inherently representative moment ought to be understood and defended against the competing claims, voiced among others by 'political constitutionalists', that also representation of 'the people' should be entrusted to elected legislative officials. We know from Rawls that such 'representative moment' realizes itself as the act of interpreting the constitutional text in the light of public reason. However, the standard for assessing that 'representation-through-interpretation' needs to be spelled out in the light of Rawls's dual normative standard of the reasonable and the 'most reasonable', as applicable now to the judgment rendered by the court qua representative of the entire

[5] This political conception of a people as bearer of constituent power is outlined in chapter 4 of a forthcoming volume, titled *Sequential Sovereignty: Constituent Power and Political Liberalism* (hereafter Ferrara, *Sequential Sovereignty*).

people in interlocution with other constituted powers that primarily represent its living segment. In contrast to Dworkin's standard of 'making the most' of the entire *corpus juris* and jurisprudential tradition of the political community in the name of which a court pronounces its judgment, and in relation to Habermas's standard of the 'betterargument' under idealized conditions that fulfil transcendental-pragmatic presuppositions of discourse, *Political Liberalism* leaves it mostly for us to spell out the exact benchmark according to which the supreme or constitutional court's interpretation of the 'will of the people' should be assessed.

The *third* facet of a reconstructed Rawlsian constitutional theory becomes visible at this juncture. If the court's interpretive judgment can never attain the degree of closure typical of subsumption under rules or logical deduction, then the guarantee that judicial review keeps clear of arbitrariness and leaves the democratic will unoccluded lies ultimately in the openness of said judgment to correction. Of course, the agent of such rectification cannot be the generations of 'the people' no longer or not yet present on the scene, but must be the *living segment* of the people—the same living segment that, qua co-author of the constitution, can amend it in new directions and that, from an empirical point of view, is indistinguishable from the electorate. Then, in the light of Rawls's remarks on the implicit entrenchment of the First Amendment and possibly of other Amendments,[6] it becomes urgent to reflect—from within the paradigm of 'political liberalism'—on the nature, source, and limits of this secondary constituent power, vested in the living segment of the people, to correct the supreme court's interpretation of the constitution and to change the constitution on the basis of the formal provisions for amending it or even beyond them. Rawls's remarks on implicit unamendability will need to be re-examined, compared with other theories of implicit unamendability, and his ultimately teleological justification for unamendability will need to be possibly strengthened by appealing to concepts derivable from other parts of the paradigm.[7] This extended reappraisal of Rawls' view of constituent and amending power will achieve its purpose when the liberal principle of legitimacy—the normative core of political liberalism—will be enriched with a full-scale reflection on its implications and the questions it raises if applied to exercises of *constituent* and of *amending* power.

Necessarily, this agenda will require future work.

[6] Rawls, *PL* 239.

[7] The limits of amending power as grounded in 'vertical reciprocity' among generations of the same people are further explored in chapter 7 of Ferrara, *Sequential Sovereignty* (n. 5).

A Liberal Limit to Constitutional Thinness

Frank I. Michelman

Reflecting on the broad sweep of constitutional politics in the United States, Mark Tushnet has written of constitutions thick and thin.[8] 'Thick' is the *corpus juris* Constitution, the lawyers' and judges' digest of clauses ('no law abridging the freedom of speech') with their doctrinal appendages of implementing rules and tests (say, 'the *Brandenburg* test' for punishable verbal incitement of civic disorder).[9] 'Thin' is a constitution composed of a few broad recitals of the liberal-democratic tenets of individual equality, liberty, and freedom of expression. Of course we do find those latter in the enacted legal instruments of 1789–91 and 1868—but those recitals there, in Tushnet's rendering (here following A. Lincoln), are to be read as secondary pointers to the real and primary thing. The founding Declaration of 1776—and specifically the affirmation there, as American creedal bedrock, of the liberal regulative idea of the equal natal dignity and inalienable rights of everyone—*that* is what counts in the end as the essential American constitution.

Tushnet drew his thick/thin distinction as part of an extended sceptical reflection on the contribution of US-style strong judicial review to this country's flourishing as a liberal democracy. Writing in 1999, taking as examples contemporaneous court battles over the thick-constitutional standing of flag-burning prosecutions and race-based affirmative action, Tushnet denied that the liberal-democratic thriving of a country like the United States should be thought to rise and fall with adjudicative outcomes in such cases. Never mind whether he, as citizen or as educated lawyer, might agree or not with those resolutions; what really and truly mattered were the terms in which the underlying issues of principle and policy were framed and discussed in our politics at large, outside the courts.

Thick adjudicative dictations of the kind Tushnet was disparaging come, after all, only in the wake of courses of political events, involving enactments of laws and so on. And as long, he thought, as those events occur through democratic processes evincing a continued attachment to the regulative liberal ideas of equality, liberty, and freedom of expression, we have the closest we are going to come on this earth to a democracy worth keeping (my words, those last,

[8] Mark Tushnet, Taking the Constitution Away from the Courts (Princeton U. Press 1999) 11.

[9] In *Brandenburg v. Ohio*, 395 U.S. 444, 447 (1969), the Supreme Court laid down an implementing rule of punishability, *pace* the First Amendment, of speech 'directed to inciting … imminent lawless action and likely to … produce such action'. On implementing rules, see Richard H. Fallon, Jr, Implementing the Constitution (Harvard U. Press 2001).

not Tushnet's). Juridicized thick constitutional oversight then is only a gratuitous blot on civic debate and collective self-rule, bearing no likelihood Tushnet could detect of a resulting closer approach over time to the Declaration's regulative idea.

Tushnet was certainly not then writing as a political hard-headed 'realist' as opposed to dreamy-eyed 'theorist'. He did push for a clear-eyed assessment of the net policy fallout from strong judicial review. He did not, though, reject the imagination, *as* real, of a publicly apprehended and commanding body of normative political ideas on which a citizenry converges, by which it collectively feels itself bound and governs itself accordingly. His urging to Americans was to claim that body as thin—as by its own principle always open to applicative debate—to a point where commitment of it to the keeping of jurists, with their special ways of arguing and plotting and deciding, should strike us as ludicrous. Writing in the year 2000, I noted that Tushnet's move in that direction would surely set off alarms among some of his liberal-minded readers. I then made bold with a suggestion that my 'some' might *not* include John Rawls.[10]

Bold the suggestion is, insomuch as Rawls seems bent on casting a country's supreme court in the role of main institutional protector of the people's higher law in a dualist democracy.[11] My full defence for it must be sought outside the pages of this book.[12] I raise it now by way of explaining my long-standing interest in questions that do lie at the heart of our explorations here: why should (or how can) a democratic regime put up for one second with subjection to substantive constraint from a constitutional higher law (whether or not judicially monitored)? How thin can a higher-law constitution get and still fill the place of a constitution in Rawlsian justification-by-constitution? How thin can it get and still be liberal? (How *thick* can it get and still be liberal?) How do these questions connect? Where does their connection leave the idea of an anti-perfectionist liberalism? Is political (not perfectionist or comprehensive or foundational) liberalism possible? Is it, then (anticipating a possible 'no'), an ideal worth holding onto, a goal worthy of pursuit?

Those are hard and serious questions. Such answers as I have begin with the duality of functions—regulatory and justificatory—that political-liberal thought ascribes to a liberal democracy's constitutional law.[13] John Rawls

[10] See Frank I. Michelman, 'Populist Natural Law (Reflections on Tushnet's "Thin Constitution")' (2000) *34 University of Richmond Law Review* 461.

[11] See this book's Introduction pp. 4–5; Rawls, *PL* 233.

[12] See e.g. Frank I. Michelman, 'The Question of Constitutional Fidelity', in Silje A. Langvatn, Mattias Kumm, and Wojciech Sadurski (eds), Public Reason and Courts (CUP 2020) 90 (hereafter Michelman, 'Question of Fidelity'). I defend the suggestion at length in a forthcoming manuscript, tentatively titled 'Constitutional Essentials: On the Constitutional Theory of Political Liberalism'.

[13] See Introduction, pp. 7, Chapter 1, pp. 8–23; Chapter 7, pp. 100–101.

supplies a philosophical scaffolding for the justificatory function of a country's body of constitutional law,[14] but a sensitivity to it spreads wide in our political culture, I would maintain, not confined to philosophers. Liberal-minded but democracy-dedicated American legal thinkers, protesting against thick constitutional obstruction of public-policy steering by current political majorities, regularly stop short of repudiation altogether of constitutionalist sensibility in the American republic. Just let's have it thin-liberal, they plead, and keep the judges off. But why have it *at all*, if some intuition of a dependence on justification-by-constitution, which we are going to find it hard to do without, is not floating somewhere in consciousness?[15]

Assume it is. Then there has to be a limit to the thinness of a higher-law corpus capable of bearing the weight of political justification. In order to sustain the regime's acceptability across a diverse country's population, the constitution's substantive terms of assurance will have to carry a core of common meanings sufficient to render coherent and persuasive the claims of citizens to each other of the worthiness of any conforming regime for continued support.[16] Nor will just any brand of substance suffice for the Rawlsian project. For *liberal* political justification, that liminal thickness of public reasonability will have to be such as to enclose some irrecusable liberal commitments, such as those proposed in this book's Chapter 9.[17] Reasonability *around here*—Rawlsian 'most reasonable for us', as Ferrara pounds home the point in our discussions[18]—is not and cannot be pure-procedural and substance-free.

But where then *does* that leave the claim to a non-perfectionist 'political' liberalism? Safe and sound, I would say, if by perfectionist we strictly mean what Rawls in *Theory of Justice* classifies as a 'teleological' theory, one that starts from a posited idea of human excellence or human good and then defines the right in politics as the pursuit of maximization of that excellence or good across society—in that way, writes Rawls, failing to take seriously 'the plurality and distinctness of individuals'.[19] But of course that does not carry us safely past the shoals of disagreement and oppression (nor has anyone recently said it does). Insist as we may on the priority of the right over the good, we still meet

[14] See this book's Introduction, pp. 3–5).

[15] See Frank I. Michelman, 'Why Not Just Say No? An Essay on the Obduracy of Constitution Fixation' (2014) *94 Boston University Law Review* 1143, 1149–1152, 1157–1160 (remarking on works of Larry Kramer, Sanford Levinson, Mark Tushnet, Jeremy Waldron, and Robin West); Frank I. Michelman, 'Michael Klarman's *Framers' Coup* (and the News from Antifidelity)' (2018) *93 Constitutional Commentary* 109, 127–128.

[16] See Chapter 9, p. 128; Michelman, 'Question of Fidelity' (n. 12) 102.

[17] See Chapter 9, p. 128.

[18] See Chapter 4, pp. 67–68.

[19] See John Rawls, A Theory of Justice (Harvard U. Press 1971) 29.

disagreement over the right. As liberal, then, we take the shovel of toleration to our own local pile of suppositious certainties.[20] We turn up and discard layer after layer of habit and prejudice that we learn to see as non-essential to our idea of the right. The circle of reasonability for us grows wider. Its base, we discover, lies deeper under the topsoil of scholastic quarrelling than we had thought. And then finally, inevitably, as liberal, we hit our spade-turning political bedrock, that truth about the right that we just do hold.

As some such truth we must; it could not possibly be otherwise. The turning of our spade cannot be a reason to conclude that the pursuit of political liberalism is wrong for us. But wait, you say, 'wrong' is the wrong question. Right as the conception may be for a world amenable to it, the pursuit of it is mistaken if impossible of achievement in the world that is ours. And is it not? And is not that so by reason of facts about the world beyond our power to change by any means permitted by the conception we would pursue? This objection, you add, might not apply with such finality to pursuit of *comprehensive* liberalism; but to *political* liberalism—the liberalism that flinches away from any slightest residue of oppression defined as coercion by law of any who stand outside the circle of the reasonable-for-us—it seems fatal.

John Rawls himself was clear on the point of the dependence of a political project's suitability for pursuit on possibility of its achievement. Legitimation-by-constitution envisages a society of citizens conducting their politics in mutually accredited submission to a *pro tempore* settled framework law ('constitution')—finding that framework law, as they do, both (i) sufficiently thick to give justificatory cover to all of the laws and policies issuing from it, and (ii) sufficiently thin to accord with principles and ideals reasonably (but variously) held by each. Now, the possibility of some constitution's co-satisfaction of conditions (i) and (ii) obviously depends on a sociological milieu in which are combined a number of special cognitive, motivational, and communicative elements that Rawls sought to capture in terms such as civility and reciprocity. Rawls was insistent that those elements would have to correlate with sociological real possibility, not just bare conceivability. If the conditions envisaged by the liberal principle of legitimacy cannot be credibly squared or fitted to other facts of society held to be strictly fixed, then that principle is not one that could be adopted by reasonable and rational citizens.[21] 'Until we bring ourselves to conceive how this could happen,' Rawls wrote, 'it can't happen.'[22]

[20] 'Political liberalism' writes Rawls, 'applies the principle of toleration to philosophy itself.' Rawls, *PL* 9–10.

[21] See Rawls, *PL* lx–lxii.

[22] John Rawls, 'Justice as Fairness: Political Not Metaphysical' (1985) *14 Philosophy & Public Affairs* 223, 231.

But Rawls maintained that it *could* happen, and by paths and means fully consistent with the basic liberties—of conscience, association, expression—laid down by the first principle of justice as fairness. As Ferrara explains at the close of our Chapter 12, it is squarely in that vein and spirit that our respective multivariate and chequerboard conceptions take shape in Part III of this book. 'This could happen,' we both speculate, through non-coercive, exemplary, and communicative processes we can work deliberately towards setting up. No doubt our speculations here fall on the optimistic side, but optimism is not tantamount to error—no more so in our case than in the case of Mark Tushnet's turn-of-century affirmation of the American thin constitution's subsistence as a historically real, sufficiently thick, and still reliable force in the conduct of our politics.

But, you say, the challenge today goes beyond questions of bare sociological possibility. For a liberalism willing to be militant (and perhaps depending on where it draws its own line on coercion), the claim of a practical and tolerable means towards inducement of a consensus on a liberally approvable constitution at least meets the logical requirements for a bid on the contract. But what distinguishes political from comprehensive liberalism is exactly, you say, the former's impulse towards extension of the tent of reasonability to take in some uncertain fraction of the obdurately counter-liberal. If we do that, and if then we take a stance of unremitting respect for reasonable difference—the avoidance of oppression at *whatever* cost to the prospect for liberal-democratic political ordering—we are dooming our liberalism to quick extinction by militant right-wing populism; just look around and see. To which I reply that your proposition surely is true as thus stated in generalized form with its two conditional clauses. What follows is that we may not accept that proposition, then, as applicable to the case of any so-called political liberalism that we could endorse. Now, I do not see where Rawls (or Ferrara or I) ever said that political-liberal reasonability and toleration would extend to views that are aggressively, incorrigibly, and dangerously anti-liberal. Liberal toleration cannot go further—it should not be read to go further—than to postpone to the outermost limit of safety the inevitable point of its descent into self-cancellation.

Bibliography

Ackerman, B., *We the People*, Vol. 1, *Foundations* (Harvard U. Press 1991).

Ackerman, B., *We the People*, Vol. 2, *Transformations* (Harvard U. Press 1998).

Ackerman, B., 'The New Separation of Powers' (2000) 3 Harvard Law Review 634–725.

Ackerman, B., *We the People*, Vol. 3, *The Civil Rights Revolution* (Harvard U. Press 2014).

Ackerman, B., *Revolutionary Constitutions: Charismatic Leadership and the Rule of Law* (Harvard U. Press 2019).

Albert, R., 'Nonconstitutional Amendments' (2009) 22 Canadian Journal of Law & Jurisprudence 5.

Albert, R., *Constitutional Amendments: Making, Breaking, and Changing Constitutions* (OUP 2019).

Archibugi, D., *The Global Commonwealth of Citizens: Toward Cosmopolitan Democracy* (Princeton U. Press 2008).

Ashbury, H., *The Great Illusion: An Informal History of Prohibition* (Greenwood Press 1968).

Balkin, J. M., *Living Originalism* (Harvard U. Press 2011).

Balkin, J. M., 'History, Rights, and the Moral Reading' (2016) 96 Boston University Law Review 1434.

Barber, B. R., *Strong Democracy: Participatory Politics for a New Age* (U. California Press 1984).

Beitz, C., *The Idea of Human Rights* (OUP 2009).

Bellamy, R., *Political Constitutionalism: A Republican Defence of the Constitutionality of Democracy* (CUP 2007).

Bellamy, R., *A Republican Europe of States: Cosmopolitanism, Intergovernmentalism and Democracy in the EU* (CUP 2019).

Bellamy, R., and Castiglione, D (eds), *Constitutionalism in Transformation: European and Theoretical Perspectives* (Blackwell 1996).

Benhabib, S., 'The Multivariate Polity or Democratic Fragmentation: On Alessandro Ferrara's *The Democratic Horizon: Hyperpluralism and the Renewal of Political Liberalism*' (2016) 42 Philosophy & Social Criticism 649.

Berger, S., 'Germany in Historical Perspective: Between Theory and Practice', in S. Berger and H. Compston (eds), *Policy Concertation and Social Partnership in Western Europe: Lessons for the 21st Century* (Berghahn 2002) 125.

Bickel, A., *The Least Dangerous Branch: The Supreme Court at the Bar of Politics* (first published 1962, 2nd edn, Yale U. Press 1986).

Bohman, J., *Democracy Across Borders: From Dêmos to Dêmoi* (MIT Press 2007).

Buchanan, A., *The Heart of Human Rights* (OUP 2013).

Caney, S., *Justice Beyond Borders: A Global Political Theory* (OUP 2005).

Chehabi, H. E., 'Religion and Politics in Iran: How Theocratic is the Islamic Republic?' (1991) 120 Daedalus 69–91.

Christiano, T., 'Democratic Legitimacy and International Institutions', in S. Besson and J. Tasioulis (eds), *The Philosophy of International Law* (OUP 2010) 119.

Congressional Record, 62d. Congr., 3d. Session, 11 December 1912.

Crisp, R. (ed.), *Griffin on Human Rights* (OUP 2014).

Cronin, C., 'On the Possibility of a Democratic Constitutional Founding: Habermas and Michelman in Dialogue' (2006) 19 Ratio Juris 342.

Derrida, J., *Of Hospitality: Anne Dufourmantelle Invites Jacques Derrida to Respond* (Stanford U. Press 2000).

Dixon, R., 'Creating Dialogue about Socioeconomic Rights' (2007) 5 International Journal of Constitutional Law 391.

Dworkin, R., *Law's Empire* (Harvard U. Press 1986).

Dworkin, R., *Justice for Hedgehogs* (Harvard U. Press 2011).

Eberhard, D. M., Simons G. F., and Fennig C. D. (eds), *Ethnologue: Languages of the World.* 23rd edition (SIL International 2020). Online version <http://www.ethnologue.com>.

Eskridge, W. N., jr, and Ferejohn, J., 'Super-statutes' (2001) 50 Duke Law Journal 1215.

Federalist Papers. By A. Hamilton, J. Madison, J. Jay (first published 1788), introd, table of contents, and index of ideas by C. Rossiter (Penguin 1961).

Ferrara, A., *Justice and Judgment: The Rise and the Prospect of the Judgment Model in Contemporary Political Philosophy* (Sage Pub. 1999).

Ferrara, A., *The Force of the Example: Explorations in the Paradigm of Judgment* (Columbia U. Press 2008).

Ferrara, A., 'The Idea of a Charter of Fundamental Human Rights', in C. Corradetti (ed.), *Philosophical Dimensions of Human Rights* (Springer 2012) 173.

Ferrara, A., *The Democratic Horizon: Hyperpluralism and the Renewal of Political Liberalism* (CUP 2014).

Ferrara, A., 'Political Liberalism Revisited: A Paradigm for Liberal Democracy in the 21st Century' (2016) 42 Philosophy & Social Criticism 681.

Ferrara, A., *Rousseau and Critical Theory* (Brill 2017).

Ferrara, A., 'Exemplarity in the Public Realm' (2018) 30 Law & Literature 387.

Ferrara, A., 'How to Accommodate *Modus Vivendi* within Normative Political Theory' (2018) 53 Biblioteca della libertà 9.

Ferrara, A., '"Most Reasonable for Humanity": Legitimation Beyond the State' (2019) 1 Jus Cogens 111.

Ferrara, A., 'Sideways at the Entrance of the Cave: A Pluralist Footnote to Plato', in V. Kaul and I. Salvatore (eds), *What is Pluralism?* (Routledge 2020) 81.

Fleming J. E., *Fidelity to our Imperfect Constitution: For Moral Readings and Against Originalisms* (OUP 2015).

Forst, R., *The Right to Justification*, tr. J. Flynn (Columbia U. Press 2012).

Frankfurt, H., *The Importance of What We Care About: Philosophical Essays* (first published 1988) (CUP 2007).

Fraser, N., 'Toward a Discourse Ethic of Solidarity' (1986) 5 Praxis International 425.

Freedom House, *Report* 2020 accessed at <https://freedomhouse.org/report/freedom-world/2020/leaderless-struggle-democracy> on 15 May 2020.

Gaus, G., *The Order of Public Reason: A Theory of Freedom and Morality in a Diverse and Bounded World* (CUP 2011).

Ginsburg, T., 'Written Constitutions Around the World' (2015) 15 Insights on Law & Society 4.

Griffin, J. G., *On Human Rights* (OUP 2008).

Gray, J., *Two Faces of Liberalism* (Polity Press 2000).

Gunther, G., 'The Subtle Vices of the Passive Virtues' (1964) 64 Columbia Law Review 1.

Habermas, J., 'Postscript to *Faktizität und Geltung*' (1994) 20 Philosophy & Social Criticism 135.

Habermas, J., *Between Facts and Norms: Contributions to a Discourse Theory of Law and Democracy* (first published 1992), tr. W. Rehg (MIT Press 1996).
Habermas, J., '"Reasonable" versus "True", or the Morality of Worldviews', in C. Cronin and P. De Greiff (eds), *The Inclusion of Other: Studies in Political Theory* (MIT Press 1998).
Habermas, J., 'Hermeneutic and Analytic Philosophy: Two Complementary Versions of the Linguistic Turn' (1999), reprinted in J. Habermas, *Truth and Justification*, tr. B. Fultner (MIT Press 2003) 51–81.
Habermas, J., 'Reply to my Critics', in J. G. Finlayson and F. Freyenhagen (eds), *Habermas and Rawls: Disputing the Political* (Routledge 2011).
Habermas, J., *Auch eine Geschichte der Philosophie*, 2 Vols (Suhrkamp 2019).
Hamm, R. F., *Shaping the Eighteenth Amendment: Temperance, Reform, Legal Culture and the Polity (1880–1920)* (U. North Carolina Press 1995).
Held, D., *Democracy and the Global Order: From the Modern State to Cosmopolitan Governance* (Stanford U. Press 1995).
Held, D., and Koenig-Archibugi, M. (eds), *Taming Globalization: Frontiers of Governance* (CUP 2005).
Horton, J., '*Modus Vivendi* and Political Legitimacy', in J. Horton, M. Westphal, and U. Willems (eds), *The Political Theory of Modus Vivendi* (Springer 2018) 131.
Jaklic, K., *Constitutional Pluralism in the EU* (OUP 2014).
Kant, I., *Critique of the Power of Judgment* (first published 1790), ed. P. Guyer (CUP 2000).
Kelly, E., and McPherson, L., 'On Tolerating the Unreasonable' (2001) 9 Journal of Political Philosophy 38.
Kelsen, H., *General Theory of Law and State* (Harvard U. Press 1949).
Korsgaard, C., *The Sources of Normativity* (CUP 1996).
Korsgaard, C., *Self-Constitution* (OUP 2009).
Larmore, C., *Les Pratiques du moi* (PUF 2004).
Levinson, S., 'How the United States Constitution Contributes to the Democratic Deficit in America' (2006-2007) 55 Drake Law Review 859.
Lindahl, H., 'Constituent Power and Reflexive Identity: Towards an Ontology of Collective Selfhood', in M. Loughlin and N. Walker (eds), *The Paradox of Constitutionalism* (OUP 2007).
Locke, J., *Two Treatises of Government* (first published 1690), introd. and notes by P. Laslett (New American Library 1965).
March, A., *Islam and Liberal Citizenship: The Search for an Overlapping Consensus* (OUP 2009).
Michelman, F., 'The Subject of Liberalism' (1994) 46 Stanford Law Review 1807.
Michelman, F., 'Always Under Law?' (1995) 12 Constitutional Commentary 227.
Michelman, F., 'Review of *Between Facts and Norms*' (1996) 93 Journal of Philosophy 307.
Michelman, F., 'Can Constitutional Democrats Be Legal Positivists? Or, Why Constitutionalism?' (1996) 2 Constellations 293.
Michelman, F., 'How Can the People Ever Make the Laws? A Critique of Deliberative Democracy', in J. Bohman and W. Rehg (eds), *Deliberative Democracy* (MIT Press 1997) 145.
Michelman, F., 'Morality, Identity, and "Constitutional Patriotism"' (1999) 76, 4 Denver University Law Review 1009–1028.
Michelman, F., 'Human Rights and the Limits of Constitutional Theory' (2000) 13, 1 Ratio Juris 63–76.
Michelman, F., 'Legitimacy, the Social Turn, and Constitutional Review: What Political Liberalism Suggests' (2015) Critical Quarterly for Legislation and Law 3.

Michelman, F., 'A Constitutional Horizon?' (2016) 42 Philosophy & Social Criticism 640.

Michelman, F., 'Political Liberalism's Constitutional Horizon: Some Further Thoughts' (2017) 4 Rivista internazionale di filosofia del diritto 599.

Michelman, F., '"Constitution (Written or Unwritten)": Legitimacy and Legality in the Thought of John Rawls' (2018) 31, 4 Ratio Juris 379.

Michelman, F., 'Political-Liberal Legitimacy and the Question of Judicial Restraint' (2019) 1 Jus Cogens 59.

Michelman, F., and Ferrara, A., *Polemika o ústave* (CAS, Institute of Philosophy 2006).

Montaigne, M., *Essais* (Garnier-Flammarion 1969).

Nässtrőm, S., 'The Legitimacy of the People' (2007) 35 Political Theory 624.

Offe, C. 'An "Empty Signifier"?' (2009) 16 Constellations 550.

Pettit, P., 'A Republican Law of Peoples' (2010) 9 European Journal of Political Theory 70.

Pogge, T., *World Poverty and Human Rights: Cosmopolitan Responsibilities and Reforms* (first published 2002) (Polity Press 2008).

Posner, E., and Vermeule, A., *The Executive Unbound: The Post-Madisonian Republic* (OUP 2011).

Putnam, H., *The Collapse of the Fact/Value Dichotomy* (Harvard U. Press 2002).

Quong, J., *Liberalism Without Perfection* (OUP 2011).

Raskin, J. B., *Overruling Democracy: The Supreme Court versus The American People* (Routledge 2003).

Resnik, J., and Dilg, L., 'Responding to a Democratic Deficit: Limiting the Powers and the Term of the Chief Justice of the United States' (2005–2006) 154 University of Pennsylvania Law Review 1575.

Rawls, J., 'Kantian Constructivism in Moral Theory' (1980) 88 Journal of Philosophy 51.

Rawls, J., *Political Liberalism* (first published 1993), expanded edn (Columbia U. Press 2005).

Rawls, J., 'The Idea of Public Reason Revisited' (1997) in *Political Liberalism* (expanded edn) 440.

Rawls, J., *The Law of Peoples* (Harvard U. Press 1999).

Rawls, J., *Justice as Fairness: A Restatement*, ed. E. Kelly (Harvard U. Press 2001).

Rousseau, J.-J., *The Social Contract* in *The Social Contract and the Discourse on the Origin of Inequality* (first published 1762), ed. L. G. Crocker (Simon & Schuster 1967).

Roznai, Y., *Unconstitutional Constitutional Amendments: The Limits of Amendment Power* (OUP 2017).

Roznai, Y., 'The Newest-Oldest Separation of Powers' (2018) 14 European Constitutional Law Review 430.

Sadurski ,W. (ed.), *Constitutional Justice, East and West: Democratic Legitimacy and Constitutional Courts in Post-Communist Europe in a Comparative Perspective* (Springer 2003).

Scanlon, T., *What We Owe to Each Other* (Harvard U. Press 1998).

Schirazi, A., *The Constitution of Iran: Politics and the State in the Islamic Republic* (Tauris 1997).

Schmitt, C., *Constitutional Theory* (first published 1928), tr. and ed. J. Seitzer, foreword by E. Kennedy (Duke U. Press 2008).

Simmel, G., 'Das individuelle Gesetz' (1913), in G. Simmel, *Das Individuelle Gesetz: Philosophische Exkurse* (Suhrkamp 1987).

Simons, G., and Fennig, C. (eds), *Ethnologue: Languages of the World*, 21st edn (SIL International), <http://www.ethnologue.com>.

Sohrabi, N., *Revolution and Constitutionalism in the Ottoman Empire and Iran* (CUP 2011).

Spencer, S., 'Progress: Its Law and Cause' (1857) in *Herbert Spencer on Social Evolution*, ed. and introd. J. D. Y. Peel (U. of Chicago Press 1972).

Swaine, L., *The Liberal Conscience: Politics and Principle in a World of Religious Pluralism* (Columbia U. Press 2006).

Taylor, C., *Sources of the Self: The Making of the Modern Identity* (Harvard U. Press 1989).

Taylor, C., *A Secular Age* (Harvard U. Press 2007).

Troper, M., 'The Development of the Notion of Separation of Powers' (1992) 26 Israel Law Review 1.

Tucker, N., 'Loving Day Recalls a Time When the Union of a Man and a Woman Was Banned', *Washington Post* (13 June 2006) online at <http://www.washingtonpost.com/wp-dyn/content/article/2006/06/12/AR2006061201716.html>.

Tushnet, M., *Taking the Constitution Away from the Courts* (Princeton U. Press 1999).

Tushnet, M., 'The Jurisprudence of Constitutional Regimes: Alexander Bickel and Cass Sunstein', in K. D. Ward and C. Castillo (eds), *The Judiciary and American Democracy: Alexander Bickel, the Countermajoritarian Difficulty, and Contemporary Constitutional Theory* (SUNY Press 2005).

Van der Walt, J., *The Concept of Liberal Democratic Law* (Routledge 2020).

Van der Walt, J., *The Horizontal Effect: Revolution and the Question of Sovereignty* (De Gruyter 2014).

Waldron, J., *Law and Disagreement* (OUP 1999).

Waldron, J., *The Dignity of Legislation* (CUP 1999).

Waldron, J., 'What a Dissenting Opinion Should Have Said in *Obergefell v. Hodges*' (2016), <http://papers.ssrn.com/sol3/papers.cfm?abstract_id=2844811>.

Walzer, M., 'Governing the Globe' (2000), in M. Walzer, *Arguing about War* (Yale U. Press 2004) 171.

Wendt, A., 'Why a World State is Democratically Necessary?' (2015), online at <http://wgresearch.org/why-a-world-state-is-democratically-necessary/>.

White, S. K., *The Ethos of a Late-Modern Citizen* (Harvard U. Press 2009).

Index

For the benefit of digital users, indexed terms that span two pages (e.g., 52–53) may, on occasion, appear on only one of those pages.